Terrorism

The Philosophical Issues

edited by

Igor Primoratz

*Department of Philosophy, The Hebrew University, Jerusalem,
and Centre for Applied Philosophy and Public Ethics,
University of Melbourne*

First published 2004 by
PALGRAVE MACMILLAN
Houndmills, Basingstoke, Hampshire RG21 6XS and
175 Fifth Avenue, New York, N.Y. 10010
Companies and representatives throughout the world

PALGRAVE MACMILLAN is the global academic imprint of the Palgrave
Macmillan division of St. Martin's Press, LLC and of Palgrave Macmillan Ltd.
Macmillan® is a registered trademark in the United States, United Kingdom
and other countries. Palgrave is a registered trademark in the European
Union and other countries.

ISBN 1–4039–1816–3 hardback
ISBN 1–4039–1817–1 paperback

This book is printed on paper suitable for recycling and made from fully
managed and sustained forest sources.

A catalogue record for this book is available from the British Library.

Library of Congress Cataloging-in-Publication Data
Terrorism : the philosophical issues / edited by Igor Primoratz.
      p.   cm.
   Includes bibliographical references and index.
   ISBN 1–4039–1816–3 (cloth) — ISBN 1–4039–1817–1 (pbk.)
   1. Terrorism—philosophy.   I. Primoratz, Igor.

HV6431.T499 2004
303.6′25′01—dc22   2004050424

10   9   8   7   6   5   4   3   2   1
13 12 11 10 09 08 07 06 05 04

Printed and bound in Great Britain by
Antony Rowe Ltd, Chippenham and Eastbourne

Contents

Part IV Cases

Acknowledgments

I would like to thank Mr Will Barrett for preparing the index. I also wish to acknowledge with gratitude a grant from the Australian Research Council Special Research Centre for Applied Philosophy and Public Ethics, the University of Melbourne division, which covered the cost of permission-to-reprint fees.

Igor Primoratz
Melbourne, April 2004

Notes on the Contributors

C.A.J. (Tony) Coady was Boyce Gibson Professor of Philosophy at the University of Melbourne from 1990 to 1998, and is now Professorial Fellow in Applied Philosophy at the University of Melbourne division of the Centre for Applied Philosophy and Public Ethics. His publications include *Testimony: A Philosophical Inquiry* and (co-edited with Michael O'Keefe) and *Terrorism and Justice: Moral Argument in a Threatened World*. He is writing a book on morality and political violence.

Nick Fotion is Professor of Philosophy, Emory University, and author of *John Searle, Military Ethics, Toleration* (with G. Elfstrom), and *Military Ethics: Guidelines for Peace and War* (with G. Elfstrom), and co-editor of *Moral Constraints on War: Principles and Cases* (with B. Coppieters).

Stephen A. Garrett is Professor, Graduate School of International Policy Studies, Monterey Institute of International Studies, and author of *Ethics and Airpower in World War II, Conscience and Power, Doing Good and Doing Well: An Examination of Humanitarian Intervention*, etc.

Virginia Held is Distinguished Professor of Philosophy, Graduate School, City University of New York, and author of *Rights and Goods: Justifying Social Action, Feminist Morality: Transforming Culture, Society, and Politics*, and *The Public Interest and Individual Interests*.

Tomis Kapitan is Professor of Philosophy, Northern Illinois University, author of papers in logic, metaphysics, philosophy of action, philosophy of language, and the Israeli–Palestinian conflict, and editor of *Philosophical Perspectives on the Israeli-Palestinian Conflict* and *Archeology, History, and Culture in Palestine and the Near East*.

Douglas Lackey is Professor of Philosophy, Baruch College and the Graduate School, City University of New York, and author of *Moral Principles and Nuclear Weapons, The Ethics of War and Peace, Ethics and Strategic Defense*, and the play, *Kaddish in East Jerusalem: An Incident in the Intifada*, produced in New York in 2003.

Burton M. Leiser is Professor Emeritus of Philosophy and Adjunct Professor of Law at Pace University. He is the author of *Custom, Law and Morality* and *Liberty, Justice and Morals*, editor of *Values in Conflict*, and co-editor of *Human Rights in Theory and Practice* (with Tom Campbell).

Igor Primoratz is Professor of Philosophy, The Hebrew University, Jerusalem, and Principal Research Fellow, Centre for Applied Philosophy and Public Ethics, University of Melbourne. He is the author of *Justifying Legal Punishment* and *Ethics and Sex*, and editor of *Human Sexuality* and *Patriotism*.

Peter Simpson is Professor of Philosophy and Classics, Graduate Center, City University of New York, and author of *A Philosophical Commentary on the Politics of Aristotle; Vices, Virtues, and Consequences: Essays in Moral and Political Philosophy*, etc.

Uwe Steinhoff is Research Associate at the CIS-Leverhulme program on 'The Changing Character of War' at the Uehiro Centre for Practical Ethics, University of Oxford, and author of *Kritik der kommunikativen Rationalität* and a number of papers in ethics. He has recently completed a book on the ethics of war and terrorism.

Leon Trotsky (1879–1940) was one of the leaders of the Russian Revolution, and author of numerous publications on political issues and contemporary history, including *The History of the Russian Revolution, Terrorism and Communism*, and *Their Morals and Ours*.

Robert Young is Reader in Philosophy, La Trobe University, Melbourne, and author of *Freedom, Responsibility and God, Personal Autonomy: Beyond Negative and Positive Liberty*, and numerous papers in ethics, political philosophy, and the philosophy of religion.

Introduction

Today no single issue of public concern seems to be quite as widely and hotly debated as that of terrorism. And with good reason: the threat of terrorism has never been as salient and as ubiquitous as it seems to be at present.

Social sciences and humanities are making an important contribution to these debates. Societies that are bearing the brunt of terrorism, whether local or international, cope by passing and enforcing laws, designing and implementing policies, making political decisions and moral choices and acting on them. Legislation and policy are better grounded, political and moral choice more judicious and effective, if they draw on the kind of understanding of terrorism proffered by sociology, psychology, and history.

Philosophy, too, has an important contribution to make to these debates. When addressing issues of morality and of value in general, philosophers seek to do two things: to analyze and clarify the concepts involved, and to analyze, clarify, and criticize arguments for and against various positions taken on those issues, and moral and other principles and values that ground those arguments. Accordingly, while social sciences study the causes, varieties, and effects of terrorism and history traces the way terrorism has evolved over time, philosophers focus on two basic questions: What is terrorism? And can it ever be morally justified? The first, conceptual question is preliminary to any discussion of terrorism, whether in philosophy itself, in any other scholarly discipline, or in public debates. The second, moral question might be thought appropriate after we have learned what we can about terrorism from history and social sciences – but before we decide just what our moral, political, and legal response to terrorism and its perpetrators should be.

What is terrorism?

What, then, is terrorism? Current ordinary usage of the word displays wide variety and considerable confusion; as a result, discussing terrorism and the array of moral, political, and legal questions it raises is difficult and often frustrating. Only two things are clear: terrorism is a type of violence, and it is a bad thing, not something to be proud of or support.

Nobody applies the word to oneself and one's own actions, nor to those one has sympathy with or whose activities one supports. As the hackneyed cliché has it, one person's terrorist is another person's freedom fighter. This suggests that in discussions of terrorism, as in so much public debate, a double standard is at work: one of the form 'us versus them.'

Another type of double standard, less obvious and thus perhaps even more of an obstacle to coming to grips with the notion of terrorism, is the tendency to accuse insurgents who resort to violence of resorting to terrorism, without pausing to take a closer look at the type of violence employed and who its victims are, coupled with an unwillingness to talk of terrorism when talking about violent actions and policies of a state, especially one's own state – even when *what* is done is the same. This indicates a double standard of the form 'the state versus non-state agents': the assumption that, whatever it is, terrorism is by definition something done by insurgents, and never by the state.

Much of this is apparent in the public debate about the use of terrorism in the Israeli–Palestinian conflict, for example. Both Palestinians and Israelis are committing what many among the uninvolved would call terrorism; both sides deny that they are engaging in terrorism; both accuse the other of doing so; and both attempt to justify the violence they employ, wholly or in part, by the terrorist acts of the other side. Palestinians claim that theirs is a just struggle to bring an end to occupation and oppression and to attain self-determination. We are morally and legally entitled to use violence to this end, they say. That is not terrorism, but fighting for freedom. Israelis retort that the State of Israel is certainly not engaging in terrorism. It is rather facing a terrorist onslaught, and is merely doing what any state in such circumstances would be morally and legally entitled and indeed bound to do: it is using its armed forces and security services in defense of the country and the security of its citizens.

Those speaking on behalf of Palestinians are thus assuming that the decisive criterion of terrorism is the ultimate goal of the agent that resorts to violence. If it is a legitimate goal, such as national liberation, that cannot be terrorism. From their point of view, 'terrorists fighting for freedom' is a contradiction in terms. Those speaking on behalf of Israel are assuming that it is the identity of the agent that determines whether an act or policy of violence is terrorism or not. If it is perpetrated by insurgents, it is terrorism; if by the state, it is either a policing action or warfare. From their point of view, 'state terrorism' is a contradiction in terms. Moreover, this denial that one's own side is guilty of terrorism while accusing the other side of resorting to it, in a conflict in which both sides engage in the same type of violent activity, suggests that an additional assumption may be at work. Both sides may well be assuming that if there is a violent conflict between two parties and one is guilty of terrorism, the other party is thereby absolved of the charge. If they are terrorists, we cannot be.

Once they are brought into the open, none of these assumptions seems plausible. There is no reason whatsoever why two parties to a conflict cannot both be using terrorism, just as two criminals can be at each other's throats, or two states at war can both be waging an unjust war. Nor will the bias in favor of the state and against insurgents withstand scrutiny. Although there is much to be said for having a state rather than living in a 'state of nature,' that is not to say that any state is to be preferred to an insurgency. We sometimes find that an insurgency is morally justified and the attempts of the state to put it down are not; this is typically the case in a struggle for national liberation. Even in such a struggle, however, not every means will do, morally speaking. We sometimes have much sympathy with a people fighting to get the occupying power off its back, but still object if its fighters seek to achieve their goal by attacking enemy civilians, rather than the military.

These remarks suggest that we will be in a better position to understand and evaluate terrorism if we discard all three assumptions, and seek a definition that does not define terrorism in terms of the agent, nor in terms of the agent's ultimate goal, and which allows for the possibility that victims of terrorism might themselves make use of it in response. Such a definition should focus on what is done and what the immediate point of doing it is, and put to one side the identity of the agent and their ultimate and allegedly justifying aim.

Both contributions to Part I: Definitions of this volume, Tony Coady's and mine, share this approach. Both highlight violence against non-combatants, civilians, the innocent, as the central defining trait of terrorism. The two accounts differ on a number of specific questions: Does only actual violence count, or should we think of threats of violence as terrorism too? Does it have to be violence against persons, or should violence against property qualify? Does terrorism necessarily induce, or seek to induce, fear (terror)? Does it have to be political, or can we speak of terrorism in a non-political – say, criminal – context as well? But by emphasizing the status of the direct victims of terrorism, both definitions capture the central moral objection to terrorism and thus prove especially useful for its moral evaluation – without, however, begging the question of its morality. To be sure, some authors doubt that a definition of terrorism can focus on the innocence of its victims without thereby also predetermining its moral status; in this collection, these doubts are voiced in particular in Robert Young's chapter.[1]

This understanding of terrorism as violence against civilians, non-combatants, the innocent, is shared by many contributors to this book. But a significant minority explicitly or implicitly dissent from this approach. They prefer a more comprehensive understanding of terrorism: as violence intended to intimidate and thereby achieve political objectives (Leon Trotsky, Robert Young), as political violence that either spreads fear or harms non-combatants (Virginia Held), or as coercive intimidation aiming at a political end (Nick Fotion). It is significant, however, that even authors who take the latter position tend to concede that terrorism that targets innocent civilians is more difficult to justify than terrorism that attacks those who can plausibly be described as complicit in the evils the terrorists are fighting.

Can terrorism be morally justified?

If terrorism – all terrorism, by definition, or much of it, as a matter of fact – uses violence against the innocent, can it ever be morally justified? The essays in Part II address this question. Positions on this issue reflect the basic division in ethics into consequentialist and non-consequentialist theories. Consequentialist ethics judges human action solely in terms of its consequences. When its consequences are good (on balance), an act is right; when they are bad (on balance), it is wrong. The same applies to rules of action, policies, practices, institutions. Nothing is right or wrong, obligatory or prohibited, in itself, but only in the light of its consequences. The goodness or badness of consequences is understood as the way they affect the people they affect. The various versions of consequentialism spell this out in different ways: in terms of causing happiness or suffering, or satisfying or frustrating preferences, or promoting or setting back interests. But they are all at one concerning the view that only consequences matter. Terrorism, too, is judged solely in terms of its consequences. That means that it, too, is not wrong in itself, but only if it has bad consequences (on balance). The innocence of its victims does not change this. Those familiar with philosophical debates about consequentialism will recall that one of the standard objections to it has been that it implies that punishment of the innocent is justified when its consequences are good (on balance). This objection can only get off the ground because consequentialism denies that in such matters a person's innocence is morally decisive in itself.[2]

To be sure, those who consider terrorism from a consequentialist point of view differ in their assessment of its morality. Their judgment on terrorism depends on two things: on their view of the good to be promoted, and on their assessment of the utility of terrorism as a means of promoting it. The two authors representing the consequentialist approach to terrorism in this volume, Leon Trotsky and Nick Fotion, differ considerably on both these questions, and accordingly also in their overall assessment of the morality of terrorism.

Trotsky's 'Defense of the "Red Terror"' is taken from his book *Terrorism and Communism*, published in 1920 as a reply to a book of the same title published by Karl Kautsky in 1919. Trotsky was one of the leaders of the Bolsheviks throughout the Russian Revolution and the Civil War that followed it. He had played a crucial role in the planning and implementation of the 'Red Terror,' and Kautsky's condemnation of the 'Red Terror' was also a condemnation of Trotsky's views and actions. Both Kautsky and Trotsky were Marxists, committed to the same view of the human good: the untrammeled flourishing of human nature, which is essentially social and therefore possible only in a 'truly human society' – society no longer plagued by class division and conflict. Where they differed was on the question of the necessity of large-scale violence, and in particular of terrorism, as a means of dismantling the existing, capitalist society and replacing it by a socialist political and economic system. While Kautsky acknowledged the violent nature of previous revolutions, he held that in the twentieth century a revolutionary transformation of society could be accomplished without imposing party dictatorship and 'a Regiment of Terror.' Yet the Bolsheviks set up a dictatorship, with revolutionary tribunals and extraordinary commissions that deliberated in secret and had extremely wide, indeed arbitrary, powers, suppressed all dissent by 'a system of wholesale execution,' and even took hostages. The means the Bolsheviks were using in order to achieve their aims were in fact compromising those aims, and the 'Red Terror' was altogether a moral disaster.[3]

In response, Trotsky rejects Kautsky's optimism concerning the possibility of avoiding violence and terrorism. Although aiming to take us beyond class society, revolution is still a product of that society and exhibits it traits and limitations. Therefore it cannot dispense with violence. The type and degree of violence is not a question of moral principle, but of expediency. The more ferociously the forces of the old order fight to preserve it, the more ferocious the revolutionary response has to be. At some point, it inevitably has to resort to terrorism. Nor is there anything particularly noxious about that. Terrorism, revolution, war are all of a piece: they are but different forms of the same thing, violence for the sake of intimidation and subjection. Whoever proposes to reject terrorism must, in consistency, reject all revolution and war as well. To the charge that by resorting to terrorism the Bolsheviks are employing the same methods as the forces of the old order and thus are no better, Trotsky's reply is that of an unflinching consequentialist and a revolutionary: the same means can be right or wrong, depending on the end they serve. 'Red Terror' is right; 'White Terror' is wrong.[4]

Although some of his remarks concerning the innocence of many direct victims of terrorism might be more at home in non-consequentialist ethics, Nick Fotion's approach remains broadly consequentialist, but he finds the usual consequentialist stance on terrorism much too permissive. He does not subscribe to an absolute moral prohibition of terrorism, but points out that if some types of terrorism are justifiable under certain circumstances, such circumstances will be extremely rare. The thrust of Fotion's critique of terrorists and their apologists is that they fail to do their calculations properly. He mentions the problematic nature of the 'higher good' that is allegedly being promoted by terrorism: it is often defined in ideological terms, rather than derived from settled preferences or interests of actual people. But he focuses for the most part on the issue of means and draws a list of what consequentialist calculations must include on the debit side, in order to show just how heavy the burden of justification is. If a terrorist act or policy is to be justified, it must be shown, first, that the end sought is good enough to justify the means; second, that the end will indeed be achieved by means of terrorism; third, that the end cannot be achieved in any other way that is morally and otherwise less costly. Terrorists not only, as a matter of fact, fail to discharge this burden; Fotion argues that, at least with regard to terrorism that victimizes innocent people, it cannot be discharged.

Non-consequentialist accounts of terrorism present an even wider range of views and arguments. Within a broadly non-consequentialist approach to morality, one might try to justify some instances or campaigns of terrorism in one of two ways. One might invoke some distinctively non-consequentialist considerations, such as justice or rights, in favor of resorting to terrorism under certain circumstances. Alternatively, one might argue that the obvious, and obviously very weighty, considerations of rights (of the victims of terrorism) and justice (which enjoins respect for those rights) may sometimes be overridden by extremely weighty considerations of consequences – an extremely high price that would be paid for *not* resorting to terrorism. For the rejection of consequentialism is of course not tantamount to denying that the consequences of our actions, policies, and practices matter to their moral assessment; what is denied is only the consequentialist's claim that *only* consequences matter.

The contributions by Robert Young and Virginia Held provide examples of the first type of argument. Young acknowledges that states, too, make use of terrorism, but puts state terrorism to one side and focuses on terrorism employed by non-state groups. Insurgent terrorism has often been defended as the sole weapon available to the politically powerless. This defense is sometimes challenged by arguing that terrorism can never be justified: when used against a non-democratic, repressive government, it cannot be efficient, while in the sole political environment where it might be efficient, namely in a democracy, it is not necessary. Young argues that both claims are false. He brings up historical examples to show that terrorism – not on its own, but combined with other methods of struggle – can be effective against a non-democratic regime. He also argues that the case of Northern Ireland shows that terrorism may be necessary, and therefore justified, in a democratic setting. Until a few years ago, the democratic political system in that province had operated in such a way as to deprive the minority Catholic population of any significant political power and influence, and thereby had also perpetuated all manner of social and economic inequality and injustice. The minority thus had serious grievances, but they could not be properly heard, let alone redressed. Non-violent methods had been tried and had failed. In such circumstances, Young argues, there may be a case for a resort to terrorism. Provided its targets are confined to property, or to the life and limb of people who cannot reasonably plead innocence of the imposition and perpetuation of the injustices at issue, and provided that such terrorism is likely to be successful, it may well be morally justified. (In the case of Northern Ireland, it seems that terrorism by groups fighting on behalf of the Catholic minority did make a crucial contribution to forcing the Protestant majority and the British government into the current political process aiming at a settlement acceptable to both sides. To be sure, this is not an example of terrorism Young's argument would justify, since as a matter of fact it was not restricted to what he would consider appropriate targets.) The argument is one of justice: it is for the sake of putting serious injustice that is being inflicted on the politically powerless on the political agenda and thus opening the way to addressing and redressing it that some forms of terrorism may be necessary, and therefore also morally justified.

Those who define terrorism as violence against the innocent are likely to remain unmoved by this. They will say that even if the argument is found convincing, what it justifies is not terrorism, but rather political assassination, guerrilla warfare and the like. That is in any case much easier to justify, since those on the receiving end are in some significant way implicated in, rather than innocent of, the injustice at issue. This kind of objection cannot be made against Virginia Held's position. She, too, operates with a broad definition of terrorism that covers two types of political violence: that which spreads fear, and that which is inflicted on non-combatants. However, the justification of terrorism she offers is meant to apply in both cases. She approaches the subject by focusing on the issue of rights. When the rights of a person or group are not respected, what can we do to ensure that they are? On one view, known as the consequentialism of rights, if the only way to ensure respect of certain rights of A and B is to violate the same rights of C, we shall be justified in doing so. Held does not think that such trade-offs in rights with the aim of maximizing their respect in a society as a whole are appropriate. Yet rights sometimes come into conflict, whether directly or indirectly, as in the above example. When that happens, there is no way we can avoid comparing the rights involved as more or less weighty, more or less important, and making certain choices between them. That is true in the case of terrorism too. Terrorism violates the human rights of its victims. But its defenders claim that in some circumstances a limited use of terrorism is the only way of bringing about a society where human rights of all will be respected. In at least some cases, this empirical claim may be true.

Held does not say that in such circumstances the use of terrorism would accordingly be justified. But she argues that it becomes justified if an additional condition is met: that of distributive justice. If there were a society where human rights of a part of the population were respected, while the same rights of another part of the population were being violated; if the only way of changing that and ensuring that human rights of all are respected were a limited use of terrorism; finally, if terrorism were directed against members of the first group, which up to now has been privileged as far as respect of human rights is concerned, then that terrorism would be morally justified. It would be justified in terms of distributive justice, applied to the problem of violations of human rights. It is more just to equalize the violations of rights in a stage of transition to a society where the rights of all are respected, than to permit the group which has already suffered large-scale violations of rights to sustain even more such violations (assuming that in both cases we are dealing with violations of the same, or equally weighty, human rights). The human rights of many are going to be violated in any case; it is more just, and thus morally preferable, that their violations should be distributed in a more equitable way.

In both Young's and Held's arguments, considerations of justice play a crucial role. It is justice that requires that certain grievances be heard, or that inescapable violations of human rights be more evenly distributed. But one could also take a different route in seeking to allow for the use of terrorism under certain circumstances within a non-consequentialist ethics of violence and war. One could say that, as far as justice and rights are concerned, terrorism (or, in the terminology preferred by Young and Held, the kind of terrorism that victimizes the innocent) is never justified. Furthermore, considerations of justice and rights carry much greater weight than considerations of good and bad consequences, and therefore normally trump them in cases of conflict. However, in exceptional circumstances considerations concerning consequences may be so extremely weighty as to override those of justice and rights. For instance, a people facing the prospect of being 'ethnically cleansed' from its land and turned into a population of refugees scattered throughout the world might turn to terrorism as the last resort. Acts of terrorism they committed would be violations of human rights of the victims and thus clearly and gravely unjust; but the need to prevent the unspeakable imminent human and moral disaster in store for it might be thought to carry even greater weight, and therefore to provide moral justification for those acts.

We come across this type of argument in Tony Coady's second contribution to this volume, albeit not as the position advanced and defended by the author, but rather as the subject of critical analysis that leads to its ultimate rejection. Coady puts the issue of terrorism firmly into the framework that many would think appropriate and indeed indispensable: that of just war theory.[5] One of the central principles of the theory, that of discrimination, enjoins us to distinguish between legitimate, military targets of lethal violence, and civilian and therefore illegitimate targets. It prohibits intentional attacks on non-combatants, civilians, the innocent. Some advocates of the theory hold this prohibition to be absolute. Others prefer to say that it is almost absolute, meaning that it obligates almost always, but that it may give way when it is only by going against it that we can hope to forestall an imminent moral disaster. Coady discusses the version of this view offered in Michael Walzer's widely influential book *Just and Unjust Wars*. Walzer deploys the argument of 'supreme emergency' in order to justify, at least up to a point in time, the terror bombing of Germany's cities and towns by the Allies in World War II. Coady argues that, if we accept this type of justification, we will in consistency have to make it available to sub-state groups that resort to terrorism as well. In doing so, however, we will be squandering its exceptional character. He also argues that the seemingly clear notion of 'supreme emergency' is actually opaque and open to a wide a variety of interpretations and misinterpretations. Allowing appeal to it in public debate about terrorism is therefore fraught with danger. Coady's conclusion is that we 'do better to condemn the resort to terrorism outright with no leeway for exemptions, be they for states, revolutionaries or religious and ideological zealots' (p. 93). In general, but especially in the present worldwide terrorism alert, the moral prohibition of terrorism ought to be understood and endorsed as absolute.

A strikingly different conclusion is reached in the final chapter of Part II, by Uwe Steinhoff. Steinhoff points out that most participants in the debates about the morality of terrorism and counter-terrorism tend to assume that civilians – civilians in general, all civilians – are innocent, and that therefore all attacks on them are terrorism and morally indefensible. Yet some civilians may ultimately be responsible for what their government and military do and therefore may constitute legitimate targets of violent resistance to oppression. To be sure, if they are attacked, that will no longer be terrorism; but if that is granted, then very many acts and campaigns of violence branded as terrorism by the media and the vast majority of participants in the public debate are not terrorism either. Moreover, some acts or campaigns properly characterized as terrorist might be justified: the duty not to harm the innocent might be overridden by the duty to attain a highly important and urgent military or political aim. Whether they are justified will depend on whether they satisfy such just war theory criteria as proportionality of harm inflicted and harm prevented, or the likelihood of success. If so, then an absolute moral rejection of terrorism can no longer be maintained. When we know that an act or policy is terrorist, we still do not know that it is morally illegitimate; we only know that it is likely to prove so, and must proceed to judge it on its merits.

The state as terrorist

When it first appeared in political discourse, the word 'terrorism' referred to the reign of terror introduced in France by the Jacobins, that is, to a case of state terrorism. Political thinkers have pointed out that tyranny usually maintains itself by inducing constant fear in its subjects and thereby coercing them into submission. Students of totalitarianism have highlighted the state's systematic use of terrorism against its own population as one of the defining traits of totalitarian rule. The paramount aim of such rule, total political control of society, could not very well be pursued by less radical means. Many non-totalitarian states, including some leading liberal democracies, have made use of terrorism in waging war. In terms of the number of victims and the scale of overall destruction, state terrorism has been much more deadly and destructive than terrorism employed by non-state and anti-state groups. Historically, the state has been the biggest terrorist. And yet, as I remarked at the outset, public discussions of terrorism typically proceed as if terrorism were the monopoly of non-state agents and 'state terrorism' a contradiction in terms.

This book is in several ways an antidote to the distorted picture dominating the public debate. Both essays on the definition of terrorism, Coady's and mine, argue for defining it in a way that allows for state terrorism. The contributions by Fotion, Young, and Held focus on insurgent terrorism, but operate with an understanding of terrorism that leaves room for the practice of state terrorism. Both Steinhoff and Coady (in his second contribution to this book) take Michael Walzer to task for a bias in favor of the state, which leads him to proffer the 'supreme emergency' argument as a justification of state terrorism, while at the same time denying it to sub-state groups and communities. Indeed, Steinhoff writes that 'terrorism is not at all the instrument of the weak, as is often claimed, but rather the routinely employed instrument of the strong, and usually only the final resort of the weak' (p. 108). Trotsky's famous (or infamous) defense of the 'Red Terror' is a defense of terrorism employed by a revolutionary regime. Of the four case studies comprising Part IV, two – those by Stephen A. Garrett and by Tomis Kapitan – deal, wholly or in a large part, with campaigns of state terrorism.

Part III is made up of two essays offering general discussions of state terrorism. My paper sketches a typology of state involvement with terrorism. I also argue that state terrorism is, by and large, morally worse than terrorism employed by non-state agents, because its record of killing, maiming, and destruction surpasses by far the record of non-state terrorism, and for further reasons. Douglas Lackey traces the development of state terrorism from the terror bombing of German and Japanese cities in World War II to American plans for nuclear war devised after the dropping of atom bombs on Hiroshima and Nagasaki and periodically updated ever since. To be sure, those plans, which provide for nuclear attacks on cities in the Soviet Union/Russia and in China under certain circumstances, were never put into effect; thus one might say that they do not amount to terrorism, but at most to a threat of terrorism. But while some authors confine 'terrorism' to a type of actual violence against non-combatants, civilians, the innocent, others expressly include the threat of such violence in the definition. (This is one of the differences between the two pieces on the definition of terrorism in this volume, Coady's and mine.) Lackey argues that the threat to launch nuclear attacks on the centers of civilian population, too, must be considered terrorist, since the moral character of doing X 'rubs off' the moral character of a threat to do X, if the threat is not a bluff – and the American threat, apparently, was no bluff.

Case studies

The final four essays in the book are studies of particular cases or campaigns of terrorism. They deploy the concepts, principles, and arguments philosophers use in their discussions of terrorism in order to help us towards a better understanding and more judicious moral evaluation of those terrorist acts and campaigns; of the conflicts, some domestic and others international, in which those acts were committed and those campaigns waged; and of the main actors, whether states or insurgent organizations, that have been involved. At the same time, these cases serve as a testing ground for those inevitably rather general concepts, principles, and lines of argument. For it is in their application to actual acts and campaigns of terrorism that the competing definitions of the term, approaches to the question of the moral standing of terrorism, and answers to that question have to prove their relevance and analytical and moral force.

The contribution by Stephen A. Garrett takes us back to World War II and the terror bombing of Germany's cities by the Royal Air Force. Garrett looks into several lines of argument that might be offered in justification of the bombing: the 'sliding scale' argument (the stronger the case for the justice of one's cause, the wider the leeway one has with regard to the way one fights), supreme emergency, military necessity, and the justification in terms of the balance of good and bad consequences. None withstands scrutiny. Moreover, since the bombing did not achieve the objectives brought up as its rationale and its (consequentialist) moral justification, and since its architects could have known that it would not achieve them, it was, in Garrett's words, 'both a crime and a blunder' (p. 157).[6] To be sure, international law subsequently came to expressly prohibit deliberate attacks on civilian population in war. A repeat of Hamburg or Dresden, Garrett believes, would be unthinkable today. But that may be a limited achievement. For, as Lackey points out, while the law prohibits it, the practice of large-scale killing and maiming civilians in war – not necessarily with intent, but certainly with foresight – is still very much with us.

However precariously, since the 1998 Good Friday Agreement, Northern Ireland seems to be on its way to a peaceful solution of the conflict between its two communities. But it was for decades one of the hotspots of violence and terrorism. Peter Simpson, whose approach is, broadly, that of natural law theory, looks into the aims and methods of both sides. He finds some of the aims of both Nationalists and Unionists just and some of the political violence the militants on both sides have employed justified. The problem is that both sides have sought to attain both just and unjust aims, and have resorted to violence way beyond what might be morally defensible. Both have engaged in terrorism too, and none of that can be justified; for Simpson argues that terrorism is necessarily unjust.[7]

Unlike the conflict in Northern Ireland, another protracted conflict that has involved large-scale use of terrorism, that between Israel and its Arab neighbors, and in particular the Palestinians, at present seems to be as far from a peaceful solution as ever. Tomis Kapitan discusses the role of terrorism in that conflict. He criticizes the view currently dominant in many circles in the West according to which only one, the Arab side, is guilty of terrorism, and terrorism is the core of the problem, as one-sided and superficial. Both sides have made use of terrorism, systematically and since the very beginning of the conflict. Moreover, terrorism is only a symptom, while the causes of the conflict are deeper. Kapitan also argues that 'the rhetoric of "terrorism"' employed by the Israeli and Western political establishments and the media actually functions as a smokescreen for Israeli state terrorism. Israel's 'reprisal actions' in which, as its Prime Minister David Ben-Gurion openly stated in 1948, no distinction is made between the guilty and the innocent, are a salient, but by no means sole example. Another function of this rhetoric is to delegitimize the Palestinian struggle for statehood, and to remove the real causes of the conflict from the public agenda.

Kapitan sees 'the rhetoric of "terrorism"' as portraying Palestinian terrorists as 'monsters unworthy of moral dialogue' (p. 183).[8] There is indeed the view that *all* terrorists are beyond the pale: like pirates of old, to be seen, and treated, as *hostes humani generis*, enemies of humankind. This view is given expression in the last contribution to this book, Burton M. Leiser's essay on September 11 and its aftermath. Terrorists, just like pirates, acknowledge the authority of no law, national or international, and act as if they were a law unto themselves. Accordingly, they forfeit all protection of law and government. Any explanation or justification of their actions they might offer should be discarded, and they should be fought, not negotiated with.[9] The perpetrators of the terrorist attacks in the US on September 11, 2001, in particular, have expressly set themselves at war with the entire international order, indeed with civilization as we know it. They must be taken at their word.

Some contributors to this book are critical of certain aspects of the 'war on terrorism' prosecuted by the United States and its allies in the wake of September 11. On the other hand, the author of the essay on September 11 and its aftermath, Burton M. Leiser, looks into the measures and policies adopted in the 'war on terrorism,' and gives them a clean bill of health. Such differences of approach, interpretation, and evaluation are characteristic of this collection as a whole; for giving a hearing to a broad variety of views was one of my main objectives in putting it together. Thus some authors insist on defining terrorism as violence against non-combatants, civilians, the innocent, while others give the term a wider scope, so that attacks on the military or political assassinations may qualify as well. Some approach the issue of its moral justification from a consequentialist point of view: they propose to evaluate terrorism by drawing a balance sheet of the harms it inflicts and the benefits it achieves or seeks to achieve. Others subscribe to a non-consequentialist ethics of one type or another; they discuss terrorism as an issue of justice, or of rights, or from the point of view of a broadly conceived, pluralist ethics, in terms of both justice and rights *and* the balance of its consequences. The authors whose essays on terrorism are assembled here also differ in their final judgment on its moral standing. Some uphold an absolute moral prohibition of terrorism; others view it as 'almost absolutely wrong,' that is, wrong in all but extreme, and extremely rare, cases; still others can envisage a somewhat wider range of circumstances in which terrorism, or a certain type of terrorism, may be morally justified. It is up to the reader to arrive at his or her own judgment on all these questions. I trust the essays brought together in this book – half of which were originally published elsewhere and have been revised and updated for this occasion, while the other half were written especially for this book – can be of considerable help.

Notes

1. In this connection, see also J. Angelo Corlett, 'Can Terrorism Be Morally Justified?' *Public Affairs Quarterly* 10 (1996), pp. 163–8, 176.
2. I discuss this objection and various attempts to rebut or circumvent it in my *Justifying Legal Punishment*, second edition (Amherst, NY: Humanity Books, 1997).

3. See Karl Kautsky, *Terrorism and Communism: A Contribution to the Natural History of Revolution*, trans. W.H. Kerridge (Westport, Conn.: Hyperion Press, 1973), especially chapter VIII.

4. For Trotsky's views, see also his *Their Morals and Ours: The Marxist View of Morality* (Sydney: Resistance Books, 2000). For an account of the discussions about means and ends in Marxism, see Steven Lukes, *Marxism and Morality* (Oxford: Oxford University Press, 1985), chapter 6.

5. For a recent statement of just war theory, see A.J. Coates, *The Ethics of War* (Manchester: Manchester University Press, 1997).

6. For a history of terrorism as a method of warfare and an argument that it has always failed to attain its objectives and is bound to be ineffectual, see Caleb Carr, *The Lessons of Terror: A History of Warfare against Civilians* (London: Little, Brown, 2002).

7. For a different view on some aspects of the Northern Ireland conflict, see David A. George, 'The Ethics of IRA Terrorism,' in Andrew Valls (ed.), *Ethics in International Affairs* (Lanham, Md: Rowman & Littlefield, 2000).

8. In this connection, see also Edward Said, 'The Essential Terrorist,' in Edward Said and Christopher Hitchens (eds.), *Blaming the Victim: Spurious Scholarship and the Palestine Question* (London: Verso, 1988).

9. For another statement of the view of all terrorists as *hostes humani generis*, see D.J.C. Carmichael, 'Of Beasts, Gods, and Civilized Men: The Justification of Terrorism and of Counterterrorist Measures,' *Terrorism* 6 (1982); for a critique of this view, see my 'On the Ethics of Terrorism,' in Elisabeth Attwooll (ed.), *Shaping Revolution* (Aberdeen: Aberdeen University Press, 1991).

Part I
Definitions

1
Defining Terrorism

C.A.J. (Tony) Coady

There are two central philosophical questions about terrorism: What is it? And what, if anything, is wrong with it? Here I propose to deal primarily with the first question, but I do so because of the importance of the second. The point is that various issues about the rights and wrongs of terrorist acts, and, for that matter, anti-terrorist responses, cannot be adequately addressed unless we are clear about what topic we are discussing. Too many debates about terrorism are at cross-purposes because of radical confusions about exactly what is being discussed.

Mathematical exactitude is not indeed to be expected in the clarification of political concepts. They will always have fuzzy edges and will be subject to contentious interpretations generated by other concepts used in the clarification. Yet we need to get as sharp a focus as we can on this difficult subject, and a much sharper one than is currently available in so much public debate. A further complication is that the definitional question is essentially irresolvable by appeal to ordinary language alone since terrorism as a concept is not 'ordinary' in even the way that intention, guilt, and dishonesty are. Nor is it a technical term belonging to some science; its natural home is in polemical, ideological, and propagandist contexts or, less alarmingly, highly political ones. Even so, there are certain contours to the confused public outcry about terrorism that can give a purchase for conceptual analysis even though the analysis must be complemented by a dose of stipulation. The success of any

An earlier, much shorter version of this chapter was published as: C.A.J. Coady, 'Terrorism,' in Lawrence C. Becker and Charlotte B. Becker (eds.), *Encyclopedia of Ethics*, second edition (New York and London: Routledge, 2001), vol. 3, pp. 1696–9. © Routledge/Taylor & Francis Books, Inc. 2001. Reproduced by permission.

such analysis must be judged both by its degree of fit with such contours and its contribution to specific and more general moral debates about violence. This latter aspect is always particularly significant in the discussion of political concepts since efforts at conceptual clarification alone in this arena can seem arid without reference to their moral and political impact.

Definitions abroad in the theoretical literature, of which there have been estimated to be more than 100,[1] fall into several groups emphasizing different aspects of the phenomena commonly referred to as terrorist. Nearly all of them take it that terrorism is, or involves, violence of a political nature as opposed to mere, as it were, mundane criminal violence, though most legal regimes would also count terrorist acts as illegal. Beyond this, they differ in the stress they put upon such things as the following.

(a) *The effect of extreme fear, either as intended or as achieved*: Definitions that focus on this element are influenced by the reference to terror in the word itself and by certain aspects of the history of its use. They sometimes go beyond the fear effect to incorporate further strategic goals that the fear is intended to produce, such as changing government policy in the community to which the victims belong.

(b) *An attack upon the state from within*: Here all violent internal attacks upon the state from political motives are regarded as terrorist and the state's own employment of violence cannot be terrorist.

(c) *The strategic purposes for which political violence is used*: Goals such as publicity-seeking or the influencing of some target group at some remove from the immediate victims of attack are often cited here.

(d) *The supposedly random or indiscriminate nature of terrorist violence*: Recourse to this feature is often prompted by the bewildering effect that terrorist attacks often have upon the community attacked, though, as we shall see, what appears random will often be a function of the perspectives of those whose comfortable world is shattered by the violence.

(e) *The nature of the targets of political violence*: This emphasis concentrates on the terrorists' selection of victims and so has a tactical dimension to it. It rejects the idea, sometimes implicit in (d), that terrorism typically has no tactical rationale.

(f) *Secrecy in the use of political violence*: This fastens upon the obvious fact that terrorists generally operate 'in the dark' as much as possible.

Some definitions combine a number of these emphases; others are more austerely concentrated. Hughes defines terrorism as 'a war in which a secret army... spreads fear,'[2] thus drawing on (a) and (f); Paskins and Dockrill say it is 'indiscriminate war of evasion,'[3] which combines (d) and apparently a version of (b); Wardlaw speaks of terrorism as 'the use, or threat of use, of violence by an individual or group, whether acting for or in opposition to established authority, when such action is designed to create extreme anxiety and/or fear-inducing effects in a target group larger than the immediate victims with the purpose of coercing that group into acceding to the political demands of the perpetrators,' thus combining (a) and (c).[4] Coady, Primoratz, Teichman, and Walzer concentrate upon the idea that terrorist violence is targeted upon non-combatants or innocents, so stressing a version of (e).[5]

This last emphasis catches a central logical and moral aspect of common discourse employing the term since terrorism is frequently objected to because 'the innocent' are attacked. Indeed, this is probably the most common public complaint about terrorism, even if there remain many unclarities and even evasions about who are to count as innocent. Both sides in the Israel – Palestine conflict, even those whose record for 'clean hands' is deeply suspect, voice this complaint about innocent victims. Yasser Arafat, for example, has stated: 'No degree of oppression and no level of desperation can ever justify the killing of innocent civilians. I condemn terrorism, I condemn the killing of innocent civilians, whether they are Israeli, American or Palestinian...'[6] The significance of the statement for my purposes lies in its acknowledgement of the understanding of terrorism in terms of attacks upon the innocent, not in Arafat's credibility in making the condemnation.

This approach also gives a handle for serious ethical discussion by linking terrorism to moral argument about war, in particular (though not exclusively) to the just war tradition which imposes strong conditions for non-combatant immunity from direct attack. In addition, I think that there are reasons of theoretical utility favoring a definition that is relatively uncommitted on the specific or ultimate purposes of terrorist violence. If we treat terrorism as the political tactic of directing violent attacks upon non-combatants, we can leave it an open empirical question for which broader purposes it is used. More exactly, I would define it as: *the organized use of violence to attack non-combatants ('innocents' in a special sense) or their property for political purposes*. This might be thought too restrictive in one direction since the threat to use such violence, even where the violence does not result, would be regarded by some as itself an instance of terrorism. If you think that plausible, you could amend the definition accordingly. I am disinclined to do so because I think that the threat to do X is generally not itself an instance of doing X, and in the present case the threat to do an act of violence is not itself an act of violence, no matter how disturbing it may be. But this depends upon the definition of violence and I have discussed that elsewhere.[7]

This definition avoids any reference to the broader purposes mentioned in (a) above, and I have already given reasons for doing that. Other theorists, however, who share my general approach are more inclined to include some reference to purposes, such as influencing government policies. So Igor Primoratz, who also includes a reference to threats, defines terrorism as 'the deliberate use of violence, or threat of its use, against innocent people, with the aim of intimidating some other people into a course of action they otherwise would not take.'[8]

The element of fear in (a) raises complex issues. There are parallel reasons for excluding it as a purpose from a definition emphasizing the targeting of non-combatants since attacks upon non-combatants may be made not to terrorize a whole population or some segment of it, but for publicity value, for 'symbolic' reasons, or merely to strike the only blow thought to be possible. On the other hand, the publicity or symbolic effect will usually operate and be expected to do so through the fear generated by the violence; the third sort of case, 'the only blow possible,' is perhaps best treated, in its pure form, as exceptional. Yet we would surely call the bombing slaughter of a busload of schoolchildren 'terrorist' even if the perpetrators intended to spread anger rather than fear, believing that an angry population and government would act foolishly and play into their hands. So, on balance, I would prefer a definition that left out the fear reference, though its incorporation would still catch a good deal that I would count as terrorism.

Some general reference to purpose is in any case required to make it clear that the tactic of terrorism has a political rather than a merely personal or criminal orientation. Spectacular criminal outrages, with no political motivations, are often enough called terrorist in the media because they frighten people and vividly set their perpetrators at odds with the state, but the major interest of terrorism, both theoretically and morally, lies in its political orientation. Terrorist acts will be illegal but their significance is deeper and more disturbing than, say, a revenge bombing of a police station by criminals. When criminals operate on a scale and with ambitions that bring them into the political arena, then the matter is different, as is illustrated by the Colombian drug syndicates of the 1980s. And the reverse tendency is also worth noting because terrorists will sometimes engage in ordinary crime, such as bank robbery and stealing arms from police stations or military barracks in order to support their political campaigns.

If we define terrorism as the tactic of intentionally directing violent attacks at non-combatants with lethal or severe violence for political purposes, we will capture a great deal of what is being discussed with such passion and we can raise crucial moral and political questions about it with some clarity. We might narrow the definition in certain respects by incorporating a reference to the idea that the attacks or threats are meant to produce political results via the creation of *fear*, and we could widen it, as I did earlier in this essay, by including non-combatant property as a target where it is significantly related to life and security. I would rather not do the former (for reasons already given) but would favor doing the latter because I think that attacks upon the property of innocent people would normally incur the charge of terrorism, though it would not usually be regarded as being as grave as attacks upon their life and limb. If an armed group seized an empty civilian airliner and blew it up as a contribution to their political campaign for liberation or whatever, this would plausibly be regarded as a terrorist act. If Israeli tanks are destroying the homes of innocent people in Palestine without actually killing the inhabitants, then this should surely count as terrorism. (Of course, it is a disputed factual question whether the inhabitants are actually non-combatants, as many of them seem to be.) In any case, we may be flexible, for present purposes, about the inclusion of either the effect of fear or the target of property within this style of definition. Let us call a definition of this type a 'tactical definition' since it is a crucial element in it that terrorism must involve the tactic of targeting non-combatants.

Such a definition will not require reference to secret armies nor, on one reading, the idea of indiscriminate violence. The adjective 'indiscriminate' is ambiguous, since it may mean something like random or irrational (as it were, wholly indiscriminate) or it may mean a particular lack of discrimination, a failure to make a relevant discrimination. Terrorism clearly does not have to be indiscriminate, in the sense of random or irrational, since terrorists may carefully weigh the worth of the victims they target for achieving the purposes they have in mind. It was presumably important to the September 11 terrorists that the World Trade Center was understood to be at the heart of the American global business domination that they hated and that it was such an important symbol of American pride. Nor need terrorists be totally bereft of any sense of morality as some commentators suggest. Wilkinson, for instance, claims that 'what fundamentally distinguishes terrorism from other forms of organised violence is not simply its severity but its features of amorality and antinomianism.' Terrorists are, he claims, 'implicitly prepared to sacrifice all moral and humanitarian considerations for the sake of some political end.'[9] Even if this were true of some terrorists, it seems to be far too strong a thesis to build into the definition of terrorism. On the other hand, a great deal of what is called 'terrorism' does deliberately violate those normal discriminations, characteristically enshrined, for example, in just war theory, favoring non-combatant immunity. This does not convict them of blindness to all moral constraints, but it does highlight their rejection of one set of highly pertinent moral values.[10] If this rejection underpins the sense of 'indiscriminate' in play, then reference to indiscriminate violence is compatible with a tactical definition.

This way of proceeding ties the widespread moral revulsion against terrorism to the fundamental prohibition in just war theory (under what is sometimes called 'the principle of discrimination') against violation of the rights of non-combatants. It avoids the pitfall of making terrorism immoral by definition, since its immorality needs to be established by argument for the acceptability of the principle of discrimination. It also helps to raise sharply the moral analogies between the state's use of violence against non-legitimate targets, either in state-to-state warfare or against its own citizens, and the political violence of non-state agencies against similarly illegitimate targets. There is a genuine case to be made in support of the common accusation of the insurgent that states, too, use terrorism. This should do nothing to excuse its use by revolutionaries, but it does point to a certain hypocrisy in much common indignation about terrorism. Those who think that the state terrorism of the World War II saturation bombing raids was justified by some argument of necessity, or other overriding moral considerations, cannot refuse to look at such arguments when mouthed by revolutionaries. A further advantage of the tactical definition is that it allows that there may be employments of revolutionary or insurgent violence that are not terrorist. This is important because if terrorism is judged to be entirely, or mostly, immoral because of its violation of the principle of discrimination, then there is still room for some non-terrorist anti-state political violence to be morally acceptable. This possibility is obscured by those definitions, in the spirit of (b) above, that treat terrorism as any form of sub-state violence directed against the state.

definitions, which I have elsewhere called political status definitions,

disadvantage that they make state terrorism impossible

This last consequence is avoided by those who define terrorism, in the spirit of (a) and (c) above, as the use of violence to spread fear for specific political purposes. For instance, Grant Wardlaw, one of the most judicious political scientists to write on this issue, defines political terrorism (as noted earlier) in this fashion. The approach captures some of what is involved in the ways that terrorism is discussed, but it has two principal defects as a theoretical tool. The first is that it suffers from being too specific about the purposes of terrorist acts since, as already suggested, such acts may aim at inducing anger rather than fear, and they may seek to achieve their political objectives by a process other than inducing the 'target group' to accede to their demands. They may, for instance, intend to demonstrate to other groups the vulnerability of the target group, so that the other groups will mobilize against the target group. The second defect is that the definition fails to discriminate sufficiently between terrorist and non-terrorist uses of political violence. Much employment of violence for political purposes in revolution or interstate warfare, that would not normally be considered terrorist, is aimed, at least in part, at creating anxiety or fear in the enemy beyond the battlefield with a view to bringing the war to an end. Inflicting defeats and losses on the enemy's troops by standard military attack is often intended to serve multiple purposes, but an important one is creating such anxiety in the enemy government and its supporters as will induce them to surrender or negotiate. But it would surely be counter-intuitive to see all or most military engagements as terrorist. This is an especially important issue from the point of view of the ethical assessment of terrorism, since, unless one is a pacifist, there will be forms of violent political struggle that may be morally legitimate whereas there seems to be at least a common presumption against the moral validity of terrorism. The tactical definition copes much better with these matters.

A difficulty with the tactical definitional approach is that the concept of non-combatant needs clarification, especially for the case of revolutionary violence. Its moral significance also needs to be established against certain natural objections. We cannot enter fully into either of these here, but the distinction between combatant and non-combatant is clearly more difficult in subversive war than 'normal' war. In 'normal' war the immunity of non-combatants is a basic principle because our justification for using lethal violence is specified by the need to deal with those who are prosecuting the evil which gives us just cause. 'Combatants' is the technical term for such agents and will include those who do so under duress, such as conscript soldiers, and agents without uniforms, such as spies and certain politicians. Non-combatants are therefore not identical with civilians, though it is an understandable shorthand to equate them. It is also common to describe non-combatants as 'innocent' and to treat them as immune to attack because of their innocence. But fully moralized notions of innocence and guilt are out of place here. They invoke ideas of free choice and full knowledge that are relevant to imputing moral blame and praise, whereas it seems that we are morally entitled to defend ourselves against an attacker even where the attacker is coerced or deluded. The sense in which non-combatants are 'innocent' is more that in which they are 'non-harming,' that is, not engaged in prosecuting the evil that justifies (or is argued to justify) the use of violence to protect or remedy. These somewhat technical uses of 'non-combatant' and 'innocent' are clearly meant to apply to contexts far removed from conventional interstate warfare. Hence, the September 11 attacks upon the World Trade Center were terrorist because their victims would count as non-combatants or innocents even though no relevant declared interstate war was then in progress. The attack upon the Pentagon was arguably different except for the fact that the passengers on the hijacked plane were clearly non-combatants, whatever the status of the victims in the Pentagon. There is an important area for debate here, and I have only scratched the surface of it, but it is receiving increasing attention from philosophers.[11]

In addition to these serious problems of philosophical clarification, there are other objections to the distinction. Supporter of doctrines of 'total war' and 'collective guilt' (notions once readily invoked in the context of formal war, notably in World War II) have tended to be contemptuous of any moral distinction between combatant and non-combatant. Under the influence of these doctrines, for instance, we find Winston Churchill saying during World War II: 'it is absurd to consider morality on this topic . . . In the last war the bombing of open cities was regarded as forbidden. Now everybody does it as a matter of course. It is simply a question of fashion changing as she does between long and short skirts for women.'[12] These attitudes of contempt or dismissal have been well critiqued elsewhere, so it is perhaps sufficient here to note the obscenity of arguing that there is no moral difference between killing soldiers who are trying to kill you and deliberately bombing a kindergarten in enemy territory. And, although the distinction is not based primarily on a consequentialist ethic, it is also worth noting the horrendous consequences of its disregard in the wars of the twentieth century where the vast carnage of that century's wars fell increasingly, as the years progressed, upon civilian populations.

Whatever the problems in understanding and applying the distinction in formal war settings, the sort of informal war often associated with terrorism increases such problems for familiar reasons. One of the most important of these is that in 'normal' war, it is fairly clear who are the obvious candidates for combatant status, namely those bearing and using arms of various kinds and those directing and assisting their military efforts. There are difficult, borderline cases, but there is a certain palpability about much of the classification into combatant and non-combatant (soldiers on the one hand, infants in prams on the other). But in guerrilla war or insurrection, a twelve-year-old girl in civilian clothes may be a suicide bomber, and there is a strong tendency for revolutionaries or militant dissidents to argue that all the civil authorities of the regime and even the ordinary submissive population are part of the evil that is being fought. None the less, some revolutionaries do try to make the discriminations both in their theory and propaganda and in their practice. The Cypriot revolutionary, General George Grivas, for instance, showed his sensitivity to the distinction in his memoirs when he wrote of the EOKA campaign, 'We did not strike, like the bomber, at random. We shot only British servicemen who would have killed us if they could have fired first, and civilians who were traitors or intelligence agents.'[13] Whether Grivas truly described EOKA practice is less important for our discussion than his acknowledgment of the possibility and desirability of directing revolutionary violence at morally legitimate targets.

It is important from the point of view of morality and often of long-term political objectives not to identify people as combatants too readily. From a moral point of view, we need good reason to use lethal violence and we cannot afford to be casual about the possession of such reasons. Politically, both revolutionaries and governments tend to lose support by slaughtering village administrators, and killing peasants or destroying villages on suspicion, not to mention the difficulties created for post-war reconstruction by such policies. A genuine reluctance to harm non-combatants will be exhibited in the reluctance to classify people as combatants even where this involves a degree of real risk to one's life and cause. Of course, in the heat of battle, combatants may lose this reluctance as fear, panic, and confusion swamp their consciousness. There is even a certain sort of madness in the midst of combat that can overcome common sense and conscience.[14] Yet not all killing of non-combatants arises in such frenzied contexts. A lot of it is planned in a cool hour, as was the Allied bombing of German cities in World War II or the Vietcong massacres of village leaders in the Vietnam war.

Here there is no excuse for the ignoring or abandoning of the reluctance in question.

This point about reluctance has another implication for the definition of terrorism. If terrorism is defined in terms of violent attacks upon non-combatants, then certain actions or policies that will not strictly count as terrorist can none the less be carried out in a terrorist spirit because they show indifference to the welfare of non-combatants. If a grenade and machine-gun attack is made against soldiers on duty in a crowd of civilians when it could have been made when they were alone, it would be understandable to describe the attack as terrorist simply because the civilian casualties were eminently avoidable. If the avoidability is sufficiently stark, it may be difficult to see the deaths and injuries as unintentional but, in some cases, they may be unintended but culpably reckless.

This suggests that the tactical definition of terrorism might be extended somewhat, while keeping much the same focus, by including acts which are not sufficiently concerned with avoiding harm to non-combatants. Another expansionary suggestion would be to define terrorism in terms of any breach of the *jus in bello* so that the refusal to give quarter to combatants, or the mutilation of corpses, for instance, would be terrorist. The first suggestion has more merit than the second, though both would make reasonable analytical and ethical tools. The second has the defect that there is room for even more debate about the other rules of war than the central dictum about non-combatant immunity. As for the first expansion, I am sympathetic to the concerns behind it, but would be inclined to resist it on grounds of conceptual economy. Intentional targeting of non-combatants is sufficiently different as a tactic to negligent or reckless behavior that harms non-combatants, that it deserves separate classification, especially as the two behaviors will generally raise somewhat different moral concerns.

All of the discussion of combatants and non-combatants assumes that there is a certain rationality or rough intelligibility about the aims and purposes which resort to political violence is meant to advance. This is not to legitimize or morally endorse them, for what is understandable can still be evil. But where an ideology of either a state or an insurgent group is sufficiently bizarre, it may be impossible to take seriously their classifications of combatant and non-combatant, just because we find their rationale for resort to violence too bizarre. Hence when they declare doctors, magistrates, or police to be perpetrators of an amorphous evil, we may be right to see their attacks upon them as just as terrorist as attacks upon postmen or office workers.

Even if we are unimpressed by the need for some form of non-combatant immunity, there remains an important problem for terrorist policies in that they face serious criticism in purely pragmatic terms, since it is by no means clear that terrorism can be expected to work. This is partly because it is sometimes obscure what goals are being pursued, but even where this is relatively clear, it is often doubtful whether there is any reasonable prospect of success. This is also true for goals provided by the view of terrorism as 'expressive' (of despair or righteous anger, perhaps), since the point of expression cannot be disconnected from the realistic possibilities of audience recognition. I called this criticism 'pragmatic,' but this is not to suggest that it is not also moral. The adoption of policies that kill or maim will be immoral if they are also futile. Prudence is a moral virtue and in the just war tradition several of the moral conditions that must be satisfied before resort to war can be legitimate are prudential, such as that of last resort and reasonable prospect of success.

Finally, it is important to stress that acts of political violence may be very wrong even where they are not terrorist. Perpetrators of an unjust war or an unjust revolution do a great wrong even where they do not kill or endanger non-combatants. Nazi troops who shoot armed Jewish resisters do evil even where they respect non-combatant immunity because they have been agents in creating the unjust situation that calls forth legitimate armed resistance to them.

Notes

1. Alex P. Schmid, *Political Terrorism: A Research Guide to Concepts, Theories, Data Bases, and Literature*, pp. 119–58, cited in Walter Laqueur, *The Age of Terrorism* (Boston: Little, Brown & Co., 1987), p. 143.
2. Martin Hughes, 'Terrorism and National Security,' *Philosophy* 57 (1982), p. 5.
3. Barrie A. Paskins and M.L. Dockrill, *The Ethics of War* (London: Duckworth, 1979), p. 89.
4. Grant Wardlaw, *Political Terrorism: Theory, Tactics and Counter-Measures* (Cambridge: Cambridge University Press, 1982), p. 16.
5. C.A.J Coady, 'The Morality of Terrorism,' *Philosophy* 60 (1985); Igor Primoratz, 'What Is Terrorism?' chapter 2 in this volume; Jenny Teichman, *Pacifism and the Just War* (Oxford: Blackwell, 1986); Michael Walzer, 'Terrorism: A Critique of Excuses,' in Steven Luper-Foy (ed.), *Problems of International Justice* (Boulder, Col.: Westview Press, 1988).
6. *The Age*, February 5, 2002 (reprinted from the *New York Times*).
7. See C.A.J. Coady, 'The Idea of Violence,' *Journal of Applied Philosophy* 3 (1986).
8. Igor Primoratz, 'What Is Terrorism?' p. 24.
9. Paul Wilkinson, *Political Terrorism* (London: Macmillan, 1974), pp. 16–17.

10. Wilkinson goes so far as to assert that, for terrorists, 'such Judaeo-Christian notions as mercy, compassion, and conscience must go with the weak to the wall of history' (p. 17). But, whatever their sins, some terrorists are surely moved to their violence by compassion for the fate of their comrades, compatriots, or co-religionists, or at least this fact should be open to investigation. Nor is it obvious that all terrrorists are bereft of conscience, even if their conscience is defective. Wilkinson's restriction of mercy, compassion, and conscience to the Judaeo-Christian tradition is simply astonishing.
11. See, most recently, David Rodin, *War and Self-Defence* (Oxford: Oxford University Press, 2002). See also Jeff McMahan, 'Self-Defense and the Problem of the Innocent Attacker,' *Ethics* 104 (1993/94), and 'Innocence, Self-Defense and Killing in War,' *Journal of Political Philosophy* 2 (1994).
12. Quoted in Stephen A. Garrett, 'Political Leadership and Dirty Hands: Winston Churchill and the City Bombing of Germany,' in Cathal J. Nolan (ed.), *Ethics and Statecraft: The Moral Dimension of International Affairs* (Westport, Conn.: Greenwood Press, 1995), pp. 80–1.
13. Quoted in Robert Taber, *The War of the Flea* (London: Paladin, 1972), p. 106.
14. Michael Walzer gives an excellent example of this frenzy by citing Guy Chapman's recounting of an episode from World War I of Allied soldiers killing Germans who were trying to surrender. See Walzer, *Just and Unjust Wars*, third edition (New York: Basic Books, 2000), pp. 306–7.

2
What Is Terrorism?

Igor Primoratz

The phenomenon of terrorism raises numerous questions. Some are theoretical: What are its causes, and what are its various effects? Others are practical: What is to be done about it? Should terrorism be tackled directly, or is the only really promising way of dealing with it to attend to the grievances that give rise to it? Still others are moral: Just what is it that makes terrorism so thoroughly morally repugnant to most of us? Could it be justifiable under certain circumstances, or is it absolutely wrong? Philosophers are likely to be most interested in the last sort of question. This chapter is an attempt at a definition of terrorism that will capture the trait, or traits, of terrorism which cause most of us to view it with repugnance.

Obviously, the definition I am after will be rather narrow in comparison to a great many definitions one finds in history and social sciences. There, the tendency seems to be to apply the word to political assassination, and sometimes even to political violence of any sort. However, a conception of terrorism that lumps together the assassination of Reinhard Heydrich, the *Reichsprotektor* of Bohemia, and the killing or wounding of a group of civilians traveling on an inter-city bus[1] can be of no use in moral thinking.

Terrorism and violence

Etymologically, 'terrorism' derives from the word 'terror.' Originally, it meant a system, or regime, of terror: at first that imposed by the

An earlier version of this chapter was published as: Igor Primoratz, 'What Is Terrorism?' *Journal of Applied Philosophy*, vol. 7 (1990), no. 2, pp. 129–38. © The Society for Applied Philosophy, Blackwell Publishing, 1990. Reproduced by permission.

Jacobins, who applied the term to themselves without any negative connotations. Subsequently, it came to be applied to any policy or regime of the sort and suggested a strongly negative attitude, as it generally does today. Since I am seeking a definition that will cover both a single act and a policy of terrorism, I suggest we put aside the notions of 'system' and 'regime,' but preserve the connection with terror. Terrorism is meant to cause terror (extreme fear) and, when successful, does so. But if someone did something likely to cause terror in others with no further aim, just for the fun of it, I think we would not see that as a case of terrorism. Terrorism is intimidation with a purpose: the terror is meant to cause others to do things they would otherwise not do. Terrorism is coercive intimidation.

This is just the definition offered by Carl Wellman in his paper 'On Terrorism Itself': 'the use or attempted use of terror as a means of coercion.'[2] Wellman remarks that violence often enters the picture, as it is one of the most effective ways of causing terror, but hastens to add that 'the ethics of terrorism is not a mere footnote to the ethics of violence because violence is not essential to terrorism and, in fact, most acts of terrorism are nonviolent.'[3] I agree that the ethics of terrorism is more than a footnote to the ethics of violence, but not for the reason adduced by Wellman. It seems to me that it would not make much sense to speak of 'non-violent terrorism' (in the sense which also excludes threats of violence). Wellman has three counter-examples, none of which strikes me as convincing. One is a judge who sentences a convicted criminal to death in order to deter potential criminals. I should think that execution is one of the more violent things we can do to a person (except, of course, if one accepts the definition of violence as 'the illegitimate use of force,' which I find most unhelpful). Then there is blackmail, in which the fear of exposure is used as a means of intimidation. I think we would need to know just how serious the harm caused by the exposure would be in particular cases. If the harm threatened were great, and if violent actions characteristically inflict great harm in a striking manner, as Wellman rightly says, then to blackmail would indeed be to threaten violence. Finally, Wellman says:

> I must confess I often engage in nonviolent terrorism myself, for I often threaten to flunk any student who hands in his paper after the due date. Anyone who doubts that my acts are genuine instances of terrorism is invited to observe the unwillingness of my students to hand in assigned papers on time in the absence of any such threat and the panic in my classroom when I issue my ultimatum.[4]

This sounds quite fanciful. But if Wellman's students are indeed as given to panic and terror as he suggests, and if to flunk his course is indeed such a great and dramatically inflicted harm that their reaction is understandable, then Wellman's threat is a threat of violence after all. It is not terrorism, though; nor is blackmail, or the meting out of the death penalty to a convicted criminal – for the reason to which I now come.

Indiscriminate violence

It is often said that the most distinctive characteristic of terrorism is that it employs violence indiscriminately. This is certainly not true if construed literally; for terrorists do not strike blindly and pointlessly, left and right, but rather plan their actions carefully, weighing the options and trying for the course of action that will best promote their objective at the lowest cost to themselves. But the claim is true and of crucial importance, if taken to refer to the terrorists' failure to discriminate between the guilty and the innocent, and to respect the immunity of the latter.

Terrorism has a certain basic structure. It has not one, but two targets: the immediate, direct target, which is of secondary importance, and the indirect target, which is really important. This indirect strategy is a feature of our everyday life, and there is nothing wrong with it as such. But when the indirect, but really important, aim is to force someone to do something they would otherwise not do, when this is to be achieved by intimidation, and when intimidation is effected by using violence against innocent people – by killing, maiming, or otherwise severely harming them – or by threatening to do so, then the indirect strategy is that of terrorism. The primary and secondary targets are different persons or groups of people. The person or persons who constitute the primary, but indirect, target of the terrorist, may or may not be innocent themselves; what is essential is that those who are made his secondary, but direct target, are. Thus terrorists may attack a group of civilians with the aim of intimidating the civilian population at large and getting it to leave a certain area. Or they may attack such a group with the purpose of cowing the government into accepting their demands, as is usually the case in airplane hijacking.

What is the sense in which the direct victims of the terrorist are 'innocent'? They have not *done* anything the terrorist could adduce as a justification of what he does to them. They are not attacking him, and thus he cannot justify his action as one of self-defense. They are not engaged in war against him, and therefore he cannot say that he is merely fighting in a war himself. They are not responsible, in any plausible sense of the word, for the (real or alleged) injustice, suffering, deprivation, which is inflicted on him or on those whose cause he has embraced, and which is so enormous that it could justify a violent response. Or, if they are, he is not in a position to know that.

I have said that one can lose one's immunity by being responsible for 'real or alleged' injustice or suffering because I am not speaking of innocence and immunity from a point of view different from, and independent of, that of the terrorist. Adopting such an approach would mean introducing an unacceptable degree of relativity into discussions of terrorism. The killing of Aldo Moro, for instance, would then be seen as a case of terrorism by most of us. For whatever we might think of Moro's policies, most of us surely do not consider them so extremely unjust and morally intolerable as to make him deserve to die on account of them; that is, most of us think of Moro as innocent in the relevant sense and therefore immune against killing. But the Red Brigades would deny that, and claim that what they did was political assassination, not terrorism; for they judged his policies quite differently. If we adopted this approach, we would have to grant that, to paraphrase *the* cliché about terrorism, one person's terrorist is another person's political assassin. I am not willing to grant that. What I am saying is that being responsible for a merely alleged injustice – an injustice that is alleged by the terrorist, but not recognized as such by anyone else – will be enough for losing one's immunity. According to the mainstream version of just war theory, immunity to deadly violence is lost not only by fighting in an unjust war, but by fighting in any war. If we accept this, we can see a grain of truth in Napoleon's notorious remark that 'soldiers are made to be killed.' Therefore, it can be lost not only by holding political office in a gravely unjust government, but by holding such office in any government. As Umberto I of Italy said after an unsuccessful attempt on his life, this kind of risk is part of the job. Of course, I am talking of 'innocence' and 'immunity' in a very specific, restricted sense: the sense relevant to the question of defining terrorism and distinguishing it from such things as war and political assassination. I am doing this to emphasize that the terrorist's victim is innocent *from the terrorist's own point of view*, i.e., innocent even if we grant the terrorist his assessment of the policies he opposes. I am not implying that as soon as opponents of a certain regime have satisfied themselves that the regime is utterly and intolerably unjust, they have a moral license to kill and maim its officials, but only that if they do so, their actions will not be terrorism, but political assassination. But nothing stands in the way of our condemning them, if we reject their judgment of the moral standing of the regime. To show that an action is not terrorism but political assassination is neither to justify nor to excuse it.

If the terrorist subscribes to some plausible understanding of responsibility, that means that he kills or maims people he himself, in his heart, believes to be innocent. This, I think, captures the distinctive obscenity of much terrorism. To be sure, there are terrorists who adhere to extremely crude notions of collective responsibility that take mere membership in an ethnic or religious group or citizenship of a state as a sufficient ground for ascription of such responsibility. The perpetrators of the attacks in New York on September 11, 2001 seem to have held such views. Still others are amoralists, and will not be bothered by questions of responsibility. Terrorists belonging to these two classes do not believe their victims to be innocent. The distinctive obscenity of their type of terrorism must be located elsewhere: in their preposterous positions on responsibility and the gory consequences these positions have in their practice.

Since terrorism is indiscriminate in the sense specified – since it does not discriminate between the guilty and the innocent – it is also indiscriminate in another sense: it is unpredictable. One can never count on keeping clear of the terrorist by not doing the things the terrorist objects to: for example, by not joining the army or the police, or by avoiding political office. One can never know whether, at any time and in any place, one will become a target of a terrorist attack.

Walter Laqueur objects to this way of defining terrorism:

> Many terrorist groups have been quite indiscriminate in the choice of their victims, for they assume that the slaughter of innocents would sow panic, give them publicity and help to destabilize the state and society. However, elsewhere terrorist operations have been quite selective. It can hardly be argued that President Sadat, the Pope, Aldo Moro or Indira Gandhi were arbitrary targets. Therefore, the argument that terrorist violence is by its nature random, and that innocence is the quintessential condition for the choice of victims, cannot be accepted as a general proposition; this would imply that there is a conscious selection process on the part of the terrorist, that they give immunity to the 'guilty' and choose only the innocents.[5]

Neither argument is convincing. To take the latter first, the way Laqueur presents it contains a contradiction: if it is claimed that terrorist violence is *random*, then it cannot also be claimed that it is directed *solely* against the innocent, while the guilty are given immunity. What *is* claimed is that the defining feature of terrorism, and the reason why many of us find it extremely morally repugnant, is its failure to discriminate between the innocent and the guilty, and its consequent failure to respect the immunity of the former and to concentrate exclusively on the latter. Terrorists do not take on the army or the police, nor do they attempt to kill a political official, but choose, say, to plant a bomb in a city bus, either because that is so much easier or, perhaps, because that will better serve their cause. They know that their victims are civilians, but that is no good reason for them not to do it. If a couple of soldiers get on the bus with the civilians and are killed as well, they will not see that as a fly in the ointment, but will either consider it irrelevant, or welcome it as an unexpected bonus. As for Laqueur's first argument, it is predicated either on a definition of terrorism that includes political assassination and is thus question-begging, or on the assumption that every act of a terrorist is a terrorist act, which is absurd. The Red Brigades, for instance, were a terrorist organization, for they committed many terrorist acts; but when they abducted and killed Aldo Moro, that was political assassination, not terrorism.

This targeting of the innocent is the essential trait of terrorism, both conceptually and morally. The distinction between guilt and innocence is one of the basic distinctions in the moral experience of most of us. Most of us require that the infliction of serious harm on someone be justified in terms of a free, deliberate action on their part. If this cannot be done, people are innocent in the relevant sense, and thus immune to the infliction of such harm. A paper on the definition of terrorism is not the right context for establishing this claim. But I would not be greatly tempted to try to prove it in any context. The belief that innocence implies a far-reaching (though perhaps not absolute) immunity against the infliction of severe harm is a brute fact of the moral experience of most of us. For those who find it compelling, it is as simple and compelling as anything, and certainly more so than anything that might be brought up as a supporting argument. Accordingly, as Walzer put it, 'the theoretical problem is not to describe how immunity is gained, but how it is lost. We are all immune to start with; our right not to be attacked is a feature of normal human relationships.'[6] One may lose this immunity by attacking someone else, or by enlisting in the army in time of war, or by joining the security services, or by holding office in a regime or an organization that is resisted by violence because of its unjust, or allegedly unjust, policies. But one who has done none of the above is innocent of anything that might plausibly be brought up as a justification for a violent attack on her, or a threat of such an attack, and is thus immune against it. When she is attacked nevertheless, with the aim of intimidating someone else and making them do something they otherwise would not do, that is terrorism. Terrorism is different, both conceptually and morally, from violence employed in self-defense, from war in general and guerrilla war in particular, and from political assassination.

The next three points are suggested by C.A.J. Coady's definition of a terrorist act as

> a political act, ordinarily committed by an organized group, which involves the intentional killing or other severe harming of non-combatants or the threat of the same or intentional severe damage to the property of non-combatants or the threat of the same.[7]

Violence against persons and against property

The violence perpetrated by terrorists is typically killing, maiming, or otherwise severely harming their victims. Must terrorist violence be directed against persons? According to Coady's definition, it need not. Suppose a terrorist organization decided to stop killing or maiming people and took to destroying valuable works of art instead. Or suppose it started destroying the crops that are the only source of livelihood of a village. Would that mean giving up terrorism for a non-terrorist struggle, or would it rather be substituting one terrorist method for another? In the latter case, I think, we would still speak of terrorism because the destruction of property would threaten people's lives. In the former case, however, the word 'terrorism' might no longer seem appropriate. As Jenny Teichman puts it, 'it may indeed be grossly unfair and unjust to destroy the property of non-combatants, but unless that property is needed for life itself it isn't terroristic. For one thing it is not likely to produce terror – only fury.'[8]

Terrorism and terror

While Wellman wants to preserve the connection between terrorism and terror, but to disconnect terrorism from violence, Coady's definition suggests the opposite: terrorism is a type of violence which, indeed, often causes terror, but this is 'an insight into the sociology of terrorism' and should not be included in the definition. The connection is merely contingent. After all, all uses of political violence effect some degree of fear.[9]

That is true, but I think there is an important difference between the sort of violence most of us would want to call terrorist and other kinds of violence, where the fear caused is either a less important objective, or not an objective at all, but merely a welcome byproduct. In terrorism proper, causing fear and coercion through fear are *the* objective. Even if the crucial role of coercion through fear is not important enough from a theoretical point of view to single out this particular type of violence, things look different from a moral point of view. Most of us feel that terrorism is so very wrong primarily, but not solely, because it is violence inflicted on the innocent; intimidation and coercion through intimidation are *additional* grounds for moral condemnation, an insult added to injury.

This should not be taken to suggest a simplistic, overly rationalistic picture of terrorism: a picture of the terrorist making a clearly specified threat to his primary target, who then rationally considers the matter and comes to the conclusion that it pays to comply. This picture may fit some cases of terrorism, but it certainly does not fit others. For terrorism very often aims at setting off long and complex social processes, involving much irrational behavior, that are meant to disorient the public and destabilize various social arrangements and institutions, if not social life in general.[10] However, intimidation plays a central role in such cases as well, while the ultimate aim of the terrorists is, again, to make those who constitute their primary target do things they would otherwise not do. Thus such cases do not call for a revision of the definition of terrorism as a type of coercion through intimidation.

Terrorism: political and non-political, state and anti-state

Terrorism is often defined in various overly restrictive ways. The identification of terrorism with political terrorism, as in the definition offered by Coady, is quite typical. But the method of coercive intimidation by infliction of violence on innocent persons has often been used in non-political contexts: one can speak of religious terrorism (e.g. that of Hizbullah) and criminal terrorism (e.g. that of the Mafia).

Even more restrictive are definitions couched in terms of *who* uses terrorism. Terrorism is often presented as a method employed solely by rebels and revolutionaries, and state terrorism is thus defined out of existence. This may be good propaganda, but it is poor analysis. The

word 'terrorism' was originally used to refer to the 'Reign of Terror
up by the Jacobins, i.e., to a particular case of *state* terrorism. And liberal
and democratic states too have engaged in terrorism: witness the bombing
of Dresden and Hamburg, Hiroshima and Nagasaki. In all these cases
the targets were neither military nor industrial, but rather major centers
of civilian population of enemy countries; the objective was to destroy
the morale and break the will of the population and in that way either
ensure victory (over Germany) or shorten the war (against Japan). This
kind of bombing has come to be known as 'terror bombing.' Furthermore,
there is a type of state, the totalitarian state, whose most fundamental
principle is permanent, institutionalized terrorism. For nothing less
than such terrorism, exercised by the omnipotent state and, in particular,
its secret police, in an utterly unpredictable manner, and embodied in
'the true central institution of totalitarian organizational power,' the
concentration camp (Hannah Arendt), would do as a means of an
attempt at total domination of society.[11]

Amoralism

A number of authors claim that terrorism is essentially amoral. Thus
Paul Wilkinson writes:

> What fundamentally distinguishes terrorism from other forms of
> organised violence is not simply its severity but its features of
> amorality and antinomianism. Terrorists either profess indifference to
> existing moral codes or else claim exemption from all such obligations.
> Political terror, if it is waged consciously and deliberately, is implicitly
> prepared to sacrifice all moral and humanitarian considerations for
> the sake of some political end.[12]

To be sure, many terrorists seem to be oblivious to the moral aspects of
their actions. Some terrorists or fellow-travelers even flaunt their amor-
alism, as did the nineteenth-century anarchist writer Laurent Tailhade
when he said: 'What do the victims matter if the gesture is beautiful!'
But such attitudes are by no means universal; terrorism of the left, at
least, can claim a rich apologetic tradition. Views on terrorism
advanced in the writings of Mikhail Bakunin, Sergei Nechaev, Leon
Trotsky, and Herbert Marcuse, were developed in response to moral
criticism; they are couched in moral terms, and exhibit the formal traits
widely considered to be definitive of moral views: they are action-guiding,
universalizable, and of overriding importance to those who hold them.

These authors do not reject morality as such, but rather conventional morality; and in the same breath they proclaim 'the interest of the Revolution' to be the supreme *moral* law. Their views may not amount to a convincing moral position (I for one am not convinced), but they do amount to *a* moral position. To think otherwise is to confuse one's own moral outlook with the moral point of view as such.[13]

Summing up

The preceding remarks lead up to the following definition of terrorism: the deliberate use of violence, or threat of its use, against innocent people, with the aim of intimidating some other people into a course of action they otherwise would not take.

Let me summarize the most important points about this definition:

1. Terrorism has a certain structure. It has two targets: the primary and secondary. The latter target is directly hit, but the objective is to get at the former, to intimidate the person or persons who are the primary target into doing things they otherwise would not do.
2. The secondary target, which is hit directly, are innocent people. Thus terrorism is distinguished both from war in general, and guerrilla war in particular, in which the innocent (non-combatants, civilians) are not deliberately attacked, and from political assassination, whose victims – political officials and police officers – are responsible for certain policies and their enforcement. This, of course, does not mean that an army cannot engage in terrorism; many armies have done so. Nor does it mean that political assassination does not often intimidate the government or the public, or is not often meant to do so.
3. The connection of 'terrorism' with 'terror' and 'terrorizing' is preserved.
4. The definition covers both political and non-political (e.g. religious or criminal) terrorism.
5. With regard to political terrorism, it makes it possible to speak both of state and non-state terrorism, of revolutionary and counter-revolutionary terrorism, of terrorism of the left and of the right. The definition is politically neutral.
6. It is also morally neutral. I believe it captures what many of us find so repugnant in terrorism: the use or threat of use of *violence* against the *innocent* for the sake of *intimidation* and *coercion*. But is does not prejudge the moral question of its justification in particular cases. For in entails only that terrorism is *prima facie* wrong, and thus does not rule out its justification under certain circumstances.

7. Some are likely to find the definition too restrictive, and to want to apply the word to other sorts of violence. It may well be that, as a matter of fact, the word is used in a wider sense most of the time. But I trust it will be generally (although not universally) agreed that the actions covered by the definition are indeed terroristic. I suspect that most of those likely to deny this will want to define terrorism in terms of who employs it and to what ultimate purpose. If so, I am not worried. Those who claim that who is a terrorist, and who a freedom fighter, depends on who is wearing the uniform, or what its color is, are not promising partners for a serious discussion anyway.

8. By highlighting the innocence of the victims of terrorism, the definition helps place the debate about the morality of terrorism in the context of the traditional discussion of the morality of war, and in particular connects it with just war theory. The main provision of that theory under the heading of *jus in bello*, the morality of ways and means of fighting in war, is the principle of discrimination, enjoining belligerents to discriminate between military and civilian targets and to refrain from harming innocent civilians.

One final remark: the definition of terrorism I have suggested is accurate and helpful with regard to the actions, policies and organizations in the twentieth and twenty-first centuries which most of us would want to describe as terrorist. Large-scale terrorism in the sense defined is very much a phenomenon of our time. To be sure, the targeting of the innocent as a means of coercive intimidation was occasionally advocated and practiced in the nineteenth century as well: advocated, for instance, by the radical democrat Karl Heinzen,[14] practiced in particular in the last decades of that century by some Irish nationalists and some of the anarchists who believed in 'propaganda by deed.' But most of those who were called, and often called themselves, terrorists, throughout the nineteenth century – most anarchists, various revolutionary groups in Russia – did not practice terrorism in this sense, but rather engaged in political assassination. Russian revolutionaries in particular were given to constant probing of the moral questions raised by their struggle. They accepted the use of violence only unwillingly, and generally insisted that it be employed sparingly; in the words of P.L. Lavrov, 'not one drop of unnecessary blood shall be spilled.' They considered assassination of some of the most prominent officials of the oppressive regime as a grave sin that must be committed, but must also be expiated by dying on the gallows. They would never contemplate deliberate killing and maiming of the innocent. If a planned assassination turned out to involve deaths of innocent people as an inevitable side-effect, they called off the action, even if that meant taking an extreme risk to themselves.[15] The moral distance between them and present-day terrorists is immense. Accordingly, I think it would be helpful to restrict the word 'terrorist' to the latter, rather than apply it to both and then distinguish between them in some such terms as 'direct' and 'indirect' or 'individual' and 'mass' terrorism.[16]

This shift away from assassination of chiefs of state and other high political officials to indiscriminate attacks on the innocent, which took place at the beginning of the twentieth century, can be explained in more than one way. Laqueur points out that 'in the twentieth century, human life became cheaper; the belief gained ground that the end justified all means, and that humanity was a bourgeois prejudice.'[17] Edward Hyams offers a different explanation: 'chiefs of state are more carefully guarded than they used to be, and revolutionaries have learnt that the elimination of individual leaders is apt to resemble driving out Satan with Beelzebub.'[18] There may be still other causes; but I will not go into this question; it is one that can be answered only by empirical research. I am mentioning this change only in order to emphasize the limited applicability of the definition of terrorism I have suggested.[19]

Notes

1. Cf. Walter Laqueur, *The Age of Terrorism* (Boston: Little, Brown & Co., 1987), pp. 21, 127.
2. C. Wellman, 'On Terrorism Itself,' *Journal of Value Inquiry* 13 (1979), p. 250.
3. Ibid., p. 251.
4. Ibid., p. 252.
5. Laqueur, *The Age of Terrorism*, pp. 143–4.
6. Michael Walzer, *Just and Unjust Wars*, third edition (New York: Basic Books, 2000), p. 145 n.
7. C.A.J. Coady, 'The Morality of Terrorism,' *Philosophy* 60 (1985), p. 52.
8. J. Teichman, *Pacifism and the Just War* (Oxford: Blackwell, 1986), p. 92.
9. Coady, 'The Morality of Terrorism,' p. 53.
10. See e.g. T.P. Thornton, 'Terror as a Weapon of Political Agitation,' in H. Eckstein (ed.), *Internal War* (New York: The Free Press, 1964).
11. See Hannah Arendt, *The Origins of Totalitarianism*, second edition (Cleveland: The World Publication Co., 1958), chapters 12–13. For more on state terrorism, see chapters 9 and 10 in this volume.
12. P. Wilkinson, *Political Terrorism* (London: Macmillan, 1974), pp. 16–17.
13. I have discussed this point in 'On the Ethics of Terrorism,' in E. Attwooll (ed.), *Shaping Revolutions* (Aberdeen: Aberdeen University Press, 1991).
14. See his essay 'Murder,' in Walter Laqueur (ed.), *The Terrorism Reader* (New York: New American Library, 1978).

15. See Z. Ivianski, 'The Moral Issue: Some Aspects of Individual Terror,' in D.C. Rapoport and Y. Alexander (eds.), *The Morality of Terrorism*, second edition (New York: Columbia University Press, 1989).
16. The first distinction is advanced e.g. by E. Hyams, *Terrorists and Terrorism* (New York: St. Martin's Press, 1974), pp. 9–11. The second is usually made in Marxist literature.
17. Laqueur, *The Age of Terrorism*, p. 84.
18. Hyams, *Terrorists and Terrorism*, p. 166.
19. Thanks to David George and Walter Sinnott-Armstrong for comments on earlier drafts of this chapter.

Part II
Justifications

3
A Defense of the 'Red Terror'

Leon Trotsky

The chief theme of Kautsky's book[1] is terrorism. The view that terrorism is of the essence of revolution Kautsky proclaims to be a widespread delusion. It is untrue that he who desires revolution must put up with terrorism. As far as he, Kautsky, is concerned, he is, generally speaking, for revolution, but decidedly against terrorism. From there, however, complications begin.

'The revolution brings us,' Kautsky complains, 'a bloody terrorism carried out by Socialist governments. The Bolsheviks in Russia first stepped on to this path, and were, consequently, sternly condemned by all Socialists who had not adopted the Bolshevik point of view, including the Socialists of the German Majority. But as soon as the latter found themselves threatened in their supremacy, they had recourse to the methods of the same terrorist regime which they attacked in the East' (p. 9). It would seem that from this follows the conclusion that terrorism is much more profoundly bound up with the nature of revolution than certain sages think. But Kautsky makes an absolutely opposite conclusion. The gigantic development of White and Red terrorism in all the last revolutions – the Russian, the German, the Austrian, and the Hungarian – is evidence to him that these revolutions turned aside from their true path and turned out to be not the revolution they ought to have been according to the theoretical visions of Kautsky. Without going into the question whether terrorism 'as such' is 'immanent' to the revolution 'as such,' let us consider a few of the revolutions as they pass before us in the living history of mankind.

The chapter 'Terrorism' (abridged) in Leon Trotsky, *Terrorism and Communism: A Reply to Karl Kautsky* (Ann Arbor, Mich.: The University of Michigan Press, 1961), pp. 48–59, 62–5. Reproduced by permission.

Let us first regard the religious Reformation, which proved the watershed between the Middle Ages and modern history: the deeper were the interests of the masses that it involved, the wider was its sweep, the more fiercely did the civil war develop under the religious banner, and the more merciless did the terror become on the other side.

In the seventeenth century England carried out two revolutions. The first, which brought forth great social upheavals and wars, brought amongst other things the execution of King Charles I, while the second ended happily with the accession of a new dynasty. The British bourgeoisie and its historians maintain quite different attitudes to these two revolutions: the first is for them a rising of the mob – the 'Great Rebellion'; the second has been handed down under the title of the 'Glorious Revolution.' The reason for this difference in estimates was explained by the French historian, Augustin Thierry. In the first English revolution, in the 'Great Rebellion,' the active force was the people; while in the second it was almost 'silent.' Hence, it follows that, in surroundings of class slavery, it is difficult to teach the oppressed masses good manners. When provoked to fury they use clubs, stones, fire, and the rope. The court historians of the exploiters are offended at this. But the great event in modern 'bourgeois' history is, none the less, not the 'Glorious Revolution,' but the 'Great Rebellion.'

The greatest event in modern history after the Reformation and the 'Great Rebellion,' and far surpassing its two predecessors in significance, was the great French Revolution of the eighteenth century. To this classical revolution there was a corresponding classical terrorism. Kautsky is ready to forgive the terrorism of the Jacobins, acknowledging that they had no other way of saving the republic. But by this justification after the event no one is either helped or hindered. The Kautskies of the end of the eighteenth century (the leaders of the French Girondists) saw in the Jacobins the personification of evil. Here is a comparison, sufficiently instructive in its banality, between the Jacobins and the Girondists from the pen of one of the bourgeois French historians: 'Both one side and the other desired the republic.' But the Girondists 'desired a free, legal, and merciful republic. The Montagnards desired a despotic and terrorist republic. Both stood for the supreme power of the people; but the Gironridist justly understood all by the people, while the Montagnards considered only the working class to be the people. That was why only to such persons, in the opinion of the Montagnards, did the supremacy belong.' The antithesis between the noble champions of the Constituent Assembly and the bloodthirsty agents of the revolutionary dictatorship is here outlined fairly clearly, although in the political terms of the epoch.

The iron dictatorship of the Jacobins was evoked by the monstrously difficult position of revolutionary France. Here is what the bourgeois historian says of this period: 'Foreign troops had entered French territory from four sides. In the north, the British and the Austrians, in Alsace, the Prussians, in Dauphine and up to Lyons, the Piedmontese, in Roussillon the Spaniards. And this at a time when civil war was raging at four different points: in Normandy, in the Vendée, at Lyons, and at Toulon' (p. 176). To this we must add internal enemies in the form of numerous secret supporters of the old regime, ready by all methods to assist the enemy.

The severity of the proletarian dictatorship in Russia, let us point out here, was conditioned by no less difficult circumstances. There was one continuous front, on the north and south, in the east and west. Besides the Russian White Guard armies of Kolchak, Denikin and others, there are attacking Soviet Russia, simultaneously or in turn: Germans, Austrians, Czecho-Slovaks, Serbs, Poles, Ukrainians, Romanians, French, British, Americans, Japanese, Finns, Estonians, Lithuanians...In a country throttled by a blockade and strangled by hunger, there are conspiracies, risings, terrorist acts, and destruction of roads and bridges.

'The government which had taken on itself the struggle with countless external and internal enemies had neither money, nor sufficient troops, nor anything except boundless energy, enthusiastic support on the part of the revolutionary elements of the country, and the gigantic courage to take all measures necessary for the safety of the country, however arbitrary and severe they were.' In such words did once upon a time Plekhanov describe the government of the – Jacobins. (*Sozial-demokrat*, a quarterly review of literature and politics. Book I, February, 1890, London. The article on 'The Centenary of the Great Revolution,' pp. 6–7).

Let us now turn to the revolution which took place in the second half of the nineteenth century, in the country of 'democracy' – in the United States of North America. Although the question was not the abolition of property altogether, but only of the abolition of property in Negroes, nevertheless, the institutions of democracy proved absolutely powerless to decide the argument in a peaceful way. The southern states, defeated at the presidential elections in 1860, decided by all possible means to regain the influence they had hitherto exerted in the question of slave-owning; and uttering, as was right, the proper sounding words about freedom and independence, rose in a slave-owners' insurrection. Hence inevitably followed all the later consequences of civil war. At the very beginning of the struggle, the military government in Baltimore imprisoned in Fort MacHenry a few citizens, sympathizers with the slave-holding South, in spite of Habeas Corpus. The question of the lawfulness or the unlawfulness of such action became the object of fierce disputes between so-called 'high authorities.' The judges of the Supreme Court decided that the President had neither the right to arrest the operation of Habeas Corpus nor to give plenipotentiary powers to that end to the military authorities. 'Such, in all probability, is the correct Constitutional solution of the question,' says one of the first historians of the American Civil War. 'But the state of affairs was to such a degree critical, and the necessity of taking decisive measures against the population of Baltimore so great, that not only the Government but the people of the United States also supported the most energetic measures.'[2]

Some goods that the rebellious South required were secretly supplied by the merchants of the North. Naturally, the Northerners had no other course but to introduce methods of repression. On August 6, 1861, the President confirmed a resolution of Congress as to 'the confiscation of property used for insurrectionary purposes.' The people, in the shape of the most democratic elements, were in favor of extreme measures. The Republican Party had a decided majority in the North, and persons suspected of secessionism, i.e., of sympathizing with the rebellious Southern states, were subjected to violence. In some northern towns, and even in the states of New England, famous for their order, the people frequently burst into the offices of newspapers which supported the revolting slave-owners and smashed their printing presses. It occasionally happened that reactionary publishers were smeared with tar, decorated with feathers, and carried in such array through the public squares until they swore an oath of loyalty to the Union. The personality of a planter smeared in tar bore little resemblance to the 'end-in-itself'; so that the categorical imperative of Kautsky suffered in the civil war of the states a considerable blow. But this is not all. 'The government, on its part,' the historian tells us, 'adopted repressive measures of various kinds against publications holding views opposed to its own; and in a short time the hitherto free American press was reduced to a condition *scarcely superior to that prevailing in the autocratic European States.*' The same fate overtook the freedom of speech. 'In this way,' Lieut.-Colonel Fletcher continues, 'the American people at this time denied itself the greater part of its freedom. It should be observed,' he moralizes, 'that *the majority of the people* was to such an extent occupied with the war, and to such a degree imbued with the readiness for any kind of sacrifice to attain its end, that it not only did not regret its vanished liberties, but scarcely even noticed their disappearance.'[3]

Infinitely more ruthlessly did the bloodthirsty slave-owners of the South employ their uncontrollable hordes. 'Wherever there was a majority in favor of slavery,' writes the Count of Paris, 'public opinion behaved despotically to the minority. All who expressed pity for the national banner...were forced to be silent. But soon this itself became insufficient; as in all revolutions, the indifferent were forced to express their loyalty to the new order of things...Those who did not agree to this were given up as a sacrifice to the hatred and violence of the mass of the people...In each centre of growing civilization (South-Western states) vigilance committees were formed, composed of all those who had been distinguished by their extreme views in the electoral struggle...A tavern was the usual place of their sessions, and a noisy orgy was mingled with a contemptible parody of public forms of justice. A few madmen sitting around a desk on which gin and whisky flowed judged their present and absent fellow-citizens. The accused, even before having been questioned, could see the rope being prepared. He who did not appear at the court learned his sentence when falling under the bullets of the executioner concealed in the forest...' This picture is extremely reminiscent of the scenes which day by day took place in the camps of Denikin, Kolchak, Yudenich, and the other heroes of Anglo-Franco-American 'democracy.'

We shall see later how the question of terrorism stood in regard to the Paris Commune of 1871. In any case, the attempts of Kautsky to contrast the Commune with us are false at their very root, and only bring the author to a juggling with words of the most petty character.

The institution of hostages apparently must be recognized as 'immanent' in the terrorism of the civil war. Kautsky is against terrorism and against the institution of hostages, but in favor of the Paris Commune. (N.B. The Commune existed fifty years ago.) Yet the Commune took hostages. A difficulty arises. But what does the art of exegesis exist for?

The decree of the Commune concerning hostages and their execution in reply to the atrocities of the Versaillese arose, according to the profound explanation of Kautsky, 'from a striving to preserve human life, not to destroy it.' A marvelous discovery! It only requires to be developed. It could, and must, be explained that in the civil war we destroyed White Guards in order that they should not destroy the workers. Consequently, our problem is not the destruction of human life, but its preservation. But as we have to struggle for the preservation of human life with arms in our hands, it leads to the destruction of human life – a puzzle the dialectical secret of which was explained by old Hegel, without reckoning other still more ancient sages.

The Commune could maintain itself and consolidate its position only by a determined struggle with the Versaillese. The latter, on the other hand, had a large number of agents in Paris. Fighting with the agents of Thiers, the Commune could not abstain from destroying the Versaillese at the front and in the rear. If its rule had crossed the bounds of Paris, in the provinces it would have found – during the process of the civil war with the Army of the National Assembly – still more determined foes in the midst of the peaceful population. The Commune when fighting the royalists could not allow freedom of speech to royalist agents in the rear.

Kautsky, in spite of all the happenings in the world to-day, completely fails to realize what war is in general, and the civil war in particular. He does not understand that every, or nearly every, sympathizer with Thiers in Paris was not merely an 'opponent' of the Communards in ideas, but an agent and spy of Thiers, a ferocious enemy ready to shoot one in the back. The enemy must be made harmless, and in wartime this means that he must be destroyed.

The problem of revolution, as of war, consists in breaking the will of the foe, forcing him to capitulate and to accept the conditions of the conqueror. The will, of course, is a fact of the psychical world, but in contradistinction to a meeting, a dispute, or a congress, the revolution carries out its object by means of the employment of material resources – though to a less degree than war. The bourgeoisie itself conquered power by means of revolts, and consolidated it by the civil war. In the peaceful period, it retains power by means of a system of repression. As long as class society, founded on the most deep-rooted antagonisms, continues to exist, repression remains a necessary means of breaking the will of the opposing side.

Even if, in one country or another, the dictatorship of the proletariat grew up within the external framework of democracy, this would by no means avert the civil war. The question as to who is to rule the country, *i.e.*, of the life or death of the bourgeoisie, will be decided on either side, not by references to the paragraphs of the constitution, but by the employment of all forms of violence. However deeply Kautsky goes into the question of the food of the anthropopithecus (see pp. 122 et seq. of his book) and other immediate and remote conditions which determine the cause of human cruelty, he will find in history no other way of breaking the class will of the enemy except the systematic and energetic use of violence.

The degree of ferocity of the struggle depends on a series of internal and international circumstances. The more ferocious and dangerous is the resistance of the class enemy who has been overthrown, the more inevitably does the system of repression take the form of a system of terror.

But here Kautsky unexpectedly takes up a new position in his struggle with Soviet terrorism. He simply waves aside all reference to the ferocity of the counter-revolutionary opposition of the Russian bourgeoisie.

'Such ferocity,' he says, 'could not be noticed in November, 1917, in Petrograd and Moscow, and still less more recently in Budapest' (p. 149). With such a happy formulation of the question, revolutionary terrorism merely proves to be a product of the bloodthirstiness of the Bolsheviks, who simultaneously abandoned the traditions of the vegetarian anthropopithecus and the moral lessons of Kautsky.

The first conquest of power by the Soviets at the beginning of November 1917 (new style), was actually accomplished with insignificant sacrifices. The Russian bourgeoisie found itself to such a degree estranged from the masses of the people, so internally helpless, so compromised by the course and the result of the war, so demoralized by the regime of Kerensky, that it scarcely dared show any resistance. In Petrograd the power of Kerensky was overthrown almost without a fight. In Moscow its resistance was dragged out, mainly owing to the indecisive character of our own actions. In the majority of the provincial towns, power was transferred to the Soviet on the mere receipt of a telegram from Petrograd or Moscow. If the matter had ended there, there would have been no word of the Red Terror. But in November 1917, there was already evidence of the beginning of the resistance of the propertied classes. True, there was required the intervention of the imperialist governments of the West in order to give the Russian counter-revolution faith in itself, and to add ever-increasing power to its resistance. This can be shown from facts, both important and insignificant, day by day during the whole epoch of the Soviet revolution.

Kerensky's 'Staff' felt no support forthcoming from the mass of the soldiery, and was inclined to recognize the Soviet Government, which had begun negotiations for an armistice with the Germans. But there followed the protest of the military missions of the Entente, followed by open threats. The Staff was frightened; incited by 'Allied' officers, it entered the path of opposition. This led to armed conflict and to the murder of the chief of the field staff, General Dukhonin, by a group of revolutionary sailors.

In Petrograd, the official agents of the Entente, especially the French Military Mission, hand in hand with the Socialist Revolutionaries and the Mensheviks, openly organized the opposition, mobilizing, arming, inciting against us the cadets, and the bourgeois youth generally, from the second day of the Soviet revolution. The rising of the Junkers on November 10 brought about a hundred times more victims than the revolution of November 7. The campaign of the adventurers Kerensky and Krasnov against Petrograd, organized at the same time by the Entente, naturally introduced into the struggle the first elements of savagery. Nevertheless, General Krasnov was set free on his word of honor. The Yaroslav rising (in the summer of 1918) which involved so many victims, was organized by Savinkov on the instructions of the French Embassy, and with its resources. Archangel was captured according to the plans of British naval agents, with the help of British warships and airplanes. The beginning of the empire of Kolchak, the nominee of the American Stock Exchange, was brought about by the foreign Czecho-Slovak Corps maintained by the resources of the French Government. Kaledin and Krasnov (liberated by us), the first leaders of the counter-revolution on the Don, could enjoy partial success only thanks to the open military and financial aid of Germany. In the Ukraine the Soviet power was overthrown in the beginning of 1918 by German militarism. The Volunteer Army of Denikin was created with the financial and technical help of Great Britain and France. Only in the hope of British intervention and of British military support was Yudenich's army created. The politicians, the diplomats, and the journalists of the Entente have for two years on end been debating with complete frankness the question of whether the financing of the civil war in Russia is a sufficiently profitable enterprise. In such circumstances, one needs truly a brazen forehead to seek the reason for the sanguinary character of the civil war in Russia in the malevolence of the Bolsheviks, and not in the international situation.

The Russian proletariat was the first to enter the path of the social revolution, and the Russian bourgeoisie, politically helpless, was emboldened to struggle against its political and economic expropriation only because it saw its elder sister in all countries still in power, and still maintaining economic, political, and, to a certain extent, military supremacy.

If our November revolution had taken place a few months, or even a few weeks, after the establishment of the rule of the proletariat in Germany, France, and England, there can be no doubt that our revolution would have been the most 'peaceful,' the most 'bloodless' of all possible revolutions on this sinful earth. But this historical sequence – the most 'natural' at the first glance, and, in any case, the most beneficial for the Russian working class – found itself infringed – not through our fault, but through the will of events. Instead of being the last, the Russian proletariat proved to be the first. It was just this circumstance, after the first period of confusion, that imparted desperation to the character of the resistance of the classes which had ruled in Russia previously, and forced the Russian proletariat, in a moment of the greatest peril, foreign attacks, and internal plots and insurrections, to have recourse to severe measures of state terror. No one will now say that those measures proved futile. But, perhaps, we are expected to consider them 'intolerable'?

The working class, which seized power in battle, had as its object and its duty to establish that power unshakably, to guarantee its own supremacy beyond question, to destroy its enemies' hankering for a new revolution, and thereby to make sure of carrying out Socialist reforms. Otherwise there would be no point in seizing power.

The revolution 'logically' does not demand terrorism, just as 'logically' it does not demand an armed insurrection. What a profound commonplace! But the revolution does require of the revolutionary class that it should attain its end by all methods at its disposal – if necessary, by an armed rising; if required, by terrorism. A revolutionary class which has conquered power with arms in its hands is bound to, and will, suppress, rifle in hand, all attempts to tear the power out of its hands. Where it has against it a hostile army, it will oppose to it its own army. Where it is confronted with armed conspiracy, attempt at murder, or rising, it will hurl at the heads of its enemies an unsparing penalty. Perhaps Kautsky has invented other methods? Or does he reduce the whole question to the *degree* of repression, and recommend in all circumstances imprisonment instead of execution?

The question of the form of repression, or of its degree, of course, is not one of 'principle.' It is a question of expediency. In a revolutionary period, the party which has been thrown from power, which does not reconcile itself with the stability of the ruling class, and which proves this by its desperate struggle against the latter, cannot be terrorized by the threat of imprisonment, as it does not believe in its duration. It is just this simple but decisive fact that explains the widespread recourse to shooting in a civil war.

Or, perhaps, Kautsky wishes to say that execution is not expedient, that 'classes cannot be cowed.' This is untrue. Terror is helpless – and then only 'in the long run' – if it is employed by reaction against a historically rising class. But terror can be very efficient against a reactionary class which does not want to leave the scene of operations. *Intimidation* is a powerful weapon of policy, both internationally and internally. War, like revolution, is founded upon intimidation. A victorious war, generally speaking, destroys only an insignificant part of the conquered army, intimidating the remainder and breaking their will. The revolution works in the same way: it kills individuals, and intimidates thousands. In this sense, the Red Terror is not distinguishable from the armed insurrection, the direct continuation of which it represents. The state terror of a revolutionary class can be condemned 'morally' only by a man who, as a principle, rejects (in words) every form of violence whatsoever – consequently, every war and every rising. For this one has to be merely and simply a hypocritical Quaker.

'But, in that case, in what do your tactics differ from the tactics of Tsarism?' we are asked, by the high priests of Liberalism and Kautskianism.

You do not understand this, holy men? We shall explain to you. The terror of Tsarism was directed against the proletariat. The gendarmerie of Tsarism throttled the workers who were fighting for the Socialist order. Our Extraordinary Commissions shoot landlords, capitalists, and generals who are striving to restore the capitalist order. Do you grasp this... distinction? Yes? For us Communists it is quite sufficient.

* * *

Kautsky, of course, is ready to 'condemn' – an extra drop of ink – the blockade, and the Entente support of Denikin, and the White Terror. But in his high impartiality he cannot refuse the latter certain extenuating circumstances. The White Terror, you see, does not infringe their own principles, while the Bolsheviks, making use of the Red Terror, betray the principle of 'the sacredness of human life which they themselves proclaimed' (p. 210).

What is the meaning of the principle of the sacredness of human life in practice, and in what does it differ from the commandment, 'Thou shalt not kill,' Kautsky does not explain. When a murderer raises his knife over a child, may one kill the murderer to save the child? Will not thereby the principle of the 'sacredness of human life' be infringed? May one kill the murderer to save oneself? Is an insurrection of oppressed slaves against their masters permissible? Is it permissible to purchase one's freedom at the cost of the life of one's jailers? If human life in general is sacred and inviolable, we must deny ourselves not only the use of terror, not only war, but also revolution itself. Kautsky simply does not realize the counter-revolutionary meaning of the 'principle' which he attempts to force upon us. Elsewhere we shall see that Kautsky accuses us of concluding the Brest-Litovsk peace: in his opinion we ought to have continued war. But what then becomes of the sacredness of human life? Does life cease to be sacred when it is a question of people talking another language, or does Kautsky consider that mass murders organized on principles of strategy and tactics are not murders at all? Truly it is difficult to put forward in our age a principle more hypocritical and more stupid. As long as human labor power, and, consequently, life itself, remain articles of sale and purchase, of exploitation and robbery, the principle of the 'sacredness of human life' remains a shameful lie, uttered with the object of keeping the oppressed slaves in their chains.

We used to fight against the death penalty introduced by Kerensky, because that penalty was inflicted by the courts-martial of the old army on soldiers who refused to continue the imperialist war. We tore this weapon out of the hands of the old courts-martial, destroyed the courts-martial themselves, and demobilized the old army which had brought them forth. Destroying in the Red Army, and generally throughout the country, counter-revolutionary conspirators who strive by means of insurrections, murders, and disorganization, to restore the old regime, we are acting in accordance with the iron laws of a war in which we desire to guarantee our victory.

If it is a question of seeking formal contradictions, then obviously we must do so on the side of the White Terror, which is the weapon of classes which consider themselves 'Christian,' patronize idealist philosophy, and are firmly convinced that the individuality (their own) is an end-in-itself. As for us, we were never concerned with the Kantian-priestly and vegetarian-Quaker prattle about the 'sacredness of human life.' We were revolutionaries in opposition, and have remained revolutionaries in power. To make the individual sacred we must destroy the social order which crucifies him. And this problem can only be solved by blood and iron.

There is another difference between the White Terror and the Red, which Kautsky today ignores, but which in the eyes of a Marxist is of decisive significance. The White Terror is the weapon of the historically reactionary class. When we exposed the futility of the repressions of the bourgeois state against the proletariat, we never denied that by arrests and executions the ruling class, under certain conditions, might temporarily retard the development of the social revolution. But we were convinced that they would not be able to bring it to a halt. We relied on the fact that the proletariat is the historically rising class, and that bourgeois society could not develop without increasing the forces of the proletariat. The bourgeoisie today is a falling class. It not only no longer plays an essential part in production, but by its imperialist methods of appropriation is destroying the economic structure of the world and human culture generally. Nevertheless, the historical persistence of the bourgeoisie is colossal. It holds to power, and does not wish to abandon it. Thereby it threatens to drag after it into the abyss the whole of society. We are forced to tear it off, to chop it away. The Red Terror is a weapon utilized against a class, doomed to destruction, which does not wish to perish. If the White Terror can only retard the historical rise of the proletariat, the Red Terror hastens the destruction of the bourgeoisie. This hastening – a pure question of acceleration – is at certain periods of decisive importance. Without the Red Terror, the Russian bourgeoisie, together with the world bourgeoisie, would throttle us long before the coming of the revolution in Europe. One must be blind not to see this, or a swindler to deny it.

The man who recognizes the revolutionary historic importance of the very fact of the existence of the Soviet system must also sanction the Red Terror. Kautsky, who, during the last two years, has covered mountains of paper with polemics against Communism and Terrorism, is obliged, at the end of his pamphlet, to recognize the facts, and unexpectedly to admit that the Russian Soviet Government is today the most important factor in the world revolution. 'However one regards the Bolshevik methods,' he writes, 'the fact that a proletarian government in a large country has not only reached power, but has retained it for two years up to the present time, amidst great difficulties, extraordinarily increases the sense of power amongst the proletariat of all countries. For the actual revolution the Bolsheviks have thereby accomplished a great work – *grosses geleistet'* (p. 233).

This announcement stuns us as a completely unexpected recognition of historical truth from a quarter whence we had long since ceased to await it. The Bolsheviks have accomplished a great historical task by existing for two years against the united capitalist world. But the Bolsheviks held out not only by ideas, but by the sword. Kautsky's admission is an involuntary sanctioning of the methods of the Red Terror, and at the same time the most effective condemnation of his own critical concoction.

Notes

1. Karl Kautsky, *Terrorismus und Kommunismus. Ein Beitrag zur Naturgeschichte der Revolution* (Berlin: Verlag Neues Vaterland, 1919). There is also an English translation: *Terrorism and Communism: A Contribution to the Natural History of Revolution*, trans. by W.H. Kerridge (London: The National Labour Press, 1920, and a reprint edition of that translation by Hyperion Press, Westport, Conn., 1973 [*editor*]).
2. *The History of the American War*, by Fletcher, Lieut.-Colonel in the Scots Guards, St. Petersburg, 1867, p. 95.
3. Ibid., pp. 162–4.

4
The Burdens of Terrorism
Nick Fotion

I

When we first come to think about terrorism, we might suppose that moralists would simply condemn the practice. If we think of terrorism as a policy of coercive intimidation designed to achieve some political end,[1] we might also suppose that moralists who cannot show that such a policy is almost always wrong are not much good for anything. It is not as if in condemning terrorism they were being asked to make close moral calls, as when in baseball the runner and the ball arrive at first base within a fraction of a second of one another. Condemning terrorism, it would seem to the ethical novitiate, is more like calling a runner out when he is still half way to first base while the ball has already nestled in the first baseman's glove.

It is disturbing, therefore, to read an account of terrorism and violence which says, 'Victimizing people is always at least prima facie wrong, indeed it is terribly wrong,' which also urges a careful consideration of all moral options including terrorism, but which, none the less, seems to open the door wider to terrorism and violence than these cautionary thoughts suggest it would.[2] It is also disturbing when this account is both biased in the direction of a particular political ideology and implies that terrorism is acceptable if it is successful.[3]

To be sure, I too will argue that victimizing people is always a *prima facie* wrong, and that one ought to look at all the options in dealing

---

An earlier version of this chapter was published as: Nicholas Fotion, 'The Burdens of Terrorism,' in Burton M. Leiser (ed.), *Values in Conflict* (New York: Macmillan, 1981), pp. 463–70. © Nicholas Fotion, 1981.

with any moral issue. None the less, I will argue that the beginner in ethical theory is nearer the mark in condemning terrorism than are some sophisticated moralists who, in the end, permit more terrorism than they should. I will hedge a bit myself by permitting some forms of terrorism. It may be, for example, that certain forms are justified in dealing with an enemy in war who is engaged in terrorism. Further, there are many forms and degrees of terrorism, and it would be foolish, in a *carte blanche* fashion, to condemn them all for all possible settings. None the less, if there are exceptions so that some forms of terrorism are justifiable, they will be extremely rare.

I will back my contention by focusing attention initially upon the recipients of the terrorists' activities rather than upon the terrorists. These recipients can be divided into those who are the direct victims of an attack and those who are terrorized because of what has happened to the victims. Of these two, I will deal with the former first.

Terrorists do not have to have victims in order to do their work. It is possible for them to terrorize a population, a class of people, a military establishment, or a government simply by displaying their power in a threatening way. One can, for example, imagine a situation in which terrorists threaten to use an atomic weapon that everyone knows they have in their possession. However, in the vast majority of the cases familiar to us, some individuals will be victimized so as to make it clear that the terrorists mean to be taken seriously.

The victims of terrorism may not be, although they are often, terrorized in (and/or following) the process of being victimized. Yet, they must be hurt in some way if they are to have the status of victims. The victims can be robbed, tortured, raped, starved, killed, or abused in any number of other ways. They may also not be 'innocent' (e.g., are in the military) or they may carry some guilt (i.e., have done something wrong). In either case, we now are tempted to hedge a bit by saying something like, 'Of course, terrorism is wrong – however, in cases like these we can see why terrorism might be acceptable.' To be sure, there seems to be nothing morally wrong with a policy of terrorism aimed at members of a military establishment provided that policy is not carried out by immoral means (e.g., by raping or torturing military personnel). However, terrorism even aimed at allegedly guilty civilians should still disturb us if for no other reason than that the victims should have been treated as if they were innocent until proven guilty. After all, in killing allegedly guilty persons, terrorists are in effect imposing the death penalty without offering their victims due process of law.

Although terrorism is bad enough when the victims chosen deserve (in some sense) the treatment they receive, it cannot help but be seen in a worse light when the victims are innocent. There are, of course, degrees of innocence and guilt; but terrorists who choose their victims in a random or near-random fashion cannot help but victimize many people who are innocent of all political or other wrongdoing. Think of a child, an uneducated peasant, a housewife, a fireman, a white-collar worker, and even a person who shares the political views of the terrorists (but is against the tactics of terrorism) who may be randomly killed, maimed, or assaulted. Each is literally treated as an object to be used – we might even say used up – to further the terrorists' ends.

In fact, in being treated as an object, innocent victims are worse off than (alleged) guilty victims. In so far as the latter are judged to have done a wrong, they are thought of as human agents. After all, it is humans, not dogs and cats, who make political errors and commit moral wrongs. For terrorists, innocent victims need not be thought of as human in this judgmental sense, or human in the sense of simply having value *as* human beings. Of course terrorists need to pick human beings as victims. But they do this because choosing human victims brings about more terror than choosing dogs or cats, or inanimate objects, for destruction. But this does not so much involve treating them *as* humans. Rather they are victimized and thereby treated as objects *because* they are humans.

No doubt terrorists could reply to these accusations by saying that they regret all the death and suffering they are causing; and in so far as they do, they show at least some respect for their human victims. Further, they might contend that they do not consider their victims to be nothing but objects. Rather, they find it necessary to sacrifice (valued) humans for a greater good.

But surely more than an expression of regret is required in order to establish that terrorists are treating their victims as humans and/or that they value them as humans. Minimally what is required is a careful set of calculations showing us just how much value they are placing on their victims and just how they made the calculations that resulted in their victims losing out to the greater good. But even this is not enough. Without some behavioral consideration, some non-verbal gesture in the direction of showing that their victims actually received some consideration, it is tempting to say that the regrets of terrorists are insincere or simply represent so much rhetoric.[4] This is especially so if their victims are selected at random without regard to their age, gender, biological and social status, past accomplishments and failures; and chosen only with regard to their racial or ethnic status (e.g., because they are Americans, Chinese, Jews, or Russians).

So the moral burden of terrorists who direct their harmful acts against innocent people is a heavy one. It is heavier still when we realize that their calculations ought to take account not only of the innocent people they are victimizing as a type, but their numbers as well. How many will they 'regretfully' sacrifice? Philosophers talk about the fallacy of the slippery slope, that is, the fallacy of assuming that when a person begins drinking, for example, he will inevitably become an alcoholic. But surely some slopes are more slippery than others, and terrorists are on one of the slipperiest. Since they have a higher calling that allows them to victimize one person, the very logic of their argument dictates that they find more victims in order to initiate and then sustain the terror. No doubt, people will eventually become inured to the terroristic killing or maiming of a mayor, policeman, or any other single individual. To restore terror in the hearts of the people, either serial victimizing will be in order and/or mass killings will be. So will governmental organized ethnic-cleansing sweeps such as those that took place in Bosnia and Kosovo just before the turn of this century.[5] Finally, using weapons of mass destruction can also help sustain terrorism. Here the city bombings of World War II and what happened on September 11, 2001 come to mind, as does threatened use of chemical, biological or nuclear weapons.[6]

But the moral burden on terrorists is heavier still. Not only are they greasing the slope with a logic that allows them to create quantitatively an almost unlimited number of victims, but they are greasing it for quality as well. If mere bombings do not terrorize because they simply maim and kill, or because people have become inured to them, terrorist logic dictates a tactical change. Why not add rape and torture to the agenda? Why not concentrate on victimizing children? Surely, terrorists might say to themselves, these 'variations' will bring about more terror. Very likely, but these variations cannot help but also increase the moral burden that terrorists must carry on their shoulders.

II

Even if terrorists were to admit that they carry all of these moral burdens, they have an effective counter-argument available. They can say that in spite of all the burdens, their tactics can and often do work. They succeed in terrorizing certain peoples and governments so that the 'greater good' is brought about. Thus, in so far as terroristic tactics are successful, they are justified. It is as simple as that.

This argument is deceptively persuasive. However, when fully understood, although it may still persuade a few, I believe most will not be moved by it. To show why, it is necessary to focus next upon the second group of people who receive the attentions of terrorists, viz. the terrorized.

The first thing to note about those who are terrorized, obvious though it is, is that they are also harmed. They too are victims. To be terrorized is at least to suffer temporary emotional trauma and, often, permanent damage as well. More than that, the terrorized may harm others. In a terrorized condition people often act violently while making demands on government officials, searching for food that belongs to others, looking for security and the like. In their irrational (terrorized) state, they may even do things that will further harm themselves.

The second thing to note, especially if the terrorism is aimed randomly at a general population, is that it will inevitably affect many innocent people. Again, this may seem obvious; but if the burdens of terrorism are to be weighed, each harm needs to be identified. So in order to reach those people or officials who must in some sense capitulate to their demands, terrorists more than likely must harm two separate layers of innocent people (i.e., their victims and those terrorized – actually three if one counts those harmed by those who are terrorized while they are in a terrorized condition). Terrorists destroy or very nearly destroy their victims and unhinge the terrorized. Along the way of getting what they consider to be the higher good, they are up to no good at all. Their means in fact are about as evil as their imagination can conceive and their powers carry out. So *successfully* terrorizing people in and of itself counts heavily against an overall assessment of what terrorists are up to. In theory at least, it is their 'higher good' alone, if and when it is achieved, which sustains their argument by counterbalancing the burdens of wrongdoing they have committed against their victims and the terrorized.

Looking, then, at the 'higher good' portion of the terrorists' argument, notice that even if the higher good is achieved, and even if it truly is a higher good, that alone does not justify their tactics. To do that they must show us that no other tactical option is available which has a reasonable chance of bringing about the higher good.[7] After all, since terrorists choose morally the worst, or just about the worst, possible means, they owe us an explanation as to why just these means are chosen over all others. Why, for instance, do they not choose to terrorize the opponent's military establishment? Certainly if the campaign against it were pressed, that establishment might be significantly damaged. It is true that military people have an unpleasant habit of shooting back when attacked, and for that reason attacking them is more dangerous than victimizing unarmed citizens. But this observation can hardly be turned into a morally convincing principle that when revolutionary work becomes hazardous it is permissible to attack children, women, and other non-combatants. In fact, when one thinks of it, the option of attacking the opponent's military establishment is always present. It is easy enough for terrorists to say that there are no other options available, but difficult to convince people that this is so. Indeed, people's feelings about this matter may be one reason why it is so difficult to sympathize with terrorists; and why terrorism is apparently counter-productive in the sense that it rarely achieves its long-term goals.[8] Be that as it may, the terrorist case is unconvincing not just because the moral burden of attacking innocent people is so heavy, but also because it is very difficult to show convincingly that there is no other less painful way to get the revolutionary job done. Given different situations, different options will likely open up. Non-violent resistance will work in some contexts; testing the laws to the limit will work in others.[9] In still others, terrorizing the offending government officials directly may be an option that, for all of its dangers, at least keeps innocent people from becoming victimized or terrorized. Still, the option of attacking the opponent's military establishment is always available; and because this is so, the terrorist tactics of attacking innocent people (so-called soft targets) at random will seem intuitively to be morally wrong to most people.

It will do terrorists little good to argue that when they talk about 'having no other choice' they do not mean this literally, but mean instead 'having no other choice *as good as* killing innocent people.' Clarifying their meaning in this manner weakens their position considerably, for it is now obvious that terrorists have a real choice. They cannot plead, after all, that the only choice they have is to kill or be killed. Such an excuse would be sufficient where one person has killed another in self-defense, having no choice but to kill in order to save herself – even where the slain victim's threat was not malicious or deliberate. The terrorists' rhetorical claim that they have no choice but to kill their innocent victims is simply false. They are not *forced* to act as they do. Rather, it is their *decision* to adopt those tactics that both victimize and terrorize innocent people.

Further, now that it is obvious their tactics are a matter of conscious and deliberate decision-making, it makes sense to ask that public calculations be made to see if the terrorists have chosen well. To be sure, it is difficult to disprove their claim to have chosen well. But this is not so much because their position is so strong as because it is so difficult to imagine how *any* overall calculation can be made of either the position's strengths or of its weaknesses. Indeed, some calculations can be made; but they hardly help terrorists to defend themselves against charges of gross immorality. It is the nature of the terrorists' tactics that some of their moral debts are calculable. We can count their victims and, in a crude fashion, measure some effects of their terror since these moral debts are so visible and are incurred by them in advance. In contrast, their credits tend to be promissory and/or often identified by them in terms of their own ideological standards rather than in terms of the standards of a wide spectrum of people. The overall calculations (which could show that the moral costs of terrorism are less than the gains) are hard to produce. In addition, terrorists must demonstrate that their form of behavior generates greater overall moral profit than does: (1) terrorizing the opponent's military establishment, and (2) choosing any of the other options available. Such a demonstration would involve putting into a set of calculations not only the value of bringing about the higher good in the first place, but also such things as: (1) the value of bringing it about a month (a year) sooner because terrorism was used rather than some other means, (2) the military and economic costs associated with terrorism as against the costs of using other means, and (3) the civilian costs associated with terrorism as against the costs of using other means. These and other difficult-to-come-by calculations leave terrorists in an awkward position, to say the least, since they need them in order to help justify their tactics.

The argument that put terrorists in such a position can be summarized as follows: Given the high moral costs of their tactics, they can say that they have (literally) no choice if they are to act to bring about their 'higher good.' But what they say here is empirically false. Terrorists always have another choice. They can choose, if no other option is available, to engage in a war of terror against their opponents' military establishment. So they must admit that they are not literally forced to adopt the tactics they do, but that they choose to do so. But their choice, which victimizes and terrorizes innocent people and thereby carries a visibly heavy moral burden, becomes even more unattractive when we realize how difficult it is to prove that it is significantly better than other choices that could have been made. Thus even if successful in bringing about their cherished goals, and even if they come to us with claims of victory and success, it would not be inappropriate for us to withhold our moral congratulations. Instead we might ask them in their moment of triumph, 'What assurance can you give us that some less bloody way was not better?'

III

Now there are many replies that terrorists can give in order to free themselves from these difficulties. I cannot deal with all of them, although I feel that they can be answered in such a way as to properly show the evils of terrorism. I will, however, present three replies that terrorists could give and deal briefly with each one.

First, they may argue that the argument against them places an undue burden of proof upon them. If they cannot prove that their tactics are the best of a bad lot, nor (they could argue) can the defenders of the other options prove that theirs are any better. However, in making this reply, terrorists forget that they carry a special burden of proof because they carry a special burden of wrongdoing. We do not ask people to justify their actions when they harm no one in the process of attempting to achieve a good or alleged good. If they fail we say, 'Too bad,' and perhaps urge them to try again. But the more their efforts clearly harm others, the more we expect an accounting that makes sense. Thus, even if terrorists are successful, it is difficult to make sense of tactics that involve such initial high costs and are also difficult to assess. A related additional argument that puts the terrorists' tactics in a still worse light is that if they fail, they are left with a heavy moral deficit with little or nothing to show for it on the positive side.

The terrorists' second response is a desperate one at best. They can deny that the calculations needed to assess the merits of their position are difficult to make by claiming that their victims and those they terrorize count for nothing. They are most likely to say this when those who are the objects of their attentions belong to a hated ethnic (racial, national, etc.) group.[10] But surely it will be difficult for them to get support for their discriminatory policies beyond their group if for no other reason than that they are violating the Universalizability Principle:

> As ethical judgements become more general, specific references to 'me', 'here' and 'now', 'them', 'there' and 'then' are eliminated, and as long as any such references remain, there is room for an appeal to a more general principle. The point at which the justification of a moral decision must cease is where the action under discussion has been unambiguously related to a current 'moral principle', independent (in its wording) of person, place and time: e.g., where 'I ought to take this book and give it back to Jones at once' has given way to 'Anyone ought always to do anything that he promises anyone else that he will do' or 'It was a promise'. If, in justifying an action, we can

carry our reasons back to such universal principles, our justification has some claim to be called 'ethical'. But, if we cannot do so, our appeal is not to 'morality' at all: if, for example, the most general principles to which we can appeal still contain some reference to us, either as individuals or as members of a limited group of people, then our appeal is not to 'morality' but to 'privilege'.[11]

Morally, then, it is a bankrupt policy to turn the hated ethnics into worthless objects. It amounts to appealing to privilege rather than to ethics.

Somewhat less desperately, terrorists could claim that their victims and those they terrorize count for something but that, in the sweep of history, the many good things produced by the revolution reduce its victims to insignificance. Aside from sounding both cavalier about other people's lives in saying this and also overly optimistic about the merits of the revolution, this reply is beside the point. The issue is, again, not just whether terrorist tactics have greater utility than doing nothing. Rather, it is whether they can be shown to be more beneficial than other options that have fewer initial moral costs.

The terrorists' third reply is not to deny the worth of those they victimize and terrorize but to deny their innocence. Whole ethnic groups or classes of people are said to share the guilt of some past deed or practice. By moving to Algeria, French citizens became 'occupiers' and so are as guilty as are the French soldiers who tried to maintain French control over that nation. Similarly by moving into Palestine, Jews of all ages are as guilty as are members of the Israeli military. And, somewhat similarly, by supporting the military 'occupation' of the sacred lands of Islam, all Americans are as guilty as are the actual military occupiers. With these kinds of argument in hand, terrorists can easily claim that they bear virtually no moral burden for their actions. Their seeming brutal actions against civilians need to be seen, so they claim, as punishments of wrongdoers. As such, they can claim responsibility for their acts of terrorism in good conscience.

In response, one may ask whether all these people are *equally* guilty. Are the terrorists implying that the hated ethnic ten-year-old is just as guilty as the hated ethnic leader? Is the hated ethnic athlete just as guilty as the hated ethnic secret agent? Whatever guilt the ten-year-old and the athlete carry must certainly be so diluted as to pale into innocence. To claim that all of 'them' are guilty equally, or even guilty enough so as to deserve becoming objects of the terrorists' attentions, is simply to be uttering half- (or quarter-) truths at best, or redefining 'guilty' in such a loose way that practically no one on the 'other' side can possibly be innocent.

IV

My arguments against terrorism are really quite simple. They attempt to make explicit why people are instinctively repelled, especially by those forms of terrorism that choose innocent people as their targets. Three basic arguments have been presented.

The first is that terrorists take upon themselves a high initial burden of moral wrongdoing. It is a two-layered burden in that they victimize some and terrorize others. This burden might possibly be overcome if there were no other way to achieve the greater good which the terrorists want so badly. However, and this is the key premise in the second argument, there is always another way. Since there is and since the other way carries with it a lesser moral burden, the terrorists' position is now doubly unattractive morally.

The third argument is that more than other tacticians, terrorists need to show us how they figure that their way is superior to all others. But this showing is difficult to come by. Terrorists are left in limbo – they need to justify themselves, but seem able to do so only by presenting weak, or half-true, arguments.

Notes

1. Kai Nielsen, 'Violence and Terrorism: Its Uses and Abuses,' in Burton M. Leiser (ed.), *Values in Conflict: Life, Liberty and the Rule of Law* (New York: Macmillan, 1981), p. 445.
2. Kai Nielsen, 'Another Look at Terrorism and Violence: A Response to Professor Edel,' unpublished manuscript.
3. Nielsen, 'Violence and Terrorism: Its Uses and Abuses.'
4. Burton M. Leiser, *Liberty, Justice, and Morals: Contemporary Value Conflicts*, revised edition (New York: Macmillan, 1979). Professor Leiser focuses on the terrorists' rhetoric in a portion of his chapter (pp. 384–8) on terrorism.
5. Carl Ceulemans, 'The NATO Intervention in the Kosovo Crisis: March–June 1999,' in Bruno Coppieters and Nick Fotion (eds.), *Moral Constraints on War* (Lanham, Boulder, New York and London: Lexington Books, 2002). In the same volume see also Boris Kashnikov, 'NATO's Intervention in the Kosovo Crisis: Whose Justice?'
6. Carl Ceulemans, 'The Military Response of the U.S.-Led Coalition to the September 11 Attacks,' in Coppieters and Fotion (eds.), *Moral Constraints on War*.
7. Nielsen, 'Violence and Terrorism: Its Uses and Abuses,' p. 440.
8. Caleb Carr, *The Lessons of Terror: A History of Warfare Against Civilians – Why It Has Always Failed and Why It Will Fail Again* (New York: Random House, 2002).

9. Nick Fotion and Bruno Coppieters, 'Likelihood of Success,' in Coppieters and Fotion (eds.), *Moral Constraints on War*.
10. Michael Walzer, *Just and Unjust Wars*, third edition (New York: Basic Books, 2000), p. 203.
11. Stephen Toulmin, *An Examination of the Place of Reason in Ethics* (Cambridge: Cambridge University Press, 1953), p. 168.

5
Political Terrorism as a Weapon of the Politically Powerless

Robert Young

Because there is so much disagreement about how *political terrorism* (hereinafter *terrorism*) should be characterized, I shall begin by setting out how I will characterize it. The concept is a highly contested one, at least in part because the phenomena covered by it are subject to dispute. In the process of outlining the characterization I will give, I will register a disagreement I have with the position of some of the other contributors to this book who advance different understandings to mine. Given that the notion is so contested, I will not offer a definition or attempt to provide a set of necessary and sufficient conditions for the correct use of the term since I do not wish to make definitional issues the focus, or to give the impression that my account is not contested. Instead, I will list the features that, I think, best capture what terrorism involves. Even then I will not attempt to provide an exhaustive list, but will concentrate on the main features. Once I have made clear how I understand *terrorism* I will focus on terrorism as it is practiced by individuals, or groups other than states. It is not my intention to rule out the idea of state terrorism (which is the subject of separate contributions by Igor Primoratz and Douglas Lackey).[1] On the contrary, I consider state terrorism to be widely practiced. This is a point of importance because state terrorism is not a weapon of the politically powerless (the concern of this chapter), but of the politically powerful. In the remaining space I will briefly consider the claim that the most promising way, morally, to defend terrorism not carried out by states is as a weapon

An earlier version of this chapter was published as: Robert Young, 'Terrorism as a Weapon of the Politically Powerless,' in Tony Coady and Michael O'Keefe (eds.), *Terrorism and Justice: Moral Argument in a Threatened World* (Melbourne: Melbourne University Press, 2002), pp. 22–30 and 127. © Robert Young, 2002.

which those who lack conventional political power can use to fight for just causes they are otherwise prevented from promoting.

Features of terrorism

Terrorist actions (whether in the form of one-off attacks or as part of an ongoing campaign) are political actions that involve either the use, or the threat of the use, of violence. The violence may be directed towards persons or property[2] – witness many of the terrorist actions of the African National Congress in South Africa or the destruction by the Tamil 'Tigers' of much of the fleet of Sri Lankan Airways. Typically, the violence will take a physical form, but it may also be psychological.

1. The use, or the threat of the use, of violence is intended to generate anxiety, fear, or terror, or to cause a breakdown in normal levels of trust in society, among some target group (even if it is not the persons or property of members of that group that are the direct objects of attack).
2. Those who thus resort to violence may act as individuals, but will, more commonly, be acting as members of an organized group. Individuals, or groups other than the state, act as insurgents when they resort to terrorism, whereas a state that employs terrorism will do so with a view to upholding its laws or maintaining the political *status quo*.
3. The purposes for which terrorism is carried out can range from intimidation or coercion of the target group to get it to accede to the political demands of the perpetrators, through to obtaining publicity for a cause, the building of morale among members of the attacking group, or even the enforcement of obedience within that group, to attempting to render a territory ungovernable or to provoking a repressive response by the state.[3]
4. Though many claim that terrorism always involves the indiscriminate or random use of violence (and some go so far as to say that it does so necessarily) this need not be the case. Not only can terrorism be directed at property, as was mentioned above, but, as well, it is worth reminding ourselves that warnings of impending terrorist actions are often given so as to preclude needless killing or maiming of individuals who are not targets but will happen to be in the vicinity where the action will occur. Moreover, terrorism is, at least on some occasions, directed at specific targets in order to achieve the particular purpose the terrorist intends. It is a general truth that the more

indiscriminate a terrorist action the harder it will be to give a moral defense of it (for reasons that will be elaborated later).[4]

5. Notwithstanding what I have just said, many believe that terrorism necessarily involves threatening to harm, or harming, non-combatants (which is code for 'innocents'), and so fails to preserve vital distinctions that have been developed through reflection on the morality of violence in war, like that between combatants and non-combatants. I reject this sort of moralized definition. Not only does a definition of this form beg the question of the moral justifiability of terrorism, it is also unwarrantedly prescriptive about which acts of political violence may be considered acts of terrorism. To take the former first: the definition implies, for instance, that where a terrorist group refrains from giving a warning to enable people to evacuate a building before it is bombed, and casualties are suffered, then an act of terrorism takes place, whereas if warnings are given and no casualties occur there is no act of terrorism but, instead, as some of those who offer such a definition would have it, merely an act of *sabotage*. As regards the latter: consider, for instance, the truck bomb attack in 1983 on the US marine barracks in Lebanon, which killed more than 200 soldiers. Lomasky takes the heroic line that the incident was only 'tangentially' a terrorist act. Other cases that have involved the killing, or attempted killing, of individuals whom it is difficult to think of as 'innocent civilians' – like the abduction and killing in 1978 by the Red Brigades of the former Italian Prime Minister, Aldo Moro, or the attempt in 1984 by the Irish Republican Army to kill the then British Prime Minister, Margaret Thatcher, and members of her Cabinet, in a Brighton hotel during their annual party conference – have been claimed to constitute *assassinations* or attempted assassinations rather than acts of terrorism. These reclassifications may save the moralized definition but are unhelpful to the careful analysis of *terrorism*.

Let us suppose (even if, for some readers, it is only for the sake of argument) that the preceding list of features provides a tolerably clear, non question-begging characterization of terrorism. That still leaves open to debate whether any particular act of terrorism can be morally justified; so I turn now to a consideration of whether individuals or groups may justifiably resort to terrorism. It is, none the less, worth saying in advance that, even on the characterization I have offered, it will be difficult to provide a convincing moral justification for such violent political action whenever it involves injuring or killing the innocent (rather than the destruction of property).

Can terrorism be morally justified?

Such defenses of non-state terrorism as there are[5] often begin from the contention that, in at least some circumstances where it is not possible for those with a serious grievance to get the political powers-that-be to give them even a hearing, terrorism may be the only remaining resort. Certain critics, like Michael Walzer,[6] dismiss the contention out of hand by suggesting that it is virtually impossible to reach a final resort because there is always something else that can be tried, even by the most seriously oppressed. (In fairness, Walzer thinks that the same holds for states which, he believes, are altogether too ready to go to war on the pretence of its being their last resort.) Walzer's is a facile response because it amounts to no more than an insistence that however unrealistic, or unlikely to succeed, the remaining options may be, they must continue to be tried. Tell that, for example, to a person from a subjugated minority group suffering serious, systematic violence at the hands of the majority (in recent times, say, those from Kosovo or Aceh), or to the citizens of a country under military occupation by another more powerful nation (say, Cyprus in the 1950s when it was occupied by British forces). Despite the commonly held view of him as exclusively a practitioner of non-violence, and certainly without wanting to suggest that he would have supported terrorism, it is worthy of note that even Gandhi contended that it was 'better to resist oppression by violent means than to submit' in the event that a non-violent response was precluded.[7]

A more promising riposte may be to suggest that the claim, made by those who assert that they have no other option than a resort to terrorism, that they do so because they are politically powerless, relies on a conflation of two very different ideas. On the one hand, there is the claim often made by members of terrorist groups that they lack power as compared with the state they oppose, and, on the other, there is the claim that they lack the ability as a group to obtain and mobilize widespread support for their cause (whether in the form of non-violent resistance, guerrilla warfare or the like).[8] Walzer's contention is that it is the second claim that we should focus on, whereas I shall suggest that it is the first. He adds that in a truly despotic and repressive situation state terrorism will be immune anyway to challenge from revolutionary terrorism or an attempt via terrorism to bring about significant societal reform, whereas, in a democratic setting, strategies other than terrorism will be available. In short, he thinks that if the cause is just, just means will be available in a democratic context.

Let us consider these claims in reverse order. Even in places when there are some of the trappings of democracy (periodic elections and the like) it may still be very difficult for some groups to get a fair hearing for their grievances. In one of the few places where terrorism could be said to have been a factor in bringing about political change, Northern Ireland,[9] the state was established with a demographic basis that made it likely that the minority[10] section of the population who wished for a unified Ireland would be regularly outvoted by the numerically larger section who wished to remain part of the United Kingdom (and so be denied access to serious political power and opportunities). There is, of course, a difference between terrorism proving effective and its being morally justified, but even with that acknowledged, it may still be that limited forms of terrorism can be justified, even where some of the features of a democracy are present, if getting a fair hearing for serious grievances would otherwise be impossible. Thus, supposing that non-violent options have proved to be to no avail, if the targets are carefully chosen and are confined to property, or to those who cannot reasonably be regarded as innocent, even in a setting with democratic features terrorism may be morally justifiable.[11]

I turn, second, to Walzer's claim that, outside of democratic settings, terrorist tactics are very likely to fail because the state will hold so much political power as to be impregnable from attack. This I simply do not accept. The Irgun Zvai Leumi (the National Military Organization) and the Stern Gang used terror tactics against the British rulers of Palestine to achieve a much different political arrangement for the birth of the State of Israel than would otherwise have been the case. The tactic could thus be said to have met with some success.[12] Similarly, terrorist acts carried out by members of the African National Congress were surely among the factors that led to the overthrow of apartheid and the introduction of the more democratic society that is present-day South Africa. In South Africa it was certainly not lack of popular support that rendered black activists politically powerless; it was, manifestly, a lack of power in relation to that of an oppressive state and its institutional apparatus. Not only did the members of the ANC who carried out terrorist acts lack political power, they also claimed to be acting on behalf of the large but politically powerless majority of the population. It is true that, on its own, terrorism would not have brought down the regime, but it played a part in that downfall. Now it is important, as I have said before, to separate the effectiveness of an act of terrorism from its moral justifiability. But, given the horrendous suffering occasioned by the way the system of apartheid operated, some of the

NO ! NEVER
MORALLY SUS EIFIED
X BUT . SomETimES NECESSARY

ANC's carefully targeted terrorist actions in South Africa are surely to be numbered among the morally justified uses of political violence. However, to make that assessment credible, I need to say how it might be supported (albeit briefly).

Does a lack of political power justify resort to terrorism, no matter what?

No, of course, it doesn't. No more, in fact, than does someone's fighting for a just cause by way of war justify whatever he or she does in the furtherance of that cause. Recourse to war may be just, and so satisfy the *jus ad bellum* (justice of war) standard, without the conduct of the war satisfying the *jus in bello* (justice in war) standard. Many who reject the moral justifiability of terrorism do so because they do not believe that terrorism can measure up to the stringent requirements of the second of these standards. It may be conceded that, like some wars, some acts of terrorism and even some campaigns of terrorism may be undertaken as a last resort, out of necessity, and have some hope of success. But those staunchly opposed to the moral justifiability of terrorism claim that terrorism cannot satisfy the central requirement of the *jus in bello* that any use of violence must discriminate between combatants and non-combatants, and respect the immunity of the latter. Precisely who is entitled to non-combatant status is a subject of dispute within just war theory,[13] but there is no need for us to enter that dispute because, as I have already indicated, terrorism does not have to involve the targeting of non-combatants.

The just war tradition appeals to non-consequentialist considerations. According to non-consequentialists, the rightness or wrongness of what we do is not determined solely by how good or bad the consequences of what we do will be. There are various possible ways of understanding what goodness and badness consist in, but, for present purposes, I will take them to be about how well or badly off a certain action leaves those whom it affects.[14] Non-consequentialists typically hold that moral judgments must take into account *prerogatives* not to maximize the good (e.g. in the pursuit of our own projects) and *constraints* on producing the best consequences overall (as when doing so would clash with the obligation not to harm others intentionally). Consequentialists, by contrast, hold that the rightness or wrongness of what we do is determined solely by whether what we do maximizes good consequences (or, for some recent writers, satisfices, that is, achieves satisfactory, even if less than maximal, good consequences, since to seek to maximize them would require difficult or costly calculations). Clearly, some terrorist actions might be said by consequentialists to be justified because they achieve more good consequences than bad.[15] This is not the occasion to argue a case for either a consequentialist or a non-consequentialist approach to ethics, let alone to consider whether in particular circumstances the most favorable balance of good over bad might be shown to have come from a terrorist action or campaign. Instead, I will merely state that I am a non-consequentialist who believes, *inter alia*, that the constraints against killing and injuring those not engaged in violent attacks against us may only be set aside when failure to do so would lead to harmful consequences of far greater significance.[16]

For my part, then, the moral justification for any particular instance of terrorism, or of any political response that includes a campaign of terrorism, will turn on whether justice can be achieved with fewer, and better targeted, killings and injuries, or less destruction, than by any of the other available alternatives (supposing always that all non-violent strategies have been exhausted). Terrorism generally is able to limit killings, injuries and destruction of property by comparison with what happens in war, though it would, of course, be a form of self-deception to suggest that it is any easier accurately to anticipate what will result from acts of terror than from acts of war.[17] For that reason, if for no other, the possibility that terrorism may sometimes be justifiable cannot be excluded.

Until the world we live in becomes a fairer one for all concerned, it seems certain that those otherwise unable to have their serious and well-founded grievances remedied will sometimes resort to terrorism. Given that few instances of terrorism are likely to be morally justifiable (even among those involving only attacks on property, or on individuals who cannot be considered innocent), and, even more fundamentally, that it would be better not to have to resort to terrorism in any case, it must be part of our responsibility to work for the fairer world that would render terrorism unnecessary. We must not lose sight of the *jus ad bellum* whenever the requirements for *jus in bello* fail to be satisfied. So, for example, even if the manner of the terrorist attack on the World Trade Center was unjustifiable it is still necessary that the justice of the cause of those who carried out the attack be investigated (since their cause may be just despite the manner of their response). When supporters of the terrorists who died in the attack say that the attack was in response to the serious affront given to the Islamic world by the US in propping up undemocratic and brutal regimes in the Middle East, including, but not only Israel; in maintaining sanctions against Iraq despite the mounting toll on civilians, especially children; and in fostering US economic interests even at the cost of impeding economic development within the predominantly Islamic nations, the US ought to consider the justice of the complaints and, if appropriate, make amends. In that direction lies the best hope that terrorism of the kind carried out in New York and Washington on September 11, 2001 or in Bali on October 12, 2002 will be rendered unnecessary.

Notes

1. Noam Chomsky has pointed out that, if the official US definition of *terrorism* is followed, the United States and many of its client states are clearly guilty of terrorism. See his *9–11* (New York: Seven Stories Press, 2001), p. 16 fn. According to that definition, an act of terrorism 'means any activity that (A) involves a violent act or an act dangerous to human life that is a violation of the criminal laws of the United States or any State, or that would be a criminal violation if committed within the jurisdiction of the United States or of any State; and (B) appears to be intended (i) to intimidate or coerce a civilian population; (ii) to influence the policy of a government by intimidation or coercion; or (iii) to affect the conduct of a government by assassination or kidnapping.'
2. *Pace* J. Teichman, *Pacifism and the Just War* (Oxford: Blackwell, 1986), p. 92, and Igor Primoratz, 'What Is Terrorism?' this volume, p. 21.
3. Cf. Grant Wardlaw, *Political Terrorism*, second edition (Cambridge: Cambridge University Press, 1989), p. 42.
4. Cf. Paul Wilkinson, *Political Terrorism* (London: Macmillan, 1974); C.A.J. Coady, 'The Morality of Terrorism,' *Philosophy* 60 (1985); Michael Walzer, 'Terrorism: A Critique of Excuses,' in S. Luper-Foy (ed.), *Problems of International Justice* (Boulder, Col.: Westview Press, 1988); Loren Lomasky, 'The Political Significance of Terrorism,' in R.G. Frey and Christopher Morris (eds.), *Violence, Terrorism and Justice* (New York: Cambridge University Press, 1991). Coady, for example, defines terrorism as 'a political act, ordinarily committed by an organized group, which involves the intentional killing or other severe harming of non-combatants or the threat of the same or intentional severe damage to the property of non-combatants or the threat of the same' (p. 52). This at least has the merit that it acknowledges that terrorism may extend to damage to property. Igor Primoratz in 'What is Terrorism?' pp. 17–19, takes a tougher line in that he considers that terrorism necessarily involves the use, or the threat of the use, of violence against 'innocent people'. Like Coady, he assumes that terrorism is seriously morally wrong. I think this is question-begging but even if he were able to show that charge to be unwarranted, terrorism, on his account, would remain impossible to justify.
5. Cf., for example, my 'Revolutionary Terrorism, Crime and Morality,' *Social Theory and Practice* 4 (1977), for one qualified defense. For a recent argument to the effect that the justifiability of modern warfare and terrorism is on a par see Andrew Valls, 'Can Terrorism Be Justified?' in Andrew Valls (ed.), *Ethics in International Affairs* (Lanham, Md.: Rowman and Littlefield, 2000). In *After the*

Terror (Edinburgh: Edinburgh University Press, 2002), and 'After the Terror: A Book and Further Thoughts,' *The Journal of Ethics* 7 (2003), Ted Honderich argues that it is inconsistent to affirm a people's (e.g., the Palestinian people's) moral right to a homeland while denying them the right to the only possible means of getting it, namely the strategic use of terrorism. His claim, of course, raises the key issue of whether terrorism is the *only* possible means of getting such a homeland. In chapter 7 of *A Delicate Balance: What Philosophy Can Tell Us About Terrorism* (Boulder, Col.: Westview Press, 2002), Trudy Govier offers an assessment of whether terrorism can be defended morally by an appeal to justice.

6. E.g., Walzer, 'Terrorism: A Critique of Excuses,' p. 239.

7. As cited in Virginia Held, 'Terrorism, Rights, and Political Goals,' this volume, p. 74.

8. Walzer, 'Terrorism: A Critique of Excuses,' p. 240.

9. So Jan Narveson, 'Terrorism and Morality,' in Frey and Morris (eds.), *Violence, Terrorism and Justice*, p. 14, relying on Edward Hyams, *Terrorists and Terrorism* (London: Dent, 1975). For helpful discussion of one element of the terrorism in Northern Ireland in the past century, see David George, 'The Ethics of IRA Terrorism,' in Valls (ed.), *Ethics in International Affairs*. George argues against the claim that the IRA has been engaged in a struggle akin to a just war.

10. I choose to speak in this way because I do not think that the use of terms like 'Catholics' and 'Protestants' adds to our understanding of what has been, and still is, a political struggle rather than a religious one. The terms 'Catholics' and 'Protestants' may serve in a rough-and-ready way to identify members of the opposing groups but they are apt to mislead as to the nature of the struggle.

11. Robert Fullinwinder has drawn attention to the way that terrorism has sometimes been used within what are considered democracies to achieve *industrial* (as against *political*) change. See 'Understanding Terrorism,' in Luper-Foy (ed.), *Problems of International Justice*, pp. 252f.

12. For helpful discussion see Neve Gordon and George A. Lopez, 'Terrorism in the Arab–Israeli Conflict,' in Valls (ed.), *Ethics in International Affairs*.

13. See, e.g., Michael Walzer, *Just and Unjust Wars: A Moral Argument with Historical Illustrations* (Harmondsworth: Penguin, 1977); James Turner Johnson, *Just War Tradition and the Restraint of War: A Moral and Historical Inquiry* (Princeton, NJ: Princeton University Press, 1981); Robert L. Holmes, *On War and Morality* (Princeton, NJ: Princeton University Press, 1989).

14. These remarks raise a number of complex issues which, unfortunately, I cannot adequately consider here. For an introduction to those issues see, e.g., Shelly Kagan, *Normative Ethics* (Boulder, Col.: Westview Press, 1998).

15. Cf., R.M. Hare, 'On Terrorism,' *Journal of Value Inquiry* 13 (1979).

16. Once again this leaves many issues unconsidered that would need consideration in a fuller discussion. It may help to give an example drawn from the realm of the law, rather than from that of morality, to illustrate what I have in mind. It is sometimes considered right to break laws or override rights in order to ensure important consequences. Thus, for instance, individual citizens may break laws, or government agencies may confiscate private property (and so override the rights of property owners), and be justified in doing so in virtue of the important social outcomes they thereby achieve.

17. It is highly unlikely, for instance, that the perpetrators of the attack on the World Trade Center (as distinct from that on the Pentagon) on September 11, 2001 would have accurately anticipated not merely how many deaths or injuries there would be and the impact of those deaths and injuries on the victims' families and friends, but the effect the attack would have on the economy of the US, and, indeed, of the world as a whole; on the resolve of the US to pursue them and so to instigate the so-called 'war against terrorism' with the consequences that that has had for Afghanistan and Iraq; the effect there would be on support for the grievances to which they were wishing to draw attention; and so on. I believe that the attack classically illustrates the claim I have made that terrorism is a weapon of those who lack the power to attack directly those they oppose since as far as the terrorists were concerned the US mainland was invulnerable to a conventional military attack. That is why they aimed at targets symbolic of US hegemony in trade and commerce, and in military and political affairs. The point was to sting the US. (Once it became harder to repeat such strikes the likelihood always was that soft targets elsewhere would become the focus, as now seems to have been true of the attack in Bali.) Of course, even if the perpetrators had been able to foresee the effects of their actions, that would not have made it any easier morally to justify what they did given the constraints against killing and injuring people, especially people engaged in innocent activities.

6
Terrorism, Rights, and Political Goals

Virginia Held

The justifiability of terrorism

I will not venture to suggest exactly what factor or combination of factors may be necessary to turn political violence into terrorism, but perhaps when either the intention to spread fear or the intention to harm non-combatants is primary, this is sufficient.[1]

A way in which usage and much popular and some academic discussion have been unhelpful in illuminating the topic of terrorism is that they have frequently built a judgment of immorality or non-justifiability into the definition of terrorism, making it impossible even to question whether given acts of terrorism might be justified. Thus news reports frequently equate terrorism with evildoing. Politicians often use the term as an automatic term of abuse. The British author Paul Wilkinson, in a book on terrorism, characterizes terrorists as persons who 'sacrifice *all* moral and humanitarian considerations for the sake of some political end.'[2] Benjamin Netanyahu goes even further. He describes the terrorist as representing 'a new breed of man which takes humanity back to prehistoric times, to the times when morality was not yet born. Divested of any moral principle, he has no moral sense, no moral controls, and is therefore capable of committing any crime, like a killing machine, without shame or remorse.'[3] The philosopher Burton Leiser says that, by definition, terrorists consider themselves above law and morality; he equates terrorism with piracy and considers it invariably criminal and

An earlier version of this chapter was published as: Virginia Held, 'Terrorism, Rights, and Political Goals,' in R.G. Frey and Christopher W. Morris (eds.), *Violence, Terrorism, and Justice* (Cambridge: Cambridge University Press, 1991), pp. 59–85. © Cambridge University Press, 1991. Reproduced by permission.

immoral.[4] Finally, Michael Walzer begins a discussion of terrorism with the assumption that 'every act of terrorism is a wrongful act.'[5]

Arguments against building unjustifiability into the definition of terrorism can follow similar arguments against holding that violence is by definition morally wrong. Not only is violence often used in ways usually accepted, as in upholding law, but one can easily cite examples of violence used against governmental authority where it makes sense to ask whether such uses of violence were morally wrong or not. The 1944 bomb plot against Hitler is one obvious candidate. Even if examples of possibly justifiable acts of terrorism, as distinct from other forms of violence, are for many persons harder to acknowledge, we should still be able to *consider* the justifiability of terrorist acts. We should be able to treat such questions as open, and this requires that we not imagine them to be answerable merely by appealing to a definition.

Many of those who use 'terrorist' as a term of denunciation apply it to their opponents and refuse to apply it to the acts of their own government, or of governments of which they approve, even when such governmental action is as clearly violent, intended to spread fear, or productive of the killing of non-combatants.[6] But one cannot effectively criticize the terrorism of those Third World revolutionaries who consider various terrorist acts to be admirable[7] unless one also criticizes the terrorist acts of campaigns of counter-terrorism carried out by one's government and the governments of states one considers 'friendly.'[8] What to consider 'original offense' and what 'retaliation' is of course a matter of political judgment. Many of those engaged in acts considered terroristic by existing governments consider themselves to be retaliating against such unjustified and violent acts by those governments as 'reprisal raids' that predictably kill civilians.

In a balanced discussion of forms of violence, the philosopher Robert Holmes concludes that terrorism *per se* is morally no worse than many conventionally accepted forms of violence. Ordinary warfare often uses terror as a tactic, and we should remember that the terror bombings of Dresden, Hiroshima, and Nagasaki undoubtedly killed far more people than have been killed by all the terrorists, as conventionally so labeled, throughout the world in all of the years since.[9]

One can further argue, as does Richard Falk, that one cannot be sincerely or consistently opposed to terrorism unless one is also opposed to the 'tactics of potential or actual warfare that rely on indiscriminate violence or that deliberately target civilians.'[10] Since those who defend preparing for nuclear war are not willing to reject such tactics, their opposition to terrorism seems more propagandistic than honest. However, the mistake of selective application can be corrected, as we become accustomed to the term 'state terrorism' and then reduce the bias so far manifest in usage concerning its application.

Some of those who define terrorism as the intentional harming of non-combatants conclude that therefore, either by definition or not, terrorism is always wrong.[11] Since we can rule out as inadequate the view that terrorism is by definition always wrong, unless all violence is, let us consider only those cases where the judgment is not one of definition but independently arrived at. Is intentionally harming non-combatants always wrong, and terrorism always wrong because it involves this?

Michael Walzer believes that at least some of the Allied bombings of German cities during World War II in which hundreds of thousands of civilians were intentionally killed were justified,[12] but many disagree. An argument can certainly be made that no absolute right of non-combatants to immunity from the violence suffered by combatants should be granted, especially when many of the combatants have been conscripted or misled into joining the armed forces. Recent reports suggest that many who serve in armies around the world are children; the Contra rebels in Nicaragua supported by the United States recruited boys as young as twelve. According to a UN report, some 200,000 members of the world's armies are youngsters. Sometimes they are forcibly rounded up; sometimes they are urged by parents 'to enlist in armies to gain food, jobs or payments if the child dies in battle.'[13] Such 'combatants' hardly seem legitimate targets while the 'civilians' who support the war in which they fight are exempt.

This is not to suggest that we should simply abandon the distinction between combatant and non-combatant. It is certainly harder to justify harming non-combatants than it is to justify harming combatants, other things equal, and we can try to combine this distinction with usefully drawn notions of 'those responsible' for a conflict. But as C.A.J. Coady notes, 'if a revolution is unjustified then any killing done in its name is unjustified whether of combatants or non-combatants.'[14] And the same thing can be said of any repression of opponents of a regime. It is often more important to keep this in mind and to apply the judgments it provides than to rely on a distinction between otherwise legitimate and illegitimate targets.

Most recent philosophical discussion avoids the mistake of making terrorism wrong by definition. R.M. Hare,[15] Carl Wellman,[16] Coady, Holmes, and others agree that, as with violence, we ought to be able to consider whether terrorism can ever be justified. The question should be open, not ruled out by definition. But then, can terrorism be justifiable?

Burleigh Wilkins argues that consequentialism provides weak defenses against terrorism.[17] To a consequentialist, terrorism would have to be justifiable if, on balance, it brings about better consequences than its alternatives. And though such consequentialists considered by Wilkins as Hare and Kai Nielsen think that terrorism is hardly ever justified, their arguments depend on empirical estimates that terrorism almost always produces results that are worse on consequentialist grounds than their alternatives. Others find the empirical claims on which such judgments rest to be questionable.

Reading the historical record is notoriously difficult. Some think, with Walter Laqueur, that terrorist violence has tended to produce 'violent repression and a polarization which precluded political progress,' rather than the changes sought by the terrorists.[18] The German philosopher Albrecht Wellmer, building on the critical theory of Jürgen Habermas, finds of the terrorism of the Red Army Faction in Germany in the 1970s that although it 'reflects and brings to a head the pathologies of the system against which it is directed,' its net effect has been reactionary: it has provided legitimation for political repression and a defamation of the entire Left.[19]

Others think, with Charles Tilly and Lewis Coser, that violent protests have been an almost normal part of the Western political process, and that they have often contributed to progressive developments.[20] Concerning effectiveness, Richard Falk points out that the bombing of the marine barracks in Lebanon in October 1983 is considered by some to be one of the most successful uses of force 'in the history of recent international relations, leading a very strong power to accede to the demands of a very weak opponent.'[21] The marines had been deployed in Lebanon as the major expression of the United States' intent to support the Gemayel government and, as a result of the bombing, were removed from Lebanon by President Reagan.

It may be almost impossible to predict whether an act of terrorism will indeed have its intended effect of hastening some political goal sought by the terrorists, or whether it will in fact do the terrorists' cause more harm than good. But as Wilkins asks, 'is there something special about acts of violence which makes them different from other acts where judgments about their consequences are concerned? We frequently do many things where the outcome is uncertain.'[22] If existing conditions are terrible, 'they might prompt a prospective terrorist to reason that *any* chance of altering these states of affairs is worth the risk of failure and the near certainty of harm to property or persons that violence involves.'[23]

Furthermore, states use violence and the threat of violence to uphold their laws, and some use terrorism. Many theorists still define the state in terms of its monopoly on the use of violence considered legitimate.[24] But if violence can be condemned on consequentialist grounds it can be condemned in state behavior as well as in the behavior of a state's opponents. On the other hand, if violence or terrorism by the state *can* be justified, it may be as impossible to predict its success as to predict the success of the violence or terrorism of its opponents. Where a legal system violates the human rights of those on whom it imposes its will, the violence or terrorism it uses to do so is surely no more justified than the violence or terrorism used against it, and quite possibly it is less so. When the security forces of an unjust regime kill or brutalize detainees to deter future opposition, or shoot at random into groups of demonstrators, they engage in acts of terrorism. Even relatively legitimate legal orders on occasion violate the human rights of some; the violence or terrorism they use to uphold their authority against those they thus mistreat is not more justified than the violence or terrorism of their opponents. In both cases, predictions of success may be impossible to make accurately, but in another sense impossible to escape making.

Terrorism and rights

In my view we cannot adequately evaluate social action in consequentialist terms alone.[25] The framework of rights and obligations must also be applied, and in the case of terrorism it is certainly relevant to ask: Are rights being violated, and can this be justified?

Against Hare and others who evaluate terrorism by applying utilitarian calculations, Wellman usefully considers the place of rights in evaluating terrorism. Wellman says that 'certain fundamental human rights, the rights to liberty, personal security, life, property, and respect, are typically violated by acts of terrorism.'[26] This means not that terrorism can never be justified, but that an adequate moral appraisal will have to take violations of rights into account along with any calculations of benefits and harms produced.[27]

Coady rightfully notes the prevalent inconsistency in many discussions of terrorism. The use of violence directed at non-combatants is judged justifiable on utilitarian grounds if carried out by one's own or a friendly state, as in many evaluations of the justifiability of bombing raids in wartime in which civilians can be expected to be killed. At the same time, when revolutionaries and rebels use violence that harms non-combatants, such acts are judged on non-utilitarian grounds to be unjustifiable violations of prohibitions on how political goals are to be pursued. As Coady observes, consistency can be achieved either by applying utilitarian evaluations to both sides or by applying non-utilitarian evaluations to both sides. He favors the latter, and concludes that terrorism is 'immoral wherever and whenever it is used or proposed.'[28] My own suggestion is for a non-utilitarian comparison of rights violations. It could reach a different conclusion.

One of the most difficult problems for political philosophy is the problem of how to evaluate situations where human rights are not being respected. What are persons justified in doing to bring about such respect, and how should these actions be judged? Should 'bringing about increased respect for human rights' be evaluated in consequentialist terms? But then how should this consequence be weighed against any violations of rights necessitated by the action to achieve this consequence? If we say that no violations of rights are justified, even in this case, this can become a disguised recipe for maintaining the *status quo*. If we permit violations, we risk undermining the moral worth of the very rights for which we are striving to achieve respect.

My suggestion is that we not yield to a merely consequentialist evaluation, but that we strive for reasonable comparative judgments. In a well-developed scheme of assured rights, rights should not be traded off against one another, or judged in comparative terms. We do not usefully speak of more of a right to vote or less of a right to vote, but of a right to vote. And we do not usefully try to determine whether a right to vote is more or is less important than a right to non-discrimination in employment. Where rights conflict, we may order them by priorities or stringency; this, however, is not a matter of maximizing, but of seeking consistency. Some rights may be deemed to have priority over others, or to be more basic than others, but our aim is not to engage in trade-offs. We seek, rather, to arrive at a consistent scheme in which all the rights of all persons can be respected and none need be violated.

In a defective society, on the other hand, where rights are not in fact being respected, we should be able to make comparative judgments about which and whose rights violations are least justifiable. Was it more important, for instance, for blacks in South Africa to gain assurance of rights to personal safety than for white South Africans to continue to enjoy their property rights undisturbed? While blacks are denied respect for their most basic rights, it seems worse to continue these violations than to permit some comparable violations of the rights of whites participating in this denial.

Such an evaluation is not a consequentialist calculation, but it does allow us to compare rights violations. It requires us not to ignore the violations involved in maintaining an existing system, since of course charges of rights violations should not be applied only to those seeking change, while those upholding an existing, and often unjust system, are exempt.

I will use the expression 'effective respect for rights' to mean that an existing legal system recognizes the rights in question and effectively upholds respect for them. Of course this does not mean that violations never occur; no legal system can secure perfect compliance with its norms. It means that violations are on the whole prevented by adequate education, socialization, and police protection, and that those who commit such violations are apprehended and dealt with to a sufficient degree to make respect for the rights is question generally high. There is no escape from the fact that effective respect for rights is a matter of degree, but it is quite possible to make an accurate empirical judgment that it is absent when a legal system does not even recognize a right in question as a legal right. When using the expression 'effective respect for rights,' we should specify the type of rights in question, and this can be done.

Let us consider the case where a certain type of right is recognized as a human right by the major international documents and bodies establishing international norms concerning rights.[29] When such a right is not recognized as a legal right for a certain group of persons in a given legal system, there will clearly then be no effective respect for those rights of those persons in that legal system. An example would be the right to non-discrimination on grounds of race recognized as a right in Articles 2 and 7 of the Universal Declaration of Human Rights adopted by the General Assembly of the United Nations on December 10, 1948. Under the system of apartheid in South Africa, especially before the reforms initiated by the government of F.W. de Klerk, this right was not recognized for South Africa's black population. Hence very clearly there was for blacks in South Africa no effective respect for this right.

Frequently, rights are recognized as legal rights in a given legal system, but respect for them is not effective because law enforcement agencies are corrupt or prejudiced, or the government is inefficient or unfair in its administration, and so forth. The empirical judgment that effective respect for rights is absent may in such cases be difficult to make, and the lack of effective respect for rights can be as serious as in those cases where the right is not even recognized in the legal system. However, an advantage for purposes of moral theorizing in choosing a case of the latter kind, where a human right is being violated and is not even acknowledged to be a legal right, is that there can be so little dispute at the empirical level that effective respect for rights is absent. So let us consider this kind of case, imagining two groups, A and B, and supposing that the failure to recognize the human rights of the members of group B as legal rights in legal system L is advantageous to the members of group A, in this case, and disadvantageous to the members of group B, in so far as further benefits and burdens accrue to them in exercising or in failing to have the rights in question. However, the evaluation of comparative justifiability of rights violations will not be made on the basis of these further benefits or burdens.

Now let us ask whether it can be morally justifiable to violate some rights to achieve effective respect for other rights. First, an aside: If there are legal rights in conflict with human rights such that we can judge that these legal rights ought not to exist, then what appears to be a violation of them will probably not be morally unjustified. That kind of case will not present the moral difficulties I wish to consider.

The difficult case is where achieving respect for the fundamental human rights of the members of one group, which rights ought to be respected, requires the violation of the fundamental human rights of the members of another group, which are also rights that seemingly ought to be respected. If terrorism can ever be justified, it would seem to present this kind of problem. Where there is a lack of effective respect for the fundamental human rights of the members of one group, and *if* there is a reasonable likelihood that limited terrorism will significantly contribute to bringing about such effective respect, and no other effective means are available, can it be justifiable to violate the fundamental human rights of those who will suffer from such terrorism? Their rights to 'life, liberty and security of person,' as specified in Article 3 of the Universal Declaration, are likely to be violated by any act of terrorism. Can this possibly be justified?

Let us specify two situations. In the first, S_1, the members of group A have a human right to x and they enjoy effective respect for this right in a given legal system, while the members of group B also have a human right to x, but suffer a lack of effective respect for this right. In situation S_2, in contrast, both the members of A and the members of B have a human right to x and they enjoy effective respect for that right. Obviously S_2 is a morally better situation than S_1. It is the process of getting from S_1 to S_2 that is in question.

We can, it seems to me, make a number of comparative judgments. First, non-violent methods not involving violations of human rights would certainly be morally superior to violent methods, other things being equal. Defenders of non-violence argue, often convincingly, that non-violent pressures are in fact more successful, and lead to the loss of fewer lives than do violent methods, in moving societies from situations such as S_1 to situations such as S_2. It seems obvious that non-violence is morally superior, if it can succeed.

I consider myself an advocate of non-violence, by which I mean one should recognize strong *prima facie* principles against the use of violence, and always place the burden of proof, in a justification, on the violent course of action if it is claimed that violence is needed to prevent or to correct serious wrongs or violations of rights. More important, one should continually champion what Sara Ruddick calls 'a sturdy suspicion of violence.'[30] One should strive to invent and to promote non-violent forms of action, and should try one's best to make non-violent approaches successful. It is often to this aim that our best efforts can be directed: to create and to sustain institutions that permit, encourage, and are responsive, when appropriate, to non-violent forms of control or protest, thus deflecting tendencies on any side of a conflict to resort to violence.

To advocate non-violence is to argue that there are *prima facie* principles against the use of violence to uphold a legal order as well as to challenge it. It may well be justifiable to intervene forcefully to prevent, say, violent assault, but force is not the same as violence, and violence usually need not and should not be used. The state has *many* means besides violence of upholding its legitimate authority and bringing about effective respect for rights, and such non-violent means should be developed far more than they have been. Strong *prima facie* arguments against violence should also apply to groups seeking changes in political and legal arrangements. Non-violence is not acquiescence; it can be a stubborn refusal to cooperate with injustice and a determination to resist oppression, but to do so non-violently. Feminists have added greatly to the case for non-violence. As the editor of one collection of essays writes: 'Put into the feminist perspective, non-violence is the merging of our uncompromising rage at the patriarchy's brutal destructiveness with a refusal to adopt its ways.'[31]

In important ways, the terrorist often shares the worst macho aspects of those he opposes, mirroring the fascination with violence and the eroticisation of force characteristic of the culture he attacks.[32] However, after this has been said, comparative judgments are still needed. If a judgment is made that in certain circumstances violence to uphold law is justifiable, cannot a judgment as plausibly be made that in certain other circumstances, violence to bring about respect for rights can be justifiable? And if violence can be justifiable, can terrorism, on occasion, also be justified? State terrorism to destroy legitimate movements of liberation exists. Can terrorism as a considered method to overcome oppression with as little loss of life as possible be, in contrast, less unjustifiable than state terrorism?

Gandhi is reported to have said that 'it is best of all to resist oppression by non-violent means,' but also that 'it is better to resist oppression by violent means than to submit.'[33] In his book on Gandhi, William Borman asserts that Gandhi 'repeatedly and explicitly makes statements preferring violence to cowardice.'[34] Gandhi wrote that 'my non-violence does not admit of running away from danger and leaving dear ones unprotected. Between violence and cowardly flight, I can only prefer violence to cowardice.'[35] This leaves us with the task of making comparative judgments concerning the use of violence by all those unwilling or unable to adopt 'the summit of bravery,' non-violence, and preferring, on their various sides of any given conflict, violence to flight. It is these comparative judgments with which I am concerned in this essay.

Let us return to my example of trying to move from S_1 to S_2. If a judgment is made, especially in special circumstances, that non-violence cannot succeed, but that terrorism will be effective in moving a society from S_1 to S_2, can engaging in terrorism be better than refraining from it? Given that it will involve a violation of human rights, can it be better to violate rights through terrorism than to avoid this violation?

Consider the situations and the alternatives. Alternative 1 is to maintain S_1 and to refrain from terrorism; alternative 2 is to employ terrorism and to achieve S_2. Both alternatives involve rights violations. The questions are: Can they be compared and can either be found to be less unjustifiable?

It has often been pointed out, in assessing terrorism, that we can almost never accurately predict that an outcome such as S_2 will be achieved as a result of the terrorism in question. But I am trying to deal with the moral issues *given* certain empirical claims. And *if* the empirical judgment is responsibly made that the transition is likely to achieve S_2, which situation is clearly morally better than S_1, and that no other means can do so, can alternative 2 be better than alternative 1? Rights will be violated in either case. Are there any grounds on which the violations in alternative 2 are morally less unjustifiable than the violations in alternative 1?

It seems reasonable, I think, that on grounds of justice, it is better to equalize rights violations in a transition to bring an end to rights violations than it is to subject a given group that has already suffered extensive rights violations to continued such violations, if the degree of severity of the two violations is similar. And this is the major argument of this chapter. If we must have rights violations, a more equitable distribution of such violations is better than a less equitable distribution.

If the severity of the violations is very dissimilar, then we might judge that the more serious violations are to be avoided in favor of the less serious, regardless of who is suffering them, although this judgment could perhaps be overridden if, for instance, many different though less serious violations were suffered by the members of group B, a situation that could outweigh a serious violation for the members of group A. But generally, there would be a *prima facie* judgment against serious violations, such as those of rights to life, to bring about respect for less serious rights, such as those to more equitable distributions of property above what is necessary for the satisfaction of basic needs.

The case on which I focus, however, involves serious violations among both groups. The human rights to personal safety of oppressed groups are, for instance, frequently violated. If a transition to a situation such as S_2 involves violations of the rights to personal safety of the oppressing groups, why would this violation be less unjustifiable than the other? Fairness would seem to recommend a sharing of the burden of rights violation, even if no element of punishment were appealed to. If punishment is considered, it would seem more appropriate for those who have benefited from the rights violations of the members of a given group to suffer, in a transition, any necessary rights violations than to allow the further rights violations of those who have already been subjected to them. But punishment need not be a factor in our assessment. We can conclude that though non-violence is always better than violence, other things being equal, terrorism carried out by the group that has reason to believe it can only thus successfully decrease the disregard of rights where such disregard is prevalent is less morally unjustifiable than terrorism carried out by the group that maintains such disregard.

That justice itself often requires a concern for how rights violations are distributed seems clear. We can recognize that some distributions are unfair, and seek to make them less so. Consider the following: The right to personal security, of freedom from unlawful attack, can be fully recognized as a right in a given legal community, and yet of course some assaults will occur. The community's way of trying to assure respect for such rights is likely to include the deployment of police forces. But if almost all the police forces are deployed in high-income white neighborhoods and almost none in low-income black neighborhoods, so that the risk of assault for inhabitants of the latter is many times greater than the risk for inhabitants of the former, we can judge without great difficulty that the deployment is unfair. Or if we take any given level of effort to protect persons from assault, and if cuts in protection are then necessary for budgetary reasons, and the cuts are all made in areas already suffering the greatest threats of attack, we can judge that such cuts are being made unfairly.

The basis for such judgments must be a principle of justice with respect to the distribution of rights violations, or of the risks of such violations. This is the principle to which I am appealing in my argument concerning terrorism, and it seems clear that it is a relevant principle that we should not ignore.

And the argument need not be limited to oppressed groups within a given legal system. If Israel fails to respect the human rights of the Palestinians in the Occupied Territories it controls, and if Palestinians seek to gain such respect for both groups, a similar argument could be used. On the other hand, when groups such as Al-Qaeda lack even goals that are acceptable, it could not. The dubious ability of terrorism to achieve a greater measure of effective respect for rights should always be kept in mind. But where the weak have few other ways to move recalcitrant oppressors, who may hold nearly all the chips in any negotiations, terrorism to change such a situation may be less unjustifiable than state counter-terrorism to prevent such change.

What all this may show is that terrorism cannot necessarily be ruled out as unjustifiable on a rights-based analysis, any more than it can on a consequentialist one. Depending on the severity and extent of the rights violations in an existing situation, a transition involving a sharing of rights violations, if this and only this can be expected to lead to a situation in which rights are more adequately respected, may well be less morally unjustifiable than continued acceptance of ongoing rights violations.

Individuals and groups

In his interesting article 'The Morality of Terrorism,' Igor Primoratz argues against my view on comparing rights violations.[36] Primoratz thinks the potential victim of terrorism will hold that his right to life should not be taken away for the sake of a more just distribution of rights violations; to do so would be to fail to recognize that he is a person in his own right, not merely a member of a group. Primoratz argues that with respect to rights to life, Robert Nozick's view of rights as 'almost absolute side constraints' is correct.[37]

My response is that to fail to achieve a more just distribution of violations of rights (through the use of terrorism if that is the only means available) is to fail to recognize that the individual whose rights are already not fairly respected is a person in his or her own right, not merely a member of a group whose interests will be furthered by some goal, or whose rights can be ignored. If we can never violate anyone's right to life in the sense that we can never kill anyone, then killing in self-defense when attacked, or in the course of law enforcement as when a convicted murderer tries to escape and is shot, could not be justified. These are not positions to which even Nozick's view would lead, and Primoratz himself makes exceptions for self-defense and punishment. But if a prohibition on all killing is not what is meant by respecting rights to life as near-absolute side-constraints, we return to questions of which rights we have, what they include, and whose rights count, or count more. Presumably everyone's rights should count equally. Respect for rights will never be perfect in practice. But it seems morally less justifiable that those who have already suffered great disrespect of their rights continue to do so than that the burden of imperfect justice be fairly shared.

Arguments for achieving a just distribution of rights violations need not be arguments, consequentialist or not, that are more than incidentally about groups. They can be arguments about the rights of individuals to basic fairness.[38]

Notes

1. For further discussion, see the original version of this chapter. In his perceptive book on terrorism, Grant Wardlaw notes that 'whilst the primary effect is to create fear and alarm the objectives may be to gain concessions, obtain maximum publicity for a cause, provoke repression, break down social order, build morale in the movement or enforce obedience to it.' *Political Terrorism* (Cambridge: Cambridge University Press, 1982), pp. 41–2.
2. Paul Wilkinson, *Political Terrorism* (London: Macmillan, 1974), p. 17 (emphasis added). In a later book, he does not build the moral judgment quite as directly into the definition, but he still concludes that terrorism is 'a moral crime, a crime against humanity.' Paul Wilkinson, *Terrorism and the Liberal State* (New York: New York University Press, 1986), p. 66.
3. Benjamin Netanyahu (ed.), *Terrorism: How the West Can Win* (New York: Farrar, Straus and Giroux, 1986). pp. 29–30.
4. Burton Leiser, *Liberty, Justice, and Morality*, second edition (New York: Macmillan, 1979), chapter 13.
5. Michael Walzer, 'Terrorism: A Critique of Excuses,' in Steven Luper-Foy (ed.), *Problems of International Justice: Philosophical Essays* (Boulder, Col.: Westview Press, 1988), p. 238. His position is effectively criticized by Robert K. Fullinwider in 'Understanding Terrorism,' in the same volume.

6. The essays collected in Netanyahu (ed.), *Terrorism*, provide many examples.
7. See John Dugard, 'International Terrorism and the Just War,' *Stanford Journal of International Studies* 12 (1976).
8. On this point see especially Richard Falk, *Revolutionaries and Functionaries: The Dual Faces of Terrorism* (New York: Dutton, 1988).
9. Robert L. Holmes, 'Terrorism and Other Forms of Violence: A Moral Perspective,' paper presented at the meeting of Concerned Philosophers for Peace, Dayton, Ohio, 16 October 1987. See also his *On War and Morality* (Princeton, NJ: Princeton University Press, 1989).
10. Falk, *Revolutionaries and Functionaries*, p. 37.
11. See, e.g., C.A.J. Coady, 'The Morality of Terrorism,' *Philosophy* 60 (1985), and Jan Schreiber, *The Ultimate Weapon: Terrorists and World Order* (New York: Morrow, 1978).
12. Michael Walzer, *Just and Unjust Wars: A Moral Argument with Historical Illustrations*, third edition (New York: Basic Books, 2000), chapter 16.
13. *The New York Times*, August 7, 1988, p. A9.
14. Coady, 'The Morality of Terrorism,' p. 63.
15. R.M. Hare, 'On Terrorism,' *Journal of Value Inquiry* 13 (1979).
16. Carl Wellman, 'On Terrorism Itself,' *Journal of Value Inquiry* 13 (1979).
17. Burleigh Wilkins, 'Terrorism and Consequentialism,' *Journal of Value Inquiry* 21 (1987).
18. Walter Laqueur, *The Age of Terrorism*, revised and expanded edition (Boston: Little, Brown, 1987).
19. Albrecht Wellmer, 'Terrorism and the Critique of Society,' in Jürgen Habermas (ed.), *Observations on 'The Spiritual Situation of the Age': Contemporary German Perspectives*, trans. A. Buchwalter (Cambridge, Mass.: MIT Press, 1984), p. 300.
20. See Charles Tilly, 'Collective Violence in European Perspective,' in Hugh Davis Graham and Ted Robert Gurr (eds.), *Violence in America: Historical and Comparative Perspectives* (New York: Bantam, 1969); and Lewis A. Coser, 'Some Social Functions of Violence,' *Annals of the American Academy of Political and Social Science* 364 (1966).
21. Falk, *Revolutionaries and Functionaries*, pp. 34–5.
22. Wilkins, 'Terrorism and Consequentialism,' p. 150.
23. Ibid.
24. The classic statement is Max Weber's: 'The state is considered the sole source of the "right" to use violence ... The state is a relation of men dominating men, a relation supported by means of legitimate (i.e. considered to be legitimate) violence' (H.H. Gerth and C. Wright Mills (trans. and eds.), *From Max Weber: Essays in Sociology* (New York: Oxford University Press, 1958), p. 78).
25. See Virginia Held, *Rights and Goods: Justifying Social Action* (New York: Free Press and Macmillan, 1984).
26. Wellman, 'On Terrorism Itself,' p. 258.
27. Ibid.
28. Coady, 'The Morality of Terrorism,' p. 58.
29. See, e.g., Committee on Foreign Affairs (comp.), *Human Rights Documents* (Washington DC: Government Printing Office, 1983). For discussion see e.g. Alan Gewirth, *Human Rights* (Chicago: University of Chicago Press, 1982), and James W. Nickel, *Making Sense of Human Rights* (Berkeley: University of California Press, 1987).

30. Sara Ruddick, *Maternal Thinking: Toward a Politics of Peace* (Boston: Beacon Books, 1989), p. 138. See also Adrienne Harris and Ynestra King (eds.), *Rocking the Ship of the State* (Boulder Col.: Westview Press, 1989).

31. Pam McAllister, 'Introduction' to Pam McAllister (ed.), *Reweaving the Web of Life: Feminism and Nonviolence* (Philadelphia: New Society, 1982), p. iii.

32. See e.g. Robin Morgan, *The Demon Lover: The Roots of Terrorism* (New York: Washington Square Press, 2001).

33. Quoted in McAllister, 'Introduction,' p. vi.

34. William Borman, *Gandhi and Non-Violence* (Albany, NY: State University of New York Press, 1986), p. xiv.

35. Quoted in ibid., pp. 252–3.

36. Igor Primoratz, 'The Morality of Terrorism,' *Journal of Applied Philosophy* 14 (1997).

37. Ibid., p. 231.

38. For further discussion of terrorism, see Virginia Held, 'Terrorism and War,' *The Journal of Ethics* (forthcoming).

7
Terrorism, Morality, and Supreme Emergency

C.A.J. (Tony) Coady

The moral issues

In this chapter, I will be using 'terrorism' in the sense of *organized use of violence to attack non-combatants ('innocents' in a special sense) or their property for political purposes.*[1] Is terrorism wrong? Given this definition – which I want to term 'tactical' – and given just war theory, the answer is, as I have argued more fully elsewhere,[2] clearly yes. Terrorism violates a central principle of the *jus in bello*, the principle of discrimination, which declares the immunity of non-combatants from direct attack. It is not just that there are good utilitarian arguments for this principle or that it has been agreed between nations. The prohibition lies at the heart of the reasoning that allows for legitimate war *in extremis* since you are entitled to wage war only against those who are doing a certain sort of harm (and then only if other conditions are fulfilled). As John Locke put it: 'they [those among the enemy population innocent of waging the war] ought not to be charged as guilty of the violence and injustice that is committed in an unjust war any farther than they actually abet it.'[3] Here Locke echoes what is common in the just war tradition.[4]

Of course, much more needs to be said about the meaning and significance of 'innocence' and non-combatant status, and the sort of wrong that terrorism constitutes. I have discussed the first issue elsewhere;[5] here, I will concentrate upon an important aspect of the second. But first let me say two things, by way of precaution. The first is that terrorism

---

A longer version of this chapter is published as: C.A.J. Coady, 'Terrorism, Morality and Supreme Emergency,' *Ethics*, vol. 114, no. 4 (July 2004) © The University of Chicago, 2004. Reproduced by permission.

is not the only wrong that political violence can commit. The intentional killing of non-combatants is morally reprehensible, but so is the bringing it about that combatants are killed in an unjust war. This is what was so morally horrible about World War I where non-combatant casualties were at a minimum. And the killing of non-combatants as 'collateral damage' can also be a great wrong. These matters deserve separate discussion but I cannot address them further here. The second thing is that the wrong of terrorism, even on my relatively restricted definition, is not an undifferentiated wrong. For one thing, attacks upon non-combatant property can be much less grave a matter than direct attacks upon life and limb. There is certainly a moral presumption against such attacks, but it may be rebuttable given grave enough reasons. Presumably, no one thinks that the property of innocent persons is of such significance that nothing could ever justify its confiscation or even destruction. Its value is of a different order to that of the life of innocent human beings. Consequently, there may be circumstances where deliberate damage to or destruction or confiscation of the property of innocent people may be justifiable if the stakes are high enough and the property not central to personal survival. There may even be 'attacks' upon persons that are slight enough to allow for justification, or for only muted condemnation, as when civilian highways are blocked by violent means in order to cause traffic delays that might serve some significant military or political objective. Or if that is not clearly enough a violent attack upon the persons (or their property) then we might consider the violent seizure of uncooperative civilians to remove them from an area where soldiers can then be attacked while the civilians are forcibly restrained temporarily elsewhere. In what follows, I shall ignore the possibility of these 'minor' terrorisms and concentrate upon major harms to persons and property.

If one takes the principle of non-combatant immunity that forms a significant part of the *jus in bello* to invoke an absolute moral prohibition upon intentionally attacking innocent people, as just war thinkers have commonly done, then major terrorism is always wrong and always impermissible.[6] Yet many contemporary moral philosophers, sympathetic to just war thinking, are wary of moral absolutes. Igor Primoratz, for instance, whose position is perhaps nearest to mine, calls terrorism 'almost absolutely wrong,' thereby endorsing a very strong moral presumption against terrorism and the targeting of non-combatants, but allowing for exceptions in extreme circumstances.[7] The situation here parallels what is sometimes said about warfare between states. So, Michael Walzer thinks that in conditions of 'supreme emergency' the violation of the normal immunity expressed by the principle of discrimination is permissible in warfare between states though only with a heavy burden of remorse. He thinks the Allied terror bombing of German cities in World War II (in the early stages) was legitimated by the enormity of the Nazi threat and the reasonable fear of its imminent triumph.[8] John Rawls recently endorsed this view while condemning the bombings of Hiroshima and Nagasaki.[9] Neither of these theorists envisages extending the supreme emergency defense to those sub-state groups who direct political violence against the state. Indeed, in a later paper,[10] Walzer's position disqualifies him from doing so (see below).

Let us look more carefully at this. The idea of exemptions from profound moral constraints has taken many different forms in modern analytical moral philosophy. Some of these are closely associated with the philosophy of utilitarianism. In its simplest form, act utilitarianism, and certain allied forms of thought, hold that all moral constraints are simply 'rules of thumb' that can and should be overruled if calculations of the overall outcomes of so doing show that it is productive of more general happiness than sorrow. This seems to me a deeply misguided view of ethics but I cannot offer a full-scale rebuttal here. Its principal defect in connection with terrorism is that, in essence, it doesn't allow that the profound moral constraints against killing the innocent are really profound at all.[11] That is why it calls them 'rules of thumb' along with all sorts of other shorthand adages in the moral life.

More subtle versions of utilitarianism, or indeed of consequentialism more generally, can perhaps avoid the charge of trivializing the deep constraint against killing or maiming the innocent by making a case for the depth of this prohibition in terms of the awful consequences of not having such a constraint. Again, I am somewhat skeptical of the success of such 'indirect' utilitarianism, but this is hardly the place to argue for that in detail. The outcome of the strategy seems to me likely to make the indirect strategist, for most, if not all, practical purposes, a bedfellow with deontologists and other believers in the intrinsic wrongness of intentionally killing the innocent. In connection with terrorism, the interesting question is how this latter group (let us call them instrinsicalists) can allow for exemptions from this basic prohibition.

Two approaches to exemption

Here, it seems possible to distinguish two positions though they have a tendency to merge. The first is that associated with many forms of modern intuitionism, as classically expressed, for instance, by W.D. Ross.[12] We might call this, 'balanced exceptionism.' The basic outlook is much more widespread amongst theorists than the intuitionist philosophy itself, but I shall use the intuitionist framework to spell it out. Here, there are various moral principles that are revealed to reflective thought and they give rise to '*prima facie* obligations' or '*prima facie* duties.' The force of these is generally independent of the calculation of consequences but whether something is *actually* obligatory will depend upon whether there are other *prima facie* obligations that outweigh it and some of these may involve the calculation of consequences, as in the case of a duty of beneficence. So the obligation not intentionally to kill the innocent, being, like all the rest, *prima facie*, may be overruled by (say) the obligation to advance the good of one's community. In this outlook, no initial prohibitions can be presumed absolute, and the final binding prohibition or obligation determines one's duty with finality, and, as it were, without loss. There may be a sense of regret that one cannot avoid doing something that was *prima facie* wrong – it would be more comfortable if one's *prima facie* duties did not conflict and therefore need resolution – but no wrong can be attributed to you if you have done the balancing conscientiously.[13] The balanced exceptionist can of course acknowledge that some *prima facie* duties are stronger than others, and hence some presumptive wrongs carry more heft than others. Indeed, the balancing story commits the outlook to this acknowledgement since there would be no point to the talk of balancing as a procedure for decision unless there were such differences of weight. But the fact remains that the granting of exemption from the prohibition on intentionally killing the innocent is part of a normal, even routine, business of balancing presumptive obligations in order to find what is finally obligatory or prohibited. If the scales tell you that it is morally permitted or even morally obligatory intentionally to kill the innocent, then in these circumstances it cannot be wrong to do so.[14]

The second exemption position emerges from the discussion of what has been called 'dirty hands.' This tradition can be traced back at least to Machiavelli, is glimpsed in Max Weber, and has found eloquent modern expression in Michael Walzer.[15] Although it has some affinities with balanced exceptionism, it seems to be distinguishable from that outlook by three things. The first is its emphasis on the political realm as the principal focus for the making of exceptions to what seem to be powerful moral prohibitions; the second is its common emphasis upon the extreme nature of the situations in which the powerful moral rule must be disregarded; and the third, and perhaps most important, is its stress upon the abiding wrongness that is done by the necessary violation of the moral prohibition. Together, these provide a distinct contrast to the intuitionist tradition and balanced exceptionism. In particular, the dirty hands theorists seem to want to treat such moral prohibitions as that upon intentionally killing the innocent as far more than *prima facie* or presumptive. They think them profound. Theorists like Walzer believe that ordinary calculations of utility cannot override these sorts of constraints, but they also hold that such constraints cannot yield at all comfortably to standard countervailing duties and obligations. This second point tends to be implicit in the dirty hands literature whereas the anti-utilitarian point is overt.[16] None the less, despite the contrast, there comes a point where the gravity of the consequences or the gravity of the conflicting duty can demand the regrettable and morally painful choice to violate such deep norms.

The 'dirty hands' tradition is a complex one and I have had to simplify it for present purposes. The basic idea that certain necessities of life, especially political life, may require the overriding of profound moral prohibitions in extreme situations is clothed in many different uniforms. Machiavelli sees it as necessity overriding morality, and Weber as a clash between the ethic of responsibility and the ethic of absolute ends. In connection with war and violence, Walzer views it in terms of 'supreme emergency' overriding (otherwise) moral absolutes. This raises the question of how such overriding is to be described. We are doing wrong because we must, but if necessity somehow legitimates our act then it seems we are right to do wrong. I have discussed this apparent paradox elsewhere,[17] and will say no more here about the conceptual problem, except to mention another possible maneuver that seems to require a less paradoxical description of what is going on. This is the position adopted by Thomas Nagel (briefly described in note 14). Nagel endorses an absolute prohibition on intentionally killing non-combatants but argues that there are certain extreme situations in which the costs of adhering to the prohibition create a moral dilemma or a 'moral blind alley.' In these situations, whatever one does is morally wrong. He envisages this as a clash between absolutist principle and very great utilitarian cost in which the agent is pulled in different directions by 'these two forms of moral intuition.' (It would presumably be possible for the moral dilemma to be created by the clash between absolute prohibition and some powerful positive duty, though Nagel says nothing on this.) This position has some affinities with the 'dirty hands' tradition but strikingly differs from it in not coming down on the side of the necessity to violate the absolute prohibition. For Nagel, it would be just as 'right' or 'necessary' to adhere to the prohibition, but that is quite against the spirit of the dirty hands tradition in either its ancient or contemporary forms. Nagel is not interested in creating a path to exemptions, but in showing certain discomforting limitations to our moral outlook. His alternative approach tells us something interesting about the dirty hands tradition and is particularly relevant to what I shall argue below is its pro-state bias.

If we are to allow exemptions from profound moral prohibitions that remain somehow in force, though rightly ignored in the particular case, then how are we to characterize the conditions under which such exemptions apply? Phrases like 'necessity' or 'supreme emergency' are very vague and open to diverse interpretations, not to mention exploitations. Machiavelli has in mind the necessity for the ruler ('the Prince') to gain and maintain power and 'glory' but although this is a powerful drive for all politicians, it is surely far too thin a value to legitimate the slaughter of innocents. More generously, we might treat him as arguing that the survival of the state is the value in question. This idea can be seen also in Weber and Walzer, but it dangerously opens the door to the identification of the state's survival with that of its political leadership. It is not only ancient French monarchs who think that their departure betokens the deluge or that they *are* the state. We shall explore this issue further below.

Dirty hands and supreme emergency

To focus our discussion. more concretely, let us take the 'supreme emergency' defense that Walzer offers for one contentious military policy, namely, the area bombing of German cities in World War II. Walzer does not defend the bombing unequivocally. He thinks that, though it was morally wrong as a violation of the principle of discrimination, it was justified by the plea of supreme emergency in the early stages of the war. In the later stages, however, it was just plain morally criminal since an Allied victory could be reasonably foreseen on the basis of morally legitimate targeting and fighting. The bombing of Dresden was therefore an outright atrocity, though the area bombing of other German cities earlier in the war was not. Walzer is a little unclear when the justification of supreme emergency ceased but it seems to be around the middle of 1942.[18] He is even less clear when it began to apply since the formal directive to attack civilians and their homes dates from February 14, 1942 though there was some city bombing in violation of the 'war convention' during the early years of the campaign.[19] He is clear that any deliberate area bombing earlier than mid-1942 was a violation of the principle of discrimination and several times refers to 'terror bombing' and twice to 'terrorism.'[20] It was morally wrong, but had to be done.

I shall consider Walzer's argument in three stages. First, I shall challenge its legitimacy in the case he chooses to motivate the category of 'supreme emergency.' This will require a brief historical detour, but it is important to see that, in what seems the strongest actual case (as opposed to philosophers' fantasies), the appeal to supreme emergency is seriously flawed. Second, I shall argue that there is an illegitimate pro-state bias built into Walzer's deployment of the argument, and that the justification of sub-state terrorism on grounds of 'supreme emergency' should therefore be more available than he allows. Third, I shall seek to show that the category of 'supreme emergency' is too opaque to do the work required of it and that its employment in the public discourse of justifying political violence is too dangerous.

Walzer's use of the category 'supreme emergency' here is grounded in three conditions. The first is that the need to defeat Nazi Germany was no ordinary necessity. Hitler's victory would have been a dire blow to civilization. The enormity of his regime and its practices was such that his extended empire would have been a disaster for most of the people living under its sway. The second condition is that of imminent threat: the prospect of Hitler's victory was present and urgent. And the third condition is that the bombing of German cities aimed directly at the civilian populations was likely to be effective in averting the threat. (Walzer also places considerable weight upon the idea that such bombing was, in the early stages, the only offensive weapon the British had – 'the bombers alone provide the means of victory,' as he quotes Churchill saying in September 1940.[21] But this is hardly relevant, even if true, unless it is coupled with some likelihood of success.)

Now, several things are worth noting about these conditions. The first is that some of the matters that Walzer seems to factor into the dire judgement on the likely results of German victory were not known to Churchill and his advisers and so did not influence the decision to use strategic bombing. In particular, the enormity of the Holocaust was not comprehended at the time. Hitler was known to be anti-Semitic and to have persecuted Jews and political opponents, but not to have a program of genocide in hand. So part of the legitimation influencing Walzer is largely *post-facto* and was not available to Churchill. Even so, had the horrors of Nazism been fully comprehended that would have given added weight to the gravity of the threat. There remain, however, the questions of the imminence of defeat and the likelihood that the terror bombing would succeed in breaking enemy morale and playing a major role in avoiding defeat. Walzer admits that respectable evidence now shows that city bombing was largely unsuccessful in its primary aim, but futile as this exercise in dirtying the hands seems to have been, Walzer thinks the British government had to gamble with innocent lives.[22]

There are two things wrong with this. First, there was good reason to believe that the prospect of imminent defeat was gone by February 1942, when the decision explicitly to adopt the policy of terror bombing was taken. The aerial Battle of Britain had been won late in 1940, the Soviet Army, in December 1941, had inflicted the first major defeat of the war on the German army by repulsing the *Wehrmacht* from the gates of Moscow and destroying Hitler's hopes of a quick victory in Russia, and the United States had entered the war against Germany three days after the Japanese attack on Pearl Harbor on December 10, 1941. Churchill himself later revealed his reaction at the time: 'So we had won after all!...Hitler's fate was sealed [and] there was no more doubt about the end.'[23] The imminent threat element in the supreme emergency justification was therefore not something Churchill could honestly invoke by the end of 1941, nor is it plausible to invoke it retrospectively for him given the realities of February 1942. After the triumph of the Spitfires in defeating enemy air power over Britain in late 1940, it is even doubtful that the very early and ambiguous resorts to terror bombing could elicit a defense of supreme emergency. Second, the success of the bombing could have been seen as highly implausible at the time, and indeed was so viewed by many senior policy advisers.[24] The murder of one's children and the destruction of one's home was bound to affect anyone's morale, but the further consequences of that were never likely to be those claimed by the advocates of terror.

In the first place, the ordinary citizens of a totalitarian, police state had no way to turn their despair into avenues of political change or serious resistance. Moreover, they were as likely to hate the bombers as to hate Hitler and hence more likely to be moved to persist with, if not enthusiastically support, the war effort. The British already had empirical evidence from their own citizens' reactions to German bombings of England that the predictions of Sir Arthur ('Bomber') Harris and the rest of the air command lobby were faulty.[25] We must conclude that the supreme emergency exemption was wrongly applied even in the restricted circumstances envisaged by Walzer and Rawls.[26] Even granting the enormity of the Nazi threat the remaining two necessary conditions were unsatisfied after December 1941 and the probability of success condition was never satisfied.[27]

The pro-state bias

A further curiosity of Walzer's argument is that it is presented only as an argument available to states and their representatives. This is not exclusively true of the tradition of the 'dirty hands' debate (it is less true of Weber, for instance) but it is a pronounced emphasis of Walzer's treatment. In Walzer's case this is particularly strange because he derived the term 'dirty hands' from Jean-Paul Sartre's play of that name and Sartre's play is concerned with the supposed need for revolutionaries to violate morality in the furtherance of their cause. In spite of this, Walzer's framework, and that of many others committed to the idea of 'dirty hands' is basically that of the duty of statesmen to preserve their polity or civilization.[28] But, if we think only of the connotations of 'supreme emergency' and the three conditions discussed above, it is not at all obvious that the issue can be so restricted. Palestinian resistance groups, for example, can mount a strong case that they face a hostile power bent upon subordination and dispossession to a degree that threatens not only their lives, but their way of life.

In his discussion of 'supreme emergency,' Walzer makes his pro-state bias quite explicit. 'Can soldiers and statesmen override the rights of innocent people for the sake of their own political communities? I am inclined to answer the question affirmatively, though not without hesitation and worry.'[29] And he goes on to speak of nations in a way that identifies political communities and nations. Of course, Walzer's language here leaves logical space for the idea that nations or political communities can be driven by necessity even where they do not possess a state or have been deprived of one. Yet it is clear that recourse by such people or their real or imagined leaders to 'supreme emergency' is far from his mind. Indeed, in another place, where he is explicitly concerned with sub-state agents employing terrorism, Walzer argues that such terrorism can *never* be justified or excused. Although he doesn't define terrorism very clearly, it is obvious that he is operating with a version of the tactical definition, saying such things as, '[terrorism] is indefensible now that it has been recognized, like rape and murder, as an attack upon the innocent.'[30] He makes his total condemnation explicit: 'I take the principle for granted: that every act of terrorism is a wrongful act.'[31] Although even this leaves theoretical room for a 'dirty hands' move to claim the wrongful act as necessary, it is clear that Walzer does not envisage such room being available for sub-state terrorists. In fact, his article is devoted to examining excuses for terrorism since he takes it as axiomatic that there can be no justifications of any sort. But he reaches the same conclusion about excuses, even though some of the excuses that he examines are formally very similar to the necessity arguments he endorses as justifications under the rubric of supreme emergency in the case of the terror bombing of World War II. Most notably, he holds that the argument that no other strategy is available is never a valid reason for terrorist acts, even though it figures so prominently in his case for the necessity of the Allied terror bombing.[32] He seems to have forgotten his description of that bombing as 'terrorism.'

But why should states enjoy the supreme emergency license when other groups do not? This is particularly pertinent when we admit, as Walzer earlier did, that states can employ terrorism (in the tactical sense). The primacy of the political community that Walzer sees as validating the special role of (most) states is highly suspect. Walzer admits of individuals that they can never attack innocent people to aid their self-defense.[33] He then adds: 'But communities, in emergencies, seem to have different and larger prerogatives. I am not sure that I can account for the difference, without ascribing to communal life a kind of transcendence that I don't believe it to have.'[34] Walzer goes on to try to locate the 'difference' in the supposed fact that 'the survival and freedom of political communities . . . are the highest values of international society.'[35] Perhaps these are the highest values of international society, but this is hardly surprising if one construes international society as a society of political communities, namely recognized states. What is needed, at the very least, is an argument that locates the survival and freedom of states as the highest *human* value, and one that is capable of justifying the overriding that 'supreme emergency' requires. I doubt that any such argument exists. We should certainly avoid the temptation to identify the survival of a state with the survival of the regime that runs it. But neither should we identify the survival of the state with the survival of its subjects. Some states may deserve to perish and their former subjects may be better for their demise. Nor is it enough to point to the undoubted value of political life for there are many other values, such as family relationships, friendship, and moral integrity that are equally if not more significant. And even if some argument could show the pre-eminent value of political community and the life it allows, this would still leave a gap between political community and state, a gap that Walzer's argument here obscures. At least some revolutionary or dissenting groups can plausibly claim to be or to represent political communities and to deploy violence in defense of a threatened political life. If so, the value that is supposed by Walzer to legitimate resort to supreme emergency should be available to them as well.

Yet this is precisely what Walzer is at pains to deny. The contrast in treatment is stark in what Walzer says of the terrorist excuse that attacking the innocent is the only option they have. Walzer objects to this that other strategies are available if you are opposing liberal and democratic states and that terrorism never works against totalitarian states.[36] In discussing what he treats as a further excuse, that 'terrorism works (and nothing else does),'[37] he adds that this efficiency excuse depends for its success on that of 'the only option' excuse or that of the structurally similar 'last resort.' Indeed, these three excuses are closely related and, as Walzer admits of the efficiency test, it goes beyond an excuse and aims to constitute a justification in consequentialist terms. If so, the question of a 'dirty hands' justification surely arises, and Walzer even mentions the 'dirty hands' of the terrorists, but he doesn't invoke any form of supreme emergency on their behalf. This must be, at least in part, because he thinks that the consequentialist considerations are defective in their own terms. As he argues: 'I doubt that terrorism has ever achieved national liberation – no nation that I know of owes its freedom to a campaign of random murder – although terrorism undoubtedly increases the power of the terrorists within the national liberation movement.'[38]

These arguments are hardly decisive as they stand, and they become still less persuasive when set against what Walzer says of the World War II bombing. As to the arguments themselves, the claim that terrorism will work (and nothing else will) need not mean that terrorism must work all by itself, as Walzer's comment about failure to achieve national liberation might suggest. The 'nothing else' claim need only mean that nothing else will fulfil the role that has been assigned to terrorism. Hence the terrorist is not committed to the view that national liberation can be achieved by terrorism alone. So understood, the question is whether terrorism has ever made a crucial, irreplaceable contribution to national liberation (or the achieving of the significant revolutionary goals, whatever they are). To say the least, this is a very difficult matter to decide. Did the terrorism of groups like the Irgun and the Stern gang play such a part in establishing the state of Israel? But, in any case, the question is structurally very similar to that Walzer poses for the legitimacy of the British bombing.

As we saw earlier, Walzer is sympathetic to the 'only option' story for the early stages of the terror bombing even while admitting that serious studies subsequently indicate the campaign to have been futile on its own terms. He thinks Churchill had to gamble because the stakes were so very high and the danger imminent. Walzer doesn't, of course, think that this means that probability has no relevance to the gamble, but just that the estimated probability doesn't have to be set so high. It can also be pretty vague. As Walzer says of the bombing, 'it makes no sense at this point to quantify the probabilities. I have no clear notion what they actually were or even how they might be calculated given our present knowledge, nor am I sure how different figures, unless they were very different, would affect the moral argument.'[39] This is strikingly at odds with what he says about non-state terrorists who argue that attacking non-combatants is the only option they have. They are given no such latitude with probabilities, no matter how imminent and awful the threat. It seems that threats to their political community can never be great enough to constitute the sort of 'immeasurable evil' that Walzer sees in the Nazi threat.[40] I am at a loss (inevitably) about gauging 'immeasurable' evils, but it would not seem impossible that various struggles against brutal, murderous, tyrannical regimes could sometimes reasonably be viewed as confronting supreme emergency. Of course, they cannot hope to succeed against a totalitarian state, according to Walzer, because terrorism never can succeed against a totalitarian state. Yet the terrorism of the bombers was itself directed against a totalitarian state and was posited on the subjects of that state being able to influence the state's policy and workings.

We should conclude that the attempt to restrict the supreme emergency exemption to states is unpersuasive. Either it applies more generally or it does not apply at all.

The third difficulty

This brings me to my third difficulty with the category of supreme emergency. If we reject Walzer's attempt to restrict the supreme emergency exemption to states, the question arises whether the broadening of the potential application of supreme emergency considerations provides a reason for skepticism about the category itself. Those in the dirty hands tradition who restrict its application to the sphere of state politics are partly moved by a certain romanticism about the superiority of the values served by states and by politics more generally. But they are also concerned to preserve the rarity value of the dirty hands exemption. As the name suggests, the supreme emergency story, as a version of the dirty hands tradition, gets its persuasiveness from the idea that its disruptive power to override profound moral prohibitions is only available in the rarest of circumstances. Any broadening of the reach of those circumstances tends to reduce the rarity value of the exemption, and hence increase the oddity of the idea that it can be right to do what is morally wrong. Why not allow that the exemption can apply to huge corporations, the existence of which is central to the lives and livelihoods of so many? Or, contrary to Walzer's declared position, to individuals when they are really up against the wall? Yet the more we move in this direction, the more the currency of supreme emergency is devalued and we seem to collapse the dirty hands position into that of balanced exceptionism.

These considerations suggest that the category of supreme emergency, in spite of its surface clarity, is conceptually opaque. This opacity is alarming enough in itself since it means that those using the concept may not be making clear sense, even to themselves. Yet, in the context of public discourse about war and terrorism, we should be particularly worried about allowing exemptions from profound moral and legal constraints under categories that are, at the very least, so open to divergent interpretations. Both the morality and legality of political violence must be concerned with the dangerous consequences of allowing justifications or exemptions that are likely to be exploited by any side to a conflict. On Walzer's own account, the 'legitimate' resort to terror in the early stages of World War II led rapidly to its illegitimate use thereafter with disastrous human consequences for hundreds of thousands of German civilians. Moreover, one party's resort to supreme emergency is likely to encourage other parties (including the current enemy) to tread the path of exemption; they are unlikely to cede the point that the original violator's resort to exemption is legitimate where their own is not.[41] In the context of the present terrorism alert the promulgation of a doctrine of supreme emergency is fraught with danger.

It may be objected that these are mere practical problems about the promulgation of what may none the less be a 'true' moral thesis. Perhaps the supreme emergency exemption states a moral truth that it would be morally disastrous to publicize. Even to concede this would be to rob the exemption of much of its point since it is supposed to form part of the publicly accessible wisdom about the waging of war and other forms of political violence. But the objection's distinction between the truth of a moral thesis and the value or disvalue of its promulgation is, in any case, debatable as a universally applicable distinction. Even those of us who think that truth, in some substantial sense, does apply to moral discourse need to acknowledge that moral truths are supported by practical reason and are dependent in complex ways on issues of practicality. This is particularly pertinent to matters of political morality where the need for public accessibility and the real possibility of rational public endorsement are rightly prominent.[42]

That completes my critique of the supreme emergency exemption. It could further be argued that it undervalues the depth and centrality of the just war prohibition on killing the innocent. I shall not attempt that argument here, since it would require an exploration of whether any prohibitions can be absolute, of the nature of moral dilemmas, and of the requirements for depth and centrality in a moral framework. The discussion of terrorism and supreme emergency does in any event clearly face us with two options. Either we insist that major terrorism (as characterized by the tactical definition) is always morally wrong and never to be allowed, or we accept that there can be circumstances in which the values served by terrorist acts are so important that it is right to do them. If the latter, then this exemption cannot be allowed only to states. Its legitimacy must in principle be more widely available, and decided on a case by case basis. My own conviction is that we surely do better to condemn the resort to terrorism outright with no leeway for exemptions, be they for states, revolutionaries or religious and ideological zealots.

Notes

1. I have argued for this definition elsewhere; see my 'Defining Terrorism,' chapter 1 in this volume.
2. Coady, 'The Morality of Terrorism,' *Philosophy* 60 (1985).
3. John Locke, *Two Treatises of Government*, ed. P. Laslett (Cambridge: Cambridge University Press, 1988), sec. II.xvi.179, p. 388.
4. As the sixteenth-century Spanish theologian and philosopher Vitoria, in similar spirit to Locke, had earlier put it: 'the foundation of the just war is the injury inflicted upon one by the enemy, as shown above; but an innocent person has done you no harm.' Francisco de Vitoria, *Political Writings*, ed. A. Pagdan and J. Lawrance (Cambridge: Cambridge University Press, 1991), pp. 314–15.
5. C.A.J. Coady, 'Terrorism and Innocence,' *Journal of Ethics*, forthcoming.
6. There is room for further discussion about the sense of 'innocent' in which non-combatants are innocent and combatants (even coerced and deluded combatants) are not. Essentially, my view is that the non-combatant innocent are those who are not themselves agents of the harm against which violent means are being deployed. Notions of the innocent as those who are not 'morally responsible' (in a rich sense of the term) are not directly to the point. The brainwashed, conscript soldier who is deliberately attacking you with a machine-gun may be forgiven by God, but you are entitled to kill him in self-defense. Of course, it is important to my position that not all civilians are non-combatants. You do not need to be personally wielding a gun or dressed in uniform to be a significant part of a chain of agency that issues in lethal violence. These are matters I have discussed elsewhere; see, in particular,

'Terrorism and Innocence.' I should add that my principal concern with the immunity of the innocent is a concern that they not be subjected to direct *attack*.

7. Igor Primoratz, 'The Morality of Terrorism,' *Journal of Applied Philosophy* 14 (1997), p. 231.

8. Michael Walzer, *Just and Unjust Wars: A Moral Argument with Historical Illustrations*, third edition (New York: Basic Books, 2000), chapter 16.

9. John Rawls, 'Fifty years after Hiroshima,' in *Collected Papers*, ed. Samuel Freeman (Cambridge, Mass.: Harvard University Press, 1999), pp. 565–72.

10. Walzer, 'Terrorism: A Critique of Excuses,' in Steven Luper-Foy (ed.), *Problems of International Justice* (Boulder, Col. and London: Westview Press, 1988).

11. I should add that my concern here with the immunity of the innocent is a concern that they not be subjected to direct *attack*. It is quite another matter whether one is entitled to take innocent life when the 'victim' requests it or can be presumed to want death, as in many cases of euthanasia. There are both utilitarian and non-utilitarian arguments in favor of euthanasia, the latter emphasizing issues of dignity, compassion, and rights. It is a very rare circumstance, though not perhaps an inconceivable one, where victims of bomb attacks will consent to being killed and maimed. Wherever I refer to 'the innocent' in this chapter I will mean the non-consenting innocent.

12. W.D. Ross, *The Right and the Good* (Oxford: Clarendon Press, 1930).

13. Ross does indeed recognize that there can be a sort of residue effect of the fact that a *prima facie* duty has been overruled. Since we still recognize the *prima facie* duty as such, then we may feel 'compunction' at not being able to fulfill it but 'not indeed shame or repentance.' And, in some cases, we may have some further duty to make up 'somehow' for the right decision not to heed the prima facie duty. (Ross, *The Right and the Good*, p. 28).

14. Thomas Nagel discusses something quite close to this sort of 'balanced exceptionism' in his paper, 'War and Massacre,' *Mortal Questions* (Cambridge: Cambridge University Press, 1979), p. 62. He calls his version 'threshold deontology' and contrasts it both with utilitarianism and absolutism. Nagel himself rejects it in favor of what he calls absolutism, but allows that some extreme situations create moral dilemmas for absolutism in which whatever one does is morally wrong. In terms of my discussion, his position is more like the 'dirty hands' tradition in some respects but differs from it in not coming down on the side of the necessity to violate the absolute prohibition.

15. Niccolò Machiavelli, *The Prince*, ed. Quentin Skinner and Russell Price (Cambridge: Cambridge University Press, 1988); Max Weber, 'Politics as a Vocation,' in *From Max Weber: Essays in Sociology*, ed. H.H. Gerth and C. Wright Mills (London: Routledge & Kegan Paul, 1948), pp.117–28; and Michael Walzer, 'Political Action: The Problem of Dirty Hands,' *Philosophy and Public Affairs* 2 (1972/73).

16. Walzer's discussions of dirty hands problems (both in 'Political Action: The Problem of Dirty Hands' and *Just and Unjust Wars*) emphasize the contrast with plain utilitarianism, but it is clear that there can be a related contrast with balanced exceptionism.

17. C.A.J. Coady, 'Messy Morality and the Art of the Possible,' *Proceedings of the Aristotelian Society* 64 (1990); 'Dirty Hands and Politics,' in Robert Goodin and Philip Pettit (eds.), *Companion to Contemporary Political Philosophy*

(Oxford: Blackwell, 1993); and 'Dirty Hands,' in Lawrence C. Becker and Charlotte C. Becker (eds.), *Encyclopedia of Ethics*, second edition (London: Routledge, 2001), vol. 1.

18. Walzer, *Just and Unjust Wars*, p. 261.
19. Stephen A. Garrett, *Ethics and Airpower in World War II: The British Bombing of German Cities* (New York: St. Martin's Press, 1993), pp. 10–11.
20. Walzer, *Just and Unjust Wars*, pp. 255, 260.
21. Ibid., p. 259.
22. Actually 'wager' is the term he uses, and he talks of wagering a 'determinate crime' against an 'immeasurable evil.' See Walzer, *Just and Unjust Wars*, pp. 259–60.
23. Cited by Garrett, *Ethics and Airpower*, p. 148.
24. For discussion of the practical doubts about the bombing and the case for alternatives to the bombing see Garrett, *Ethics and Airpower*, especially chapter 6.
25. Churchill himself had put the argument well in 1917 as Minister of Munitions when discussing the resorts to bombing civilian populations in World War I. 'It is improbable that any terrorization of the civil population which could be achieved by air attack would compel the government of a great nation to surrender...In our own case, we have seen the combative spirit of the people roused, and not quelled, by the German air raids.' Quoted in Garrett, *Ethics and Airpower*, p. 46. And, as early as autumn 1941, Churchill wrote: 'it is very disputable whether bombing by itself will be a decisive factor in the present war. On the contrary, all that we have learnt since the war began shows that its effects, both physical and moral, are greatly exaggerated.' Quoted in Garrett, *Ethics and Airpower*, p. 14.
26. This is no insignificant conclusion since even in the brief period between the policy being officially endorsed in February 1942 and the July date that Walzer seems to see as ending the exemption, devastating raids were carried out on Lübeck, Rostock, and Cologne with great loss of life and over 150,000 people rendered homeless. See Garrett, *Ethics and Airpower*, pp. 14–15. Furthermore, since the failure of the probability of success condition rules out the sporadic and more informal terror bombing that had preceded the formal directive of February 14, 1942, we can add the deaths and homelessness caused by that earlier bombing to the tally of unjustified terrorism.
27. It is worth noting that Walzer makes the issue of Germany's possible victory a matter of supreme emergency but not that of Japan's. This is a further sign of the difficulties of interpreting the doctrine of supreme emergency since those who suffered the depredations of the Japanese Army could hardly think of their aggression as 'a more ordinary sort of military expansion' as Walzer calls it (*Just and Unjust Wars*, p. 268). Japan's war really began with the Japanese invasion of China in the 1930s, and it is soberly estimated that more than 400,000 Chinese civilians were massacred in Nanjing alone in a racist rampage of raping, beheading and bayoneting that lasted six weeks. (For the horrible details, see Iris Chang, *The Rape of Nanking: the Forgotten Holocaust of World War II*, New York: Basic Books, 1997.)
28. Walzer does give one example that hardly involves the salvation of the State, but again it is heavily state-oriented. It is the example of the politician running for high political office who does a deal with a dishonest ward boss and his

contractor friends in order to ensure his election. For several reasons, I don't think this is a convincing example of dirty hands, but the story gets what plausibility it has from the supposition that it is very important politically that the candidate be elected. See 'Political Action: The Problem of Dirty Hands,' pp. 165–6.

29. Walzer, *Just and Unjust Wars*, p. 254.
30. Walzer, 'Terrorism: A Critique of Excuses,' p. 238. Walzer's understanding of terrorism as an attack upon the innocent also includes the idea that the attack is intended to spread fear amongst other members of the group attacked. This would clearly include acts and policies of state terrorism such as the British bombing of German cities as well as the attacks by sub-state groups.
31. Walzer, 'Terrorism: A Critique of Excuses,' p. 238.
32. Ibid., p. 239.
33. Walzer *Just and Unjust Wars*, p. 254. At least this seems to be what he is saying. The issue is confused by his tendency here as elsewhere to put the point as though he is reporting common opinion: 'it is not usually said of individuals in domestic society that they necessarily will or that they morally can strike out at innocent people, even in the supreme emergency of self-defence. They can only attack their attackers.'
34. Walzer, *Just and Unjust Wars*, p. 254.
35. Ibid., p. 254.
36. Walzer, 'Terrorism: A Critique of Excuses,' pp. 239–40.
37. Ibid., p. 240.
38. Ibid., p. 240.
39. Walzer, *Just and Unjust Wars*, p. 259.
40. Ibid., p. 259.
41. It is true that the objection is an argument from tendencies or likely consequences, but like many other 'consequentialist' considerations, it is open to use by non-consequentialists.
42. There are connections here with Kant's principle of publicity and Rawls's related, though rather different, appeal to publicity in his elaboration of an idea of public reason but this is not the place to explore the matter further. See Immanuel Kant, *Perpetual Peace*, Appendix II, in *Kant on History*, ed. Lewis White Beck (Indianapolis: Bobbs-Merrill, 1963), especially pp. 129–30; and John Rawls, 'The Idea of Public Reason Revisited,' *The Law of Peoples* (Cambridge, Mass.: Harvard University Press, 1999).

8
How Can Terrorism Be Justified?
Uwe Steinhoff

Can terrorism be justified? Nowadays, whoever seriously poses this question runs a good chance of being excommunicated from the so-called discourse community, and of not even being listened to in the first place. This explains why several pre-existing philosophical analyses of the phenomenon of terrorism, some of which well antedate September 11, 2001, are paid practically no attention at all in the current public debate. The reason they are ignored is this: these philosophical investigations have as their goal the critique and questioning of socially promoted modes of discussion and prejudices, *not* their docile acceptance.

In the following I will attempt to defend such analyses and bring out that which is valid in them. To this end one can appeal to a sense of justice, as well as to reason. The appeal to reason may be made with the simple remark that abstinence from reflection surely cannot be an appropriate method for solving problems. The appeal to a sense of justice may be made with reference to, for example, public opinion in the United States, which denounces terrorism as unjustifiable on the one hand, but, when it comes to the moral questions surrounding the dropping of the atomic bomb on Nagasaki and Hiroshima, sees the matter quite differently. When, therefore, certain analysts in the United States are given ample opportunity in the serious press to develop views alternative to a moral condemnation of the directed mass killing of civilians in Hiroshima and Nagasaki – a position for which there might be good arguments and which one cannot at all reject out of hand – one should not be wroth to grant a similar opportunity to speak also to those philosophers who seek to approach the phenomenon of terrorism as soberly as possible, even when it happens to be directed against the West.

I

I will take Igor Primoratz's definition of terrorism as basis for the following discussion:

> [Terrorism is] the deliberate use of violence, or threat of its use, against innocent people, with the aim of intimidating some other people into a course of action they otherwise would not take.[1]

Thus, the ethical problem of terrorism is, of course, that it consists in a deliberate attack on innocents. How could such attacks possibly be justified? An important proposal for a justification comes from Virginia Held:

> It seems reasonable, I think, that on grounds of justice, it is better to equalize rights violations in a transition to bring an end to rights violations than it is to subject a given group that has already suffered extensive rights violations to continued such violations, if the degree of severity of the two violations is similar.... If we must have rights violations, a more equitable distribution of such violations is better than a less equitable distribution.[2]

The attack on non-combatants would be legitimized here by means of reference to *groups* as recipients of a supposedly just distribution of rights violations. Since Held explicitly understands this strategy of legitimization as based on rights and not on utility, a question from the logical point of view suggests itself right away: How can one have recourse to rights in order to legitimize their infraction? This is a difficulty Held could solve simply by giving a more carefully worded version of her argument. But it is quite appropriate, especially in light of certain extreme situations, to rethink the logic of rights. Rights violations can be justified.[3] Be that as it may, one may readily assume that a position such as Held represents would not be unattractive for many members of groups which fall victim to oppression and rights violations. The concept of 'poetic justice' plays a certain role here. The ethnologist James C. Scott reports the reaction of many black people to the sinking of the *Titanic*: 'The drowning of large numbers of wealthy and powerful whites...in their finery aboard a ship that was said to be unsinkable seemed like a stroke of poetic justice to many blacks.... "Official" songs about the loss of the *Titanic* were sung ironically ("It was *saaad* when the great ship went down").'[4]

Naturally, similar reactions could be seen in the wake of the destruction of the World Trade Center – and in fact, such reactions are indeed natural. In reaction to them certain persons, especially in the German and American press, pointed the moral finger and condemned the lack of compassion on the part of many in the Arab world. (The level of compassion in a significant portion of the Latin American population was not much greater, but the established press chose to keep silent about that.) Herein is another injustice to be found: the oppressed not only have to bear an unequal distribution of rights violations, one also demands of them more compassion for those who profit from this unequal distribution than the privileged are required to show for the oppressed. Thus Ron Hirschbein remarks on public opinion in the United States during the first Gulf War: 'There was no public outcry, for example, when the popular press cited the conclusion of a Harvard Medical School study: 75,000 Iraqi children would die due to the destruction of the Iraqi infrastructure. The civic celebration continued as Bush's popularity soared.'[5]

And yet, though such a lack of compassion in the public opinion of the United States was manifest, moral fingers were pointed neither there, nor in Germany. Apparently, Americans who do not let the death of 75,000 children rain on their parade for the bombs are more acceptable than Arabs who, in view of 3,000 American casualties, are glad that misfortune hit the other side for a change. Such discrepancies understandably increase the willingness of oppressed peoples to see whole groups as enemies and thus to have recourse to an argumentative strategy such as Held's.

Igor Primoratz, however, objects to Held's argument:

Faced with the prospect of being killed or maimed on the grounds of this ... justification, might I not draw on Nozick's view of rights, and say that I am a person in my own right, that my life is the only life I have and all I have, and that nobody may take it away, nor ruin it by making me a cripple, for the sake of a more just distribution of, and subsequently more general respect for, the right to life and bodily security within a group of people? ... The value and significance of my life is not derived from my membership in a group. Nobody may sacrifice it to the group.[6]

On the other hand, Primoratz thinks it legitimate if an artillery unit fires at a village and hence kills innocents as long as it fulfils the requirements of the doctrine of double effect, that is, 'those casualties were unintended, inevitable, reduced to a minimum, and proportionate to the military aim achieved.'[7] Since, of course, the doctrine of double effect is quite controversial, he adds a second consideration, trying to restate the point he wishes to make with an appeal to the difference between positive and negative duties:

> The military need of putting an end to the activities of the enemy unit may have been so strong and urgent that it prevailed over the prohibition of killing or maiming a comparatively small number of civilians. . . . On the other hand, if our gunners shelled the village in order to destroy it and kill or maim the villagers, they simply disregarded one of the basic moral duties of a soldier, the duty not to attack civilians, without any moral reason for doing so. Their action can be neither justified nor excused, and is a crime of war. If it was done as a way of intimidating other people into doing something they otherwise would not do, it was also a case of terrorism.[8]

But if the negative duty not to kill innocents can be overridden by a positive duty to kill enemy soldiers, why could this negative duty not also be overridden by a positive duty to intimidate other people into doing something they otherwise would not do by means of killing innocents? Primoratz just presupposes here that this cannot be the case, but he does not give any argument for his claim. Apart from this, it is also rather one-sided of Primoratz to put himself into the role of the victim when he is dealing with terrorism, but not do so when he is dealing with the bombing of villages by the military. For the victim of such a bombing could say the following:

> Faced with the prospect of being killed or maimed on the grounds of the doctrine of double effect (or on the grounds of someone else's presumably having a positive duty to do this to me), might I not draw on Nozick's view of rights, and say that I am a person in my own right, that my life is the only life I have and all I have, and that nobody may take it away, nor ruin it by making me a cripple, for the sake of achieving the military aim of killing enemy soldiers? The value and significance of my life is not conditional on my being near to some group of soldiers. Nobody may sacrifice it in killing such a group.

Here the life of the complainer is sacrificed in order to make other people *worse* off (namely: to kill them). As long as these people are not aggressors (but soldiers of the just side) there is, one would suppose, an even stronger reason to complain than in the case in which one's death at least results in something good. Thus, if, as Primoratz holds, one of the two things is legitimate – the Heldian terrorism or the Primoratzian artillery fire – it will be the Heldian terrorism.

II

Nevertheless, Held's argument is wrong. Its point is, in contrast to purely consequentialist or utilitarian arguments, to play off rights against rights. While mere interests can hardly override a right, conflicting rights can do this much more easily. But the Achilles' heel of Held's argument is precisely that the postulated right to an equalization of violence risks or rights violations does not exist in the way which is relevant here. The example given by Held is in more than one respect misleading:

> The right to personal security, of freedom from unlawful attack, can be fully recognized as a right in a given legal community, and yet of course some assault will occur. The community's way of trying to assure respect for such rights is likely to include the deployment of police forces. But if almost all the police forces are deployed in high-income white neighborhoods and almost none in low-income black neighborhoods...we can judge without great difficulty that the deployment is unfair.[9]

This is correct, but what she has to show is not the injustice of these unequal risks induced by the unjust distribution of the police forces, but rather that the order described in the example is less just than one in which some poor blacks (or their helpers) go over to the rich whites in order to equalize the risk of being the victim of violence by killing some of them. Indeed, this *can* be more just, namely in circumstances in which the whites themselves have seen to this unjust distribution of the police forces. Then they are *aggressors*, they *violate the rights* of the blacks. Consequently, however, they are not innocent any more; but it is the attack on innocents that we are supposed to be dealing with here.

Secondly, the example of the distribution of existing police forces does not do justice to the fact that in the case of the distribution of rights violations there is no determined quantity of such violations such that in order to distribute them we only have to select the victims who will receive them. If it is a determined fact that each year 1,000 murders are committed and one is forced to distribute them in some way, it would probably be best to let a lottery decide (provided, of course, that one does not know who will be the murderers). Thus, a distribution which would exempt all whites from the role of the victim would certainly be unjust. In the face of such a distribution it would seem justified that the blacks divert part of the violence to the whites, even if the whites themselves are completely innocent of the manipulation. In fact, however, the 'distribution' of rights violations is not a zero-sum game. This means that if the blacks march off to kill some whites, they do not thereby redistribute 'pre-existing' acts of violence, but they produce new ones. And while it may be just to distribute a fixed total suffering or total rights violations burden equally on all shoulders, it is not just to equalize the suffering of one innocent by making the other innocents suffer, too. 'If one group is having a bad time, the others shall also have a bad time' does not look like a particularly commendable principle of justice. If someone objects against this that Held does not want to end up with a heavier, but more equally distributed burden of suffering and rights violations, he misunderstands her argument. For the decisive point is *how* the redistribution – also against innocents – is to be justified. After all, she does not want to justify it with an appeal to a better end result – this would be a utilitarian or consequentialist argument – but with an appeal to distributive justice. She claims that the redistributive measures are not only conducive to a certain ideal state, but above all *more just*. And for the reason given this claim is not correct.

Moreover, there is a third reason. This reason consists in the difficulty of identifying a suitable 'receiver group' for the redistribution of the rights violations. For let us assume that Joe, Jim and Jill (group 1) as well as Frank, Fred and Fran (group 2) live in the poor neighborhood, while Bob, Bill and Berta (group 3) live in the rich one. Let us further assume that the members of group 1 have already been robbed and bear a high risk of being robbed again, while this is not true for the members of groups 2 and 3. (Frank and Fred are monks, Fran is a nun, and this is respected by the criminals in the neighborhood as sufficient reason not to assault them – apart from the fact that they do not have any valuables anyway.) Why, now, should the redistribution of rights violations or of risks of becoming a victim of violence proceed from group 1 to group 3 – which is probably what Held has in mind – instead of proceeding from group 1 to group 2? Again one cannot argue that the latter redistribution may lead to an absolute lowering of the rate of rights violation because this, as already mentioned, would not be a rights based argument. There is only one convincing distribution principle in such cases, namely responsibility (here for the unequal distribution). But *ex hypothesi* responsibility is not involved here. Profit is no convincing principle, either. First, group 2 does not profit less from the unequal distribution than group 3, and secondly, someone's profiting *innocently* is hardly a sufficient reason to violate his rights.

III

Questing the Nature of Innocent

But what happens if the receiver group is *not* innocent? Well, one could say, we are not dealing with terrorism any more. This is a correct observation. It has, however, the important consequence that many acts that are hastily called 'terrorism' and condemned as such are not terrorism at all. For just because certain human beings are civilians they are not yet automatically innocent. They may still be engaged in or contributing to an attempt to destroy you, or they may be the responsible causers of such an attempt. Let us consider the following example given by Jeff McMahan:

> Suppose there is a group of your enemies who wish you to be killed, since they will profit from your death. They build a device that can be programmed to transmit irresistible commands to a person through a receiver implanted in his brain. Once programmed and activated the device requires no further guidance or intervention. Your enemies then kidnap an innocent person, install the implant in his brain ... and activate the [controlling] device. ... Your only recourse [to save yourself], other than killing the innocent pursuer, is to coerce your enemies to deactivate or reveal the location of the device. You soon realize, however, that the only way to do this is to begin killing them, one by one, until one of them is sufficiently intimidated to tell you where the device is located. ... Assuming that killing the enemies would be equally effective in averting the threat and other things are equal, it is clearly morally preferable to kill the enemies – and to kill as many of them as necessary – rather than to kill the innocent pursuer.[10]

McMahan is certainly correct. Now, the important point with this example is that the control device was activated in the past. The group of enemies is at the moment neither attacking nor supporting an attack nor preparing one. Rather, the endangered person is endangered by the consequences of an already *past* act. Nevertheless, he is obviously justified to divert the harm – death – to those who are responsible for it.[11] Let us now turn to another, but similar case. In Israel, a democracy, the people votes with a large majority for a suspected war criminal, terrorist, militarist, and racist, namely Ariel Sharon. Sharon is comparable here to the control device in McMahan's example. Once such a person is prime minister, the people does not need to demand brutality and crimes against the Palestinians – he will do this of his own accord, which is precisely the reason why the Israelis trustingly elected him. We are dealing here with a case of hired murder, hired mutilation, and hired deprivation of liberty. The Israelis who voted for Sharon are therefore as guilty of the crimes he commits against the Palestinians as the enemies in McMahan's example are for the persecution of the threatened person. If by killing them one by one, one could cause them to end the criminal Israeli policies against Palestine and to recognize the human rights of Palestinians and their right to self-determination (for example, by voting for a very different prime minister), this would be justified. Of course, by attacks against civilians innocents would be killed too – for example, Israelis who have emphatically spoken out for the rights of Palestinians. But these deaths of innocents would be 'collateral damage' – they happen in the course of the attack on an aggressor (since the large majority of the Israelis voted for Sharon). Direct attacks on school buses, kindergartens or similar targets, however, would still be terrorist, for the children did not vote for Sharon.

Naturally, one might doubt whether the premise (the 'if' clause) of this justification is fulfilled. And this is indeed doubtful. There are good reasons to think that the Palestinians do more harm than good to their cause by their attacks on civilians. However, with the said premise I kept completely to McMahan's interpretation. But in fact, I would contradict him with regard to a decisive point: it would be legitimate for me to kill the enemies one by one even if I knew with certainty that in the end I cannot escape the persecutor with the implant, that is, if the just war criterion of the probability of success were not met. This is simply an application of my liberal right to punish aggressors (if there is no superior punishing power, or if it neglects its duties or is not able to meet them in this case and my right to punish overrides my duty to abstain from private justice because of the gravity of the crime). On the other hand, it is to be emphasized that it is illicit to give the punishment of the guilty priority over the protection of innocents. Since attacks on civilians in some coffee-houses will inevitably also kill innocents, the probabilities of success remain relevant. Depending on which probabilities of success a responsible calculation can come up with here, the Palestinian attacks on Israeli voters are either justified or not.

Even if they are not justified, however, for the reasons given they would not be terrorist.

IV

A further strategy for the legitimization of terrorism may be developed from Michael Walzer's argument of 'supreme emergency,' though very much against his intentions. He thinks that sub-national terrorism is neither to be legitimated, nor to be excused. In accordance with this position is the manifesto signed by 58 scholars in the United States, in which we read that 'no appeal to the merits or demerits of specific foreign policies can ever justify...the mass slaughter of innocent persons.'[12] And yet, in his book on *Just and Unjust Wars*, he considers the war waged by the German government and armed forces as sufficient justification for the terror bombing of German cities (Walzer himself uses this term). Supposedly, German aggression threatened the survival and freedom of the political community of Britain in such a way as to justify this use of the only potent offensive weapon the British possessed in the years 1940 and 1941.[13] And Walzer is 'inclined,' as he says, to accept this justification not only in the face of Nazi-like threats against the whole of humanity: 'Can soldiers and statesmen override the rights of innocent people for the sake of their own political community? I am inclined to answer this question affirmatively, though not without hesitation and worry.'[14]

Walzer's further remarks and his very high esteem of political communities,[15] however, demonstrate that these worries are somewhat limited, for 'the survival and freedom of political communities – whose members share a way of life, developed by their ancestors, to be passed on to their children – are the highest values of international society.'[16]

Andrew Valls, who criticizes Walzer's double moral standard, asks the obvious question: 'But why is it that the territorial integrity and political independence of, say, Britain, justify the resort to...violence that targets civilians – but the right of self-determination of a stateless nation never does?'[17] Apparently, there is no reason for this, especially since Walzer explicitly deduces the rights of states from those of communities, and the rights of these from those of individuals.[18]

Let me adduce a further example for the justificatory force of supreme emergency. Imagine a head of family whose family is kidnapped by slave traders. A direct attack on them would be doomed to failure because of the superior weapons technology of the slave traders. For the father there is no other possibility to save his family than to use an opportunity to kidnap the innocent daughter of the leader of the slave traders and to threaten to kill her if his family is not released. Can he really be blamed for the calculated violence against an innocent, or do not rather the slave traders bear the responsibility for the escalation? In order to prevent any doubts: Yes, he violates the rights of the innocent daughter by kidnapping her (as Primoratz's artillery unit that abides by the doctrine of double effect violates the rights of the innocents by killing and maiming them), and yes, he makes himself guilty (as does the artillery unit). But, in my view, he does not bear the brunt of the guilt. His positive duties towards his family may override here the negative duties against the leader's daughter. It would be a justified or at least an excusable action. The application to politics is obvious.

V

Whoever seeks to legitimize certain *particular* acts of terrorism carries the burden of proof, for the protection of innocents is indeed an extraordinarily precious right and legal good. To outweigh this right in any particular situation there must be very good and very carefully examined reasons. On the other hand, whoever claims that terrorism can *never* be justified also carries the burden of proof, as shown by the availability of the legitimization strategy just outlined. This claim – that terrorism is never justified – would only be valid under the ethical premise that direct attack on civilians in acceptance of risking the lives of innocent victims is *absolutely* forbidden. Regrettably, such a premise is hardly plausible in the context of an ethics of responsibility.[19] Besides, this premise is also rejected by the great majority of those who now loudly denounce terrorism as absolutely evil and bad: when such persons want to justify the terrorism which they think is good, they often have recourse to the patterns of argumentation described above. Of course, they do not call it terrorism – they may call it a 'war against terror,' as in the case of the massive bombing in Afghanistan or Clinton's rocket strike in Sudan, or they may also call it a 'war-shortening measure,' as in the case of the dropping of the atomic bomb on Hiroshima and Nagasaki.

A first result of these considerations is that the inference from the terrorist character of an attack to its illegitimacy is not valid. At best, the inference of the probability of the act's illegitimacy would be valid. But this in turn means that, according to the criteria of just war, if a state falls victim to a terrorist attack, it must first examine the reasons motivating the attack and can certainly not dismiss out of hand the question of

motivation as irrelevant, before it has the right to take a bellicose coun-
ter-measure. And even if this examination reaches the conclusion that
the attack was illegitimate, it still opens the possibility of recognizing
that the perpetrators did not act out of purely evil intentions, but rather
more probably out of desperation – a desperation for which the victim
state is perhaps not completely unaccountable. And this recognition
could possibly lead to a certain amount of moderation in the application of counter-measures. Herein lies precisely the purpose and meaning of a theory of just war (or at least, it should do so today): to limit
war – and not to promote self-righteousness and dispense warrants
to destroy.

A second, substantial conclusion of these considerations results from
the nature of the patterns of justification outlined. As previously mentioned, these are also used by the apologists for state terrorism. However,
these patterns do not fail to recognize the validity of proportionality
and of the probability of success as criteria in the judgment of the justification of an act of violence. For this reason, too, the constraints of these
schemes are not just difficult to fulfill but are, in fact, *more difficult for
strong parties to fulfill than for weak ones*. Let us take the pattern of argument
borrowed from Walzer as an example. The freedom of the political community of the Palestinians is not only threatened by Israel, but has in
effect been prevented for some decades, and the creation of a Palestinian
state or even a truly autonomous political entity has been foiled. The
Palestinians are not standing with their backs to the wall: they are being
smashed against the wall. But has the existence of Israel ever been
threatened by the *intifada* or by the Palestinian Authority, or would the
existence of Israel be threatened by a Palestinian state? In consideration
of the military might of Israel and its American ally, such a thought
seems utterly absurd. The idea that Al-Qaeda or the Taliban could
threaten the existence or freedom of the United States is just as absurd.
A similar asymmetry is to be found in other patterns of argumentation,
as could easily be shown. Nevertheless, most 'serious' commentators
tend to excuse the violence committed by the stronger party. (One
could consider the mild, even positive reactions to the American bombing
of Tripoli in 1986 and of a pharmaceutical factory in Sudan in 1998; the
frequent retaliation measures of Israel against Palestinian civilians; or
the devastating sanctions against Iraq which have cost the lives of
hundreds of thousands of civilians, half of which were children. At least
the reactions to Israel's massive attacks against the Palestinians since
December 2001 give occasion for some glimmer of hope.) This is not
only immoral and hypocritical, it defies all logic.

Bad Def of
Terrorism.

Terrorism is not at all the instrument of the weak, as is often claimed, but rather the routinely employed instrument of the strong, and usually only the final resort for the weak. (This is true of secular terrorism, not of that kind of terrorism which is motivated by apocalyptic visions such as may be found in the Aum sect, certain racist militias in the US, and apparently also in Al-Qaeda.) As such a final instrument, terrorism is, to cite Annette Baier, 'a demonstration of this power to make resentment at exclusion felt.'[20] We may add: resentment at exclusion from justice and freedom. Even if the United States were to succeed in their 'war against terrorism' and were to annihilate all such terrorism which is neither promoted, supported nor approved of by them, and thus were to remove the last resort of those who are excluded to put up some resistance – even then there would be only a little less violence in the world. There would certainly not be more justice. This 'war against terrorism' – waged by state terrorists and with terrorist means – does not have as its object universal values, but rather undisputed power.

If strong states really want to fight sub-national terrorism, then there are only three legitimate and commendable means at their disposal: the rejection of a double moral standard, focused prosecution of crimes (in so far as the committing of a punishable crime – and not of an act of justifiable resistance – may be demonstrated) and, finally, the inclusion of the excluded.[21]

Notes

1. Igor Primoratz, 'What is Terrorism?', this volume, p. 24.
2. Virginia Held, 'Terrorism, Rights, and Political Goals,' this volume, pp. 74–5.
3. Compare Thomas Nagel, 'War and Massacre,' and Michael Walzer, 'Political Action: The Problem of Dirty Hands,' in Marshall Cohen et al. (eds.), *War and Moral Responsibility* (Princeton, NJ: Princeton University Press, 1974); Michael Walzer, *Just and Unjust Wars*, third edition (New York: Basic Books, 2000), pp. 225–32, 251–63, 323–7. See also the excellent article by Arthur Isak Applbaum, 'Are Violations of Rights ever Right?' *Ethics* 108 (1997/8).
4. James C. Scott, 'Domination, Acting, and Fantasy,' in Carolyn Nordstrom and Jo-Ann Martin (eds.), *The Paths to Domination, Resistance, and Terror* (Berkeley: University of California Press, 1992), p. 67.
5. R. Hirschbein, 'A World without Enemies (Bush's Brush with Morality),' in Deane C. Curtin and Robert Litke (eds.), *Institutional Violence* (Amsterdam: Rodopi, 1999), p. 344.
6. Igor Primoratz, 'The Morality of Terrorism,' *Journal of Applied Philosophy* 14 (1997), p. 231.
7. Ibid., p. 228.
8. Ibid.
9. Held, 'Terrorism, Rights, and Political Goals,' pp. 75–6.

10. Jeff McMahan, 'Innocence, Self-Defense and Killing in War,' *Journal of Political Philosophy* 2 (1994), pp. 202–3.

11. Cf. also Phillip Montague, 'Self-Defense and Choosing among Lives,' *Philosophical Studies* 40 (1981); and 'The Morality of Self-Defense: A Reply to Wasserman,' *Philosophy & Public Affairs* 18 (1989).

12. 'What We're Fighting for,' electronic resource, cited February 2, 2002 under: www.propositionsonline.com/Fighting_For/fighting_for/html.

13. Walzer, *Just and Unjust Wars*, pp. 255–63.

14. Ibid., p. 254.

15. See also Michael Walzer, 'The Moral Standing of States,' in Charles Beitz et al. (eds.), *International Ethics* (Princeton, NJ: Princeton University Press, 1990). One must not forget that Walzer is a communitarian.

16. Walzer, *Just and Unjust Wars*, p. 254.

17. Andrew Valls, 'Can Terrorism Be Justified?', in Andrew Valls (ed.), *Ethics and International Affairs* (Lanham, Md: Rowman and Littlefield, 2000), p. 73.

18. Walzer, *Just and Unjust Wars*, pp. 53–5, 254.

19. Max Weber distinguishes between *Verantwortungsethik* (ethics of responsibility) and *Gesinnungsethik* (ethics of principled conviction). While in the former the consequences of one's actions are to be carefully considered, the latter is concerned with purity of heart and absolutist moral norms. Its motto is 'fiat justitia et pereat mundus.' A notorious example of *Gesinnungsethik* is Kant's insistence that lying is never allowed, not even when the life of an innocent person can only be saved by telling a lie. See Max Weber, 'The Profession and Vocation of Politics,' *Political Writings*, trans. and ed. P. Lassman and R. Spiers (Cambridge: Cambridge University Press, 1994), pp. 359ff.

20. A. Baier, 'Violent Demonstrations,' in R.G. Frey and C.W. Morris (eds.), *Violence, Terrorism, and Justice* (Cambridge: Cambridge University Press, 1991), p. 54.

21. I owe thanks to Colin King for translating an earlier draft of this paper, and to him and Igor Primoratz for checking the amendments.

Part III
State Terrorism

9

State Terrorism and Counter-terrorism

Igor Primoratz

Introduction

When it first entered political discourse, the word 'terrorism' was used with reference to the reign of terror imposed by the Jacobin regime – that is, to describe a case of state terrorism. Historians of the French Revolution have analyzed and discussed that case in great detail. There are also quite a few historical studies of some other instances of state terrorism, most notably of the period of 'the Great Terror' in the Soviet Union.

In a contemporary setting, however, state terrorism is apparently much more difficult to discern. Discussions of terrorism in social sciences and (to a lesser degree) in philosophy tend to focus on non-state terrorism. In common parlance and in the media, terrorism is as a rule assumed to be an activity of non-state agents in virtue of the very meaning of the word. If one suggests that the army or security services are doing the same things that, when done by insurgents, are invariably described and condemned as terrorist, the usual reply is: 'But these are actions done on behalf of the state, in pursuit of legitimate state aims: the army, waging war, or the security services, fending off threats to our security.' In other words,

> Throwing a bomb is bad,
> Dropping a bomb is good;
> Terror, no need to add,
> Depends on who's wearing the hood.[1]

As far as everyday discourse and the media are concerned, this can perhaps be explained by two related tendencies. One is the widely shared assumption that, at least normally, what the state does has a certain kind of legitimacy, while those challenging it tend to be perceived as the forces of disorder and destruction, engaged in clearly unjustifiable pursuits. The other is the double standard of the form 'Us vs. Them.' In states facing insurgency, the general public and the media find themselves on the side of the state. This tends to affect the usage. An offshoot of this tendency is that when insurgents abroad are sponsored by our state, we do not call them terrorists, but rather guerrillas, freedom fighters, and the like.

The focusing on non-state terrorism in social sciences is given a different explanation: that whatever the similarities between state and non-state terrorism, the dissimilarities are more prominent and instructive. Walter Laqueur, a leading authority on the history and sociology of terrorism, tells us that the two 'fulfil different functions and manifest themselves in different ways,' and that 'nothing is gained by ignoring the specifics of violence.'[2] I am not convinced that this approach is to be preferred in social science;[3] but be that as it may, it certainly will not do in philosophy. If some acts of state agents are basically similar to and exhibit the same morally relevant traits as acts of non-state agencies commonly termed terrorist, that will clearly determine our moral understanding and evaluation of both. Thus philosophers have been less reluctant than sociologists and political scientists to recognize and discuss state terrorism.[4]

But the philosophical work on the subject done so far leaves room, and indeed suggests the need, for a typology of state involvement in terrorism, and a fuller statement of the argument for the claim philosophers sometimes make in passing, that state terrorism is worse, morally speaking, than terrorism by non-state agents. My aim in this chapter is to offer some comments on these two topics. In the light of these comments I will then make a few remarks on counter-terrorism.

I have argued elsewhere that, for the purposes of philosophical discussion, terrorism is best defined as the deliberate use of violence, or threat of its use, against innocent people, with the aim of intimidating some other people into a course of action they otherwise would not take.[5] This is the sense in which I will be using the word 'terrorism' throughout this chapter.

Varieties of state involvement with terrorism

Philosophers tend to be perceived as given to introducing all manner of distinctions where none were acknowledged before. With respect to state terrorism this has been the case to a lesser degree than on most other issues. Thus Alan Ryan discusses the claim that 'a terrorist state' is logically impossible by virtue of the definition of 'state,' and brings up Nazi Germany and Stalin's Soviet Union as obvious counterexamples. Further on he writes: 'If Syria paid for, protected, equipped, and assisted hijackers and would-be bombers of El Al aircraft, that makes the Syrian regime a terrorist regime.'[6] This looks rather like a leaf from the US State Department's book; for the purpose of moral assessment, it is clearly much too rough. However repugnant Syria's sponsorship of Palestinian terrorism may have been, it is certainly not in the same moral league as the regimes of Hitler and Stalin. Surely we ought to differentiate more carefully.

When speaking of state involvement in terrorism, there are distinctions to be made both in terms of degree of such involvement and with regard to its victims.

Concerning the degree of state involvement in terrorism, we should withstand the temptation to classify every state that has made use of terrorism, either directly or by proxy, as a *terrorist state*. I suggest that we reserve this label for states that do not merely resort to terrorism on certain occasions and for certain purposes, but employ it in a lasting and systematic way, and indeed are defined, in part, by the sustained use of terrorism against their own population. These are *totalitarian states*, such as Nazi Germany, Soviet Union in Stalin's day, or Cambodia under the rule of the Khmer Rouge.

A totalitarian regime aims at total domination of society and total unanimity of its subjects. Such an aim can be pursued only by appropriately radical means: incessant terrorism, inflicted by an omnipresent and omnipotent secret police on an atomized and utterly defenseless population. Its efficiency is due, for the most part, to its arbitrary character: to the unpredictability of its choice of victims. Students of totalitarianism have pointed out that both in the Soviet Union and in Nazi Germany, the regime at first brutally suppressed all its opponents; when it no longer had any opposition to speak of, it deployed its secret police against 'potential opponents.' In the Soviet Union, it was eventually unleashed on masses of victims chosen at random. In the words of Carl J. Friedrich and Zbigniew K. Brzezinski, totalitarian terrorism

aims to fill everyone with fear and vents in full its passion for unanimity. Terror then embraces the entire society...Indeed, to many it seems as if they are hunted, even though the secret police may not touch them for years, if at all. Total fear reigns.... The total scope and the pervasive and sustained character of totalitarian terror are operationally important. By operating with the latest technological devices, by allowing no refuge from its reach, and by penetrating even the innermost sanctums of the regime...it achieves a scope unprecedented in history. The atmosphere of fear it creates easily exaggerates the strength of the regime and helps it achieve and maintain its façade of unanimity. Scattered opponents of the regime, if still undetected, become isolated and feel themselves cast out of society. This sense of loneliness, which is the fate of all but more especially of an opponent of the totalitarian regime, tends to paralyze resistance...It generates the universal longing to 'escape' into the anonymity of the collective whole.[7]

While only totalitarian states use terrorism in this way and with such an aim, many states that are clearly not totalitarian, including many basically democratic and liberal states, have used terrorism on a much more limited scale and for more specific purposes. They have done so directly, or by sponsoring non-state agents whose *modus operandi* is, or includes, terrorism. But as their resort to terrorism is occasional rather than sustained, let alone essential, they should not be termed terrorist states. When they are, an important moral, political, and legal divide is blurred.

Another distinction is that between the use of terrorism by a state *against its own citizens*, and the use of terrorism *abroad*, as a means of foreign policy, war, or occupation. Other things being equal, state terrorism of the former type seems worse, morally speaking, than that of the latter type. For in the former case the state is attacking the very population for which it should be providing order, security, and justice.

Quite a few non-totalitarian states have made use of terrorism against their own population. Some have done so directly, by having state agencies such as the armed forces or security services employ terrorism. Many military dictatorships in South America and elsewhere are examples of this; the most extreme cases are, of course, Chile under Augusto Pinochet and Argentina under the generals. Other states have done the same indirectly, by sponsoring death squads and the like.

Many states, both totalitarian and non-totalitarian, have used terrorism abroad, as a means of achieving foreign policy objectives, in the course of waging war, or as a method of maintaining their occupation of another people's land.

These types of state involvement in terrorism are not mutually exclusive; indeed, they are often complementary. A terrorist state will see no moral reason for hesitating to use terrorism beyond its borders too, whether in the course of waging war or in peacetime, as a means of pursuing its foreign policy objectives. Both Nazi Germany and the Soviet Union provide examples of that. But the same is true of states that do not qualify as terrorist, but do resort to terrorism against their own population on certain occasions and for some specific purposes. Such states, too, are not likely to be prevented by moral scruples from using terrorism abroad as well, whether directly or by proxy, when that is found expedient.

On the other hand, the fact that a state has resorted to terrorism in the international arena need not make it more prone to do the same at home, as there is a fairly clear line between the two. But it might. Since its establishment, Israel has often made use of terrorism in its conflict with the Palestinians and the neighboring Arab states. The suppression of the second Palestinian uprising (*intifada*) has been carried out, in part, by state terrorism. (Israel's neighbors, on their part, have supported Palestinian terrorism against Israel.) The way Israeli police put down the demonstrations of Palestinians living in Israel proper, as its citizens, in October 2000 – by shooting at them with rubber-coated and live ammunition and killing thirteen – may well qualify as state terrorism. If it does, that shows how the willingness to resort to terrorism abroad can eventually encourage its use at home.

To be sure, in practice the dichotomy of state and non-state terrorism does not always readily apply. Attempts at drawing hard-and-fast lines cannot succeed because of the widespread phenomenon of terrorist organizations receiving various types and degrees of support by states. Since in such cases a simple division of terrorism into state and non-state is no longer feasible, the moral assessment too becomes much more complex.

State terrorism is morally worse than non-state terrorism

All terrorism is *prima facie* extremely morally wrong. But not everything that is extremely morally wrong is wrong in the same degree. State terrorism can be said to be morally worse than terrorism by non-state agents for at least four reasons.

First, although unwilling to extend the scope of his discussion of terrorism to include state terrorism, Laqueur remarks that 'acts of terror carried out by police states and tyrannical governments, in general, have been responsible for a thousand times more victims and more misery than all actions of individual terrorism taken together.'[8] He could also have mentioned terrorism employed by democracies (mostly, but not exclusively, in wartime), although that would not have affected the striking asymmetry very much. Now this asymmetry is not just another statistical fact; it follows from the nature of the state and the amount and variety of resources that even a small state has at its disposal. No matter how much non-state terrorists manage to enrich their equipment and improve their organization, planning, and methods of action, they stand no chance of ever significantly changing the score. No insurgent, no matter how well funded, organized, determined, and experienced in the methods of terrorism, can hope to come close to the killing, maiming, and overall destruction on the scale the Royal Air Force and US Air Force visited on German and Japanese cities in World War II, or to the psychological devastation and subsequent physical liquidation of millions in Soviet and Nazi camps.

The terrorist attacks in the US carried out on September 11, 2001 were in some respects rather unlike what we had come to expect from non-state terrorism. The number of victims, in particular, was unprecedented. Mostly because of that, I suspect, the media have highlighted these attacks as 'the worst case of terrorism ever.' So have quite a few public intellectuals. Thus Salman Rushdie, in his monthly column in the Melbourne daily *The Age*, wrote of 'the most devastating terrorist attack in history.'[9] The number of people killed, believed to be approaching 7,000 at the time, was indeed staggering. Yet 'the worst case of terrorism ever' mantra is but another instance of the tendency of the media to equate terrorism with non-state terrorism. When we discard the assumption that only insurgents engage in terrorism – as I submit we should – the overall picture changes significantly. Let me give just one example from the Allies' terror bombing campaign against Germany. During the night of July 27, 1943, the RAF carried out the second of its four raids on Hamburg, known as the 'Firestorm Raid.' In the morning, when both the attack itself and the gigantic firestorm it had created were over, some 40,000 civilians were dead.[10]

Second, in one way or another, state terrorism is bound to be compounded by secrecy, deception, and hypocrisy. When involved in terrorism – whether perpetrated by its own agencies or by proxy – a state will be acting clandestinely, disclaiming any involvement, and declaring its adherence to values and principles that rule it out. Or, if it is impractical and perhaps even counterproductive to deny involvement, it will do its best to present its actions to at least some audiences in a different light: as legitimate acts of war, or acts done in defense of state security. It will normally be able to do that without much difficulty, given the tendencies of common usage mentioned above.

Those engaging in non-state terrorism, on the other hand, need not be secretive, need not deceive the public about their involvement in terrorism (except, of course, at the operational level), and need not hypocritically proclaim their allegiance to moral principles that prohibit it. Some of them are amoralists, possibly of the sort exemplified by the notorious declaration of the nineteenth-century anarchist writer Laurent Tailhade: 'What do the victims matter if the gesture is beautiful!' Others exhibit what Aurel Kolnai has called 'overlain conscience':[11] conscience completely subjected to a non-moral absolute (the Leader, the Party, the Nation), which will permit and indeed enjoin all manner of actions incompatible with mainstream moral views, including terrorism. Still others adhere to some version of consequentialist moral theory, which will readily justify terrorism under appropriate circumstances.[12] In none of these cases will there be a need for deception and hypocrisy concerning the performance of specific terrorist acts or the adoption of policies of terrorism.

Third, virtually all actions that constitute terrorism are prohibited by one or another of the various international human rights declarations or conventions and agreements that make up the laws and customs of war. The latter provide for immunity of civilians in armed conflict and thus prohibit terrorism by belligerent sides. Most, if not all, remaining types of terrorism – terrorism in wartime perpetrated by groups not recognized as belligerent parties, and terrorism in time of peace perpetrated by anyone at all – are covered by declarations of human rights. Now those engaging in non-state terrorism are not signatories to these declarations and conventions, while virtually all states today are signatories to most if not all of them. Therefore, when a state is involved in terrorism, it acts in breach of its own solemn international commitments. This particular charge cannot be brought against those resorting to non-state terrorism.

Fourth, non-state terrorism is often said to be justified, or at least that its wrongness is mitigated, by the argument of no alternative. In a case where, for instance, a people is subjected to foreign rule with the usual attendant evils of oppression, humiliation, and exploitation, which is utterly unyielding and deploys overwhelming power, a liberation movement may claim that the only effective method of struggle at its disposal is terrorism. To refrain from using terrorism in such circumstances would be tantamount to giving up the prospect of liberation altogether.

This argument is often met with criticism. First, since terrorism is extremely morally wrong, the evils of foreign rule, grave as they may be, may not be enough to justify, or even mitigate, resort to it. After all, its victims would by definition be innocent people, rather than those responsible for these evils. Second, one can hardly ever be confident that terrorism will indeed achieve the aims adduced as its justification or mitigation. Which people has ever succeeded in liberating itself by terrorism?

These objections are weighty, and may be enough to dispose of most attempts at justifying particular cases and policies of terrorism; but they do not show that the 'no alternative' argument will *never* work. Persecution and oppression of an ethnic, racial, or religious group can reach such an extreme point that even terrorism may properly be considered. And the question of its efficiency, being an empirical one, cannot be settled once and for all. So it is possible that a liberation movement should be facing such circumstances where resort to terrorism is indeed the only feasible alternative to the continuation of persecution and oppression so extreme as to amount to an intolerable moral disaster. In such a situation, the 'no alternative' argument would provide moral justification for terrorism, or at least somewhat mitigate our moral condemnation of its use. On the other hand, it seems virtually impossible that a state should find itself in such circumstances where it has no alternative to resorting to terrorism.

The only counterexample that comes to mind is the terror bombing campaign of the RAF against the civilian population of Germany in World War II, inasmuch as it can be seen as a case of 'supreme emergency' allowing one to set aside even an extremely grave moral prohibition in order to prevent an imminent moral catastrophe.[13] Yet even this example is of a very limited value. The supreme emergency argument may have been valid only during the first year of the campaign: in 1942, the victory of Nazi Germany in Europe – a major moral disaster by any standard – might have been thought imminent. However, after German defeats at El Alamein (November 6, 1942) and Stalingrad (February 2, 1943), that was clearly no longer the case. But the campaign went on almost to the very end of the war. As Michael Walzer says, 'the truth is that the supreme emergency passed long before the British bombing reached its crescendo. The greater number by far of the German civilians killed by terror bombing were killed without moral (and probably also without military) reason.'[14]

My argument might be challenged by pointing out that what I have called terrorist regimes can maintain themselves only by employing sustained, large-scale terrorism against their own population. Furthermore, a state that would not qualify as terrorist in this sense may be waging a war whose aims can be achieved only by means of terrorism. The successive Serbian onslaughts on Croatia, Bosnia-Herzegovina, and Kosova in the 1990s are a clear example. Their aim was conquest, 'ethnic cleansing,' and annexation of territories whose inhabitants included a non-Serb majority or large minority. Under the circumstances, and given the constraints of time, the 'cleansing' had to be accomplished by large-scale terrorism. The Serbs had no alternative.[15]

All this is true, but not to the point. In such cases terrorism is indeed the only efficient option and, if the aim is to be achieved, there is no alternative to its use. But in such cases, unlike at least some conceivable cases of non-state terrorism justified or mitigated by the 'no alternative' argument, the aim itself – the continuation of a Nazi or Stalinist regime, or the setting up of a greatly expanded *and* 'ethnically homogeneous' Serbia – can justify or mitigate nothing. Its achievement, rather than failure to achieve it, would amount to an intolerable moral disaster.

Another objection would refer to the 'balance of terror' produced by the mutual threat of nuclear attack that marked the Cold War period. The type of such threat relevant here was the threat of attacking the other side's civilian population centers. (In Cold War jargon, this was known as 'counter-value deterrence.') If that threat was morally justified, it was a case of state terrorism justified by the 'no alternative' argument.

I am not convinced that it was justified. Clearly, carrying out the threat and actually destroying major population centers of the enemy and killing hundreds of thousands, if not millions, of enemy civilians, could never be morally justified. But does that mean that a threat to do so – made with the aim of preventing the chain of events that would make such destruction a serious option – is also morally impermissible? A positive reply to this question assumes that, if it is wrong to do X, it is also wrong to intend to do X, and therefore also to threaten to do X. This assumption has been questioned.[16] I have not made up my mind on this matter. Perhaps the problem can be circumvented by arguing that the threat need not involve the intention of ever carrying it out; a bluff will do. Yet one might well wonder if a threat of this sort can be both credible and a bluff. Of course, if the threat is not credible, it will not be morally justified either.

But this is too large a subject to go into on this occasion. Therefore, I will say in conclusion only that even if the 'balance of terror' generated by the threat of use of nuclear weapons against civilian targets turned out to be a convincing counterexample to my fourth argument for the claim that state terrorism is morally worse than terrorism employed by non-state agents, the first three arguments would still stand and, I trust, suffice.

Counter-terrorism

This discussion of state terrorism has some fairly straightforward implications with regard to moral assessment of and constraints on counter-terrorist measures in general, and the 'war against terrorism' the US and its allies are currently waging in particular.

One concerns the moral high ground the state usually claims in the face of insurgent terrorism. What is at issue is a certain policy contested by the insurgents or a certain political setup the state wants to maintain and the insurgents want to do away with. But at the same time the conflict is seen as much more basic: since the insurgents have resorted to terrorism, the conflict is also about the very fundamentals of the political and social order, and indeed about certain moral values and principles, which terrorists are challenging and the state is defending. Now it is true that terrorism challenges some of our fundamental moral beliefs and rides roughshod over some highly important moral distinctions. Therefore, opposition to terrorism can and indeed should be motivated, above all, by moral concern.

But that is not the only condition for claiming the moral high ground in the face of terrorism. The other, equally necessary condition is that of moral standing. A thief does not have the moral standing required for condemning theft and preaching about the paramount importance of property. A murderer does not have the moral standing necessary for condemning murder and pontificating about the sanctity of life. By the same token, a state which has made use of terrorism, or sponsored it, or condoned it, or supported governments that have done any of the above – in a word, a state which has itself been involved in or with terrorism to any significant degree – lacks the moral standing required for *bona fide* moral criticism of terrorism.

This simple point bears emphasizing. More often than not, it is completely ignored. As a result, we are treated, time and time again, to moral condemnations of terrorism by representatives of states that have much to answer for on the same count. Much of the quaint moralistic rhetoric that accompanies the 'war against terrorism' currently waged by the US and its allies is as good an example as any.

Another point has to do with the nature of counter-terrorism. Insurgency that makes use of terrorism poses a difficult challenge to the state. Not only does it contest the state's monopoly of violence – any violent opposition activity does that – but also demonstrates that the state is no longer capable of performing efficiently enough its most important task, that of providing basic security to its citizens. For the indiscriminate nature of terrorism poses a threat of deadly violence to virtually everyone; there is next to nothing a citizen can do to ensure his or her lasting physical security.

Faced with such a challenge to its very *raison d'être* and the difficulties of fighting terrorism while remaining within the bounds of morality and the law, the state may well be tempted to resort to terrorism itself, as Israel has done in response to Palestinian terrorism. Since the 1950s, a central part of Israel's response to terrorism have been reprisals in which civilian targets in the neighboring countries were attacked in order to force their governments to deal ilestinian terrorists operating from their soil. Israel occasi{ed the terrorist nature of its strategy, most memorabl{ister (and Defense Minister) Yitzhak Rabin explain{elling and bombing south Lebanon was 'to ma'{hereby force the Lebanese Government to {he Palestinian liberation movement on {ade extensive use of state terrorism in i{ries occupied in 1967 and its fight agai{sm; it is doing so at the time of writi{terrorism with terrorism ought to be{rrorism may well prove a dismal failu{ in the Israeli case. More to the point,{...ucreisidle from the moral point of view. Israel has certainly had other options, and so does virtually every state.

What of the current 'war against terrorism' prosecuted by the US and its allies? It raises a number of serious moral, political, and legal concerns about citizens' rights at home and the treatment of enemies taken prisoner.[17] But surely, it will be said, it does not present an example of state terrorism. There have been civilian casualties in the course of attacks on the Taliban and Al-Qaeda targets in Afghanistan. But the innocent have not been attacked intentionally; civilian casualties have been foreseen, but not intended side-effects of attacks on legitimate military targets. Such casualties – known as 'collateral damage' in US military jargon – are inevitable in modern war. Actions that bring them about do not qualify as terrorism, on my own or any other definition of 'terrorism' I find helpful, and do not constitute a violation of the relevant principle of just war theory, that of discrimination. If the principle ruled out unintentional harming of civilians too, given the conditions of modern warfare, the theory would enjoin renunciation of all war. It would no longer deserve the name of just *war* theory, since it would turn out to be, for all practical purposes, indistinguishable from pacifism.

It is true that the US and its allies are not guilty of state terrorism, since terrorism is by definition *intentional* attack on the innocent. But that is not the end of the matter. Concerns about the scale of 'collateral damage' the 'war on terrorism' has been inflicting surfaced early on, as the war was initially conducted exclusively from the air, and from very high altitudes at that. By January 2002, these concerns appeared to be based on good grounds. Under the heading 'News of Afghan Dead is Buried,' the US correspondent of *The Age* reported:

> University of New Hampshire economics professor Marc Herold was so disturbed by the lack of coverage of civilian deaths in the war in Afghanistan that he began keeping a tally.... Professor Herold says, on average, 62 Afghan civilians have died each day since bombing began. The total was now close to 5000, far more than the 3000 killed in the terrorist attacks in America on September 11.... According to Professor Herold, America's strategy of using air strikes to support local ground forces is designed to minimize American casualties. Only one American soldier has died from enemy fire.[18]

Now just war theory does not prohibit harming the innocent *simpliciter*. In this matter it applies the doctrine of double effect, and accordingly prohibits harming them intentionally, while leaving room for deliberate attacks on military targets that also have the foreseen but unintended effect of harming the innocent. But it does not leave room for unintentionally harming *any number* of civilians. Acts of war that unintentionally harm civilians must also satisfy another requirement of the doctrine: the harm must be proportionate to the importance and urgency of the military objective that cannot be attained in any other way. It will not do, say, to shell a village in order to take out a handful of enemy soldiers who have taken up position in it if that also involves the unintended, but foreseen killing of scores of innocent villagers.

This much is clear in any mainstream version of just war theory. The version elaborated by Walzer in his influential book *Just and Unjust Wars* adds an important qualification. When performing an act of war that will also have the unintended but foreseen consequence of harming the innocent, we must seek to reduce that harm to a minimum, and must accept risk to life and limb of our own soldiers in order to do so:

> Simply not to intend the death of civilians is too easy... What we look for in such cases is some sign of a positive commitment to save

civilian lives. Not merely to apply the proportionality rule and kill no more civilians than is militarily necessary – that rule applies to soldiers as well; no one may be killed for trivial purposes. Civilians have a right to something more. And if saving civilian lives means risking soldiers' lives, the risk must be accepted.[19]

Mark the words 'right' and 'must': taking risks to ensure that harm to the innocent is reduced to a minimum is not a matter of supererogation, but rather a *duty* of soldiers and a correlative *right* of civilians. The right of the innocent not to be killed or maimed is the point of departure of just war theory and, indeed, of any plausible ethics of war. Since it is the soldiers who put the civilians' life and limb in danger, it is only fair that they should accept some risk in order to minimize that danger.[20]

Now our repugnance of terrorism is generated, primarily, by the value we place on human life and bodily integrity, and in particular by our commitment to the right of the innocent not to be killed or maimed. This right is violated in the most radical way when the terrorist intentionally kills or maims them in order to achieve his or her aims. But it is also violated in a morally unacceptable way when their death or grave physical injury is not brought about as a means, but as an anticipated side-effect, if the harm they sustain is out of all proportion to the aim achieved, and those who do the killing and maiming refuse to take any chance of being harmed themselves in the process. The latter is not terrorism and is less repellent, morally speaking, than the former. But not *much* less.

If this is granted, it means that terrorism may not be fought by terrorism. Nor may it be fought by means of a strategy that does not amount to terrorism, but must be condemned on the ground of the same moral values and principles that provide the strongest reasons for our rejection of terrorism. In this respect, so far the record of the 'war on terrorism' has been very poor indeed.[21]

Notes

1. R. Woddis, 'Ethics for Everyman,' quoted in C.A.J. Coady, 'The Morality of Terrorism,' *Philosophy* 60 (1985), p. 52.
2. W. Laqueur, *The Age of Terrorism* (Boston: Little, Brown & Co., 1987), p. 146. In a more recent book, *The New Terrorism: Fanaticism and the Arms of Mass Destruction* (New York: Oxford University Press, 1999), Laqueur remains faithful to this approach. The book includes a chapter on 'State Terrorism,' but its scope is clearly circumscribed in its first sentence: 'State-*sponsored* terrorism, warfare by proxy, is as old as the history of military conflict' (p. 156, emphasis

added). State terrorism in the strict sense is still beyond Laqueur's ken: 'Terrorism seldom appeared in brutal dictatorships such as in Nazi Germany or Stalinist Russia, for the simple reason that repression in these regimes made it impossible for the terrorists to organize' (p. 6).

3. For a sample of social science research illustrating a different approach, see M. Stohl and G. A. Lopez (eds.), *The State as Terrorist: The Dynamics of Governmental Violence and Repression* (Westport, Conn.: Greenwood Press, 1984).

4. See J. Glover, 'State Terrorism' and A. Ryan, 'State and Private; Red and White,' in R.G. Frey and C.W. Morris (eds.), *Violence, Terrorism and Justice* (Cambridge: Cambridge University Press, 1991); P. Gilbert, *Terrorism, Security and Nationality* (London: Routledge, 1994), chapter 9; R. B. Ashmore, 'State Terrorism and its Sponsors,' in T. Kapitan (ed.), *Philosophical Perspectives on the Israeli–Palestinian Conflict* (Armonk, NY: M.E. Sharpe, 1997); D. Lackey, 'The Evolution of the Modern Terrorist State,' chapter 10 in this volume.

5. See my 'What Is Terrorism?', chapter 2 in this volume.

6. Ryan, 'State and Private; Red and White,' p. 249.

7. C.J. Friedrich and Z.K. Brzezinski, *Totalitarian Dictatorship and Democracy*, second edition (Cambridge, Mass.: Harvard University Press, 1965), pp. 169–70.

8. Laqueur, *The Age of Terrorism*, p. 146.

9. Salman Rushdie, 'How to Defeat Terrorism,' *The Age*, October 4, 2001, p. 15.

10. See M. Middlebrook, *The Battle of Hamburg* (Harmondsworth: Penguin, 1984), chapter 15.

11. A. Kolnai, 'Erroneous Conscience,' *Ethics, Value and Reality* (London: Athlone Press, 1977), pp. 14–22.

12. See my 'The Morality of Terrorism,' *Journal of Applied Philosophy* 14 (1997).

13. See M. Walzer, *Just and Unjust Wars: A Moral Argument with Historical Illustrations*, third edition (New York: Basic Books, 2000), chapter 16.

14. Ibid., p. 261. For an account of the terror bombing of Germany, see J. Friedrich, *Der Brand. Deutschland im Bombenkrieg 1940–1945* (Munich: Propyläen Verlag, 2002), and the accompanying volume of photographs, J. Friedrich, *Brandstätten. Der Anblick des Bombenkriegs* (Munich: Propyläen Verlag, 2003). For a discussion of the moral issues involved, see S.A. Garrett, *Ethics and Airpower in World War II: The British Bombing of German Cities* (New York: St. Martin's Press, 1993).

15. See N. Cigar, *Genocide in Bosnia: The Politics of 'Ethnic Cleansing'* (College Station, Texas: Texas A & M University Press, 1995), chapter 5.

16. See e.g. G. Kavka, 'Some Paradoxes of Deterrence,' *Journal of Philosophy* 75 (1978).

17. See, e.g., R. Dworkin, 'The Threat to Patriotism,' *The New York Review of Books*, February 28, 2002; 'The Trouble with the Tribunals,' *The New York Review of Books*, April 25, 2002; 'Terror and the Attack on Civil Liberties,' *The New York Review of Books*, November 6, 2003.

18. G. Alcorn, 'News of Afghan Dead is Buried,' *The Age*, January 12, 2002, p. 17.

19. Walzer, *Just and Unjust Wars*, pp. 155–6.

20. Ibid., p. 152.

21. An earlier, shorter version of the first three sections of this chapter was read at the workshop 'Terrorism and Justice' at the Centre for Applied Philosophy and Public Ethics, University of Melbourne, on November 2, 2001, and published in T. Coady and M. O'Keefe (eds.), *Terrorism and Justice* (Melbourne:

Melbourne University Press, 2002). The present version has benefited from the discussion at the conference on 'Ethics of Terrorism and Counterterrorism,' held at the Zentrum für interdisziplinäre Forschung (ZiF), University of Bielefeld, on October 28–30, 2002, and from correspondence with Stephen Nathanson.

10
The Evolution of the Modern Terrorist State: Area Bombing and Nuclear Deterrence

Douglas Lackey

Britain and the area bombing campaigns

In the winter and spring of 1942, Allied fortunes in the war were at a low ebb. Germany had conquered most of Europe; Italy held large areas of Africa; Japan held sway over much of China, Southeast Asia, and the South Pacific. The battles of Midway, Stalingrad, el-Alamein were yet to come.

In the skies over England, British Spitfires had achieved some success against German fighters and bombers. But defense of the homeland is not offense, and all offensive measures against German forces had failed. British bombing attacks against German military facilities, in particular, had been costly and unsuccessful. The German submarine yards and other military targets selected by British bombers were hard to hit, difficult to damage, and easy to repair. British bombers were poorly armed and easily brought down by German fighters.[1] The Red Army was bearing the brunt of the fighting, and Stalin was calling for second front in Europe. But Churchill had no interest in a second Gallipoli. Some less costly offense had to be found.

In February 1942, Churchill decided on the new offensive strategy: British bombers would raid at night, safe from fighters under cover of darkness.[2] Since little can be seen at night, British planes would bomb designated 'areas,' not specific military targets. In these designated areas, civilians resided. If the areas were objects of attack, then the civilians were objects of attack. The new British strategy was a strategy of terror, and cause terror it did. Giulio Douhet in 1921 had advocated 'terror from the air' as an alternative to the war of attrition in the trenches.[3] The new strategy made Douhet's terror a reality. By the war's end,

595,000 German civilians had been killed by Allied bombings, victims of Churchill and the new head of Bomber Command, Arthur Harris.[4]

The accusation that British area bombing was terrorist bombing, in violation of the international laws of war, was repeatedly made on the German radio by Josef Goebbels. The British responded that area bombing was a legitimate military operation, necessary to defeat the enemy in a just war.[5] The goal, the British said, was not to kill civilians, but to defeat Germany. The fact that Goebbels called British bombing 'terror' bombing has been one of the reasons historians have been reluctant to apply the label. If Goebbels said it, it must be wrong. But consider:

(a) No document or memorandum can be found that indicates that the British, in their targeting choices, made any effort to minimize civilian casualties. In high-level memoranda, for example, circulating before the bombing of Dresden, various German *cities* are named as targets.[6] (One *sotto voce* quip among Bomber Command pilots after targeting briefings was 'Target Point: Cathedral.')[7] Size and accessibility of cities seem to have been controlling factors in target selection, not the presence or absence of military facilities on the ground.

(b) When the American Eighth Air force arrived in England in 1943, a debate broke out between the Americans, who favored daylight precision bombing,[8] and the British, who insisted on the superiority of nighttime raids. That is, in 1943 the British explicitly rejected taking military facilities as targets. Similarly, in 1945, Harris argued ferociously *against* shifting the bombing campaign from German cities to quasi-military targets like oil refineries.[9]

(c) On those few occasions when the RAF did aim at a specific target rather than at areas, they chose non-military targets over military targets. On May 17–18, 1943, for example, the British bombed German dams on the Möhne, Eder, and Sorpe, even though such dams could not be considered military facilities.[10]

(d) On the night of July 24–25, 1943, British bombing, which included the use of incendiary bombs, set off an unprecedented firestorm in Hamburg, destroying the city center and taking tens of thousands of civilian lives. Fire does not discriminate between military and civilian targets. The British continued to use incendiary weapons against German cities, perhaps in the hope of igniting similar firestorms. They showed no interest is discontinuing the use of incendiary bombs even after a study of what had happened to Hamburg.[11]

(e)   In the closing months of the war, depleted *Luftwaffe* fighter forces were pulled back to defend Berlin. Despite the fact that it was no longer necessary for British planes (in most cases) to fly under cover of darkness, they continued to do so, bombing the largely undefended city of Dresden during the night February 13–14, 1945, killing at least 70,000 people.[12]

Points (a)–(e) are part of the evidence that the British knowingly targeted German civilians in their bombing campaigns in World War II, and that the campaign is properly described as terrorism. We can reach this judgement without complicated analyses of British intentions. The bombings were as indiscriminate as the fires they caused. The common soldier is not a terrorist, because the majority of his victims are soldiers and a minority of his victims are civilians. In the British bombing campaign, the majority of those killed were civilians, and a small minority of those killed were German soldiers.

Consider the following thought experiment. Suppose that nation A is engaged in a just war against nation B. In location B1 are 999 B soldiers and 1 B civilian. In location B2 are 999 B civilians and 1 B soldier. A has the capacity to obliterate B1 or B2 with bombs. If A bombs B1 *or* B2, A is 'killing civilians.' If A bombs B1 *or* B2, A is 'killing enemy soldiers.' But bombing B1 is a legitimate act of war, and bombing B2 is a terrorist act. The distinction is not found in A's intention or goals, or in the fact that civilians are killed or the fact that soldiers are killed, or in finely tuned talk about regretted side-effects. The difference is found in the ratio of military to non-military damage. I will apply this Ratio of Damage Test in what follows.

Though British bombing was terror bombing, history has not labeled Churchill a terrorist. It is interesting to consider why the historians are wrong.

To begin, heads of state are given special status by historians, and Churchill in approving area bombing was acting as head of state. But if Churchill is exempt from moral judgement as a head of state, then all heads of state are exempt from moral judgement, and there is no moral case against Hitler.

Second, the decision to begin area bombing took place in the middle of a war, while the more easily labeled terror events, like the September 11 attacks, take place in peacetime. People get psychologically brutalized by war, develop hatred of 'the enemy,' introduce the morally irrelevant observation that 'the Germans did it first,' and deploy the dismissive response that 'bad things happen in war.' But even the 'bad things happen' response implies that killing civilians in this ratio is a bad thing, and historians in the comfort of their studies should not share the prejudices of the psychologically brutalized.

Third, the area bombings were viewed as acts against 'Nazi Germany' and if the Nazis were utterly bad, it follows, in the minds of many, that anything done against 'Nazi Germany,' even terrorism, was utterly good. But those who insist that terrorism against Nazi Germany is a morally good thing are admitting the main point, that the bombing campaign was terrorism.

The United States and the bombing campaign against Japan

The Eighth Air Force arrived in England determined to do the morally right thing. American B-17s had more guns than British Lancasters, and American bombardiers had the Norden bombsight that made precision bombing possible – at least on sunny days. The Americans paid a high price for their principles. In one raid on the Schweinfurt ball-bearing factories in 1943, 10 per cent of the US bombers were shot down, and in attacks on the Ploesti synthetic oil refineries in 1943 and 1944, US forces suffered even greater losses.

Indeed, the loss rates were so high in 1943 and 1944 that it was imperative to look for alternatives. The model of area bombing, rejected with scorn by the Americans in 1943, was embraced in 1945. The Americans still bombed during the day, but the targets had become cities; the RAF bombed Dresden at night, the Americans bombed Dresden the next day, churning up rubble with high explosives.

The switch from precision bombing to area bombings in Europe had come about by slow steps. In the Pacific campaign, the change was abrupt.[13] The campaign again the Japanese mainland began in October 1944 when the XXI Bomber Command under Haywood Hansell launched B-29 bombing raids from Saipan. The raids of 1944 were precision raids against such targets as Japanese aircraft engine factories, and achieved modest success. But in 1945, when US ground forces were suffering heavy losses taking island after island, Hap Arnold, commander of the Twentieth Air Force in the Pacific Theater, recommended that the XXI Bomber Command consider taking the RAF as their model and commencing incendiary attacks on Japanese cities. When Hansell protested the requested targeting changes (echoing the 1943 American protests against British policy), he was replaced by Curtis LeMay, a man with no scruples about city attacks. The fact that a change of command was necessary in order to initiate city bombing against Japan shows that the change of policy was a deliberate choice, not a matter of target creep.

The devastation wrought by the RAF on Dresden was matched by the devastation rained on Tokyo on March 9–10, 1945, when American incendiary bombs ignited a firestorm killing at least 80,000 people and destroying 250,000 buildings.[14] Other incendiary raids followed, culminating in the attacks on Hiroshima and Nagasaki on August 6 and 9, 1945.

It has been remarked, in response to widespread moral condemnation of the Hiroshima attack, that 'the raid on Tokyo killed even more people.' Such remarks ignore the possibility that *both* attacks were immoral. But I will not, in this essay, develop arguments about the morality of these attacks, *all things considered*. My concern here is simply to assess whether such raids on cities were terrorist attacks.

In his radio address to the nation following the Hiroshima bombing, President Truman spoke of 'destroying Japan's power to make war.'[15] This remark depicts attacks on cities as attacks on the Japanese power to wage war. But if the 'power to make war' means the power to attack another nation, Japan's power was destroyed by US fighting forces before these city attacks began. And if the 'power to make war' means the power to engage in armed resistance, then that power persisted irrespective of the raids on Japanese cities. Suppose counterfactually that every major Japanese city had been obliterated by fire bombing as early as February 1945. Despite this, the entrenched Japanese forces on Iwo Jima and Okinawa could have, and would have, presented the same degree of furious resistance that they in fact mounted in February and April 1945. Even on the mainland, the Japanese capacity for armed resistance survived the attacks: a kamikaze squadron planned to attack the USS *Missouri* as it sailed into Tokyo harbor for the surrender ceremony on August 14. The squadron was disarmed, not by American bombing, but by a personal appeal from the brother of the Emperor.

By the Ratio of Damage standard the fire raids of 1945 were terrorist attacks. The vast majority of people killed were civilians; the vast majority of structures destroyed were non-military structures. The intent of the raids was to induce surrender by inflicting death and pain on the civilian population. About 500,000 Japanese civilians died in these raids. In nine months American bombing had killed almost as many civilians as British bombing had killed in three and a half years. If American criticisms of British bombing policy in 1943 were valid, then those criticisms apply to American attacks on Japan in 1945.

American plans for nuclear war

Terror bombing was employed by the United States during the Korean War, the Vietnam War, the Gulf War, and the action against Serbia in 1999. Rather than explore these later cases I wish to examine a prong of the issue stemming from the use of nuclear weapons. In the years following Hiroshima, there was considerable interest in the integration of small-size nuclear weapons into the equipment of American fighting forces. By the Ratio of Damage argument, such small nuclear weapons could be used in non-terrorist ways. But despite the deployment, or at least the storage, of thousands of tactical nuclear weapons fit for use in battle, the main post-Hiroshima use of nuclear weapons was the use of strategic (i.e. very large) nuclear weapons for the purposes of 'deterrence.' The root idea of nuclear deterrence was simple: leader L from nation A is led to believe, if he does bad act B, that American bombers or missiles will drop nuclear weapons on A. Fearing this, L does not do B. Note that this is not a potential use of nuclear weapons: this is an actual use, even if the weapons do not explode.

A nuclear attack is a serious business, and American planning restricted thinking about nuclear deterrence to serious bad acts. I believe that developed scenarios for counter-attacks using strategic nuclear weapons existed for (a) a Soviet attack on Western Europe, (b) a Chinese invasion of Taiwan, (c) a North Korean or Chinese attack on South Korea, and (d) an attack by either the Soviet Union or China against the territory of the United States. Of these, I will dismiss as implausible (a) to (c). The United States considered and failed to use nuclear weapons against China in response to Chinese intervention in the Korean War, an intervention that killed thousands of US troops. The fear was that if the United States began using nuclear weapons against a foreign power, then nuclear allies of that foreign power might respond by using nuclear weapons against the United States. As Henry Kissinger remarked, nations are not going to commit suicide in defense of somebody else.

The prime deterrence scheme was (d). Even here the logic was vague. Deterrence is always conditional: *if* B happens, a nuclear attack will follow against A. There were problems with the details of B, and the details of the response against A. Suppose that Soviet land forces invaded Alaska, for example. Would the United States respond with a nuclear attack on Russia? That might produce a nuclear counter-attack on New York, which had thus far been spared. But one thing seemed clear and credible: if there were a Soviet nuclear attack on the American mainland, the response would be an American nuclear attack on the Soviet Union.

In the 1950s the design of the US nuclear response to a Soviet attack on the United States was largely left to the Strategic Air Command, organized in 1946 and commanded by General LeMay from 1947 to 1958.[16] The attacks planned by SAC on Russia in the 1940s and 1950s were city-busting attacks along the lines of Hiroshima and Nagasaki. One must suppose that the thought patterns of the general who had designed city attacks on Japan carried over to the design of the Apocalypse.

In the early 1960s, when deterrence options expanded with the introduction of submarine launched missiles, the Defense Department decided to integrate US nuclear forces into a single coordinated multi-service response. The first such Single Integrated Operational Plan, or SIOP, was introduced for 1962. In the event of a bad act B, considered worthy of nuclear response, the 1962 SIOP called for massive nuclear retaliation against the Soviet Union *and China*, resulting in the deaths of at least 400 million people.

Evaluating the character of 1962 SIOP is like wrestling with the devil. Surely the attacks envisioned in the SIOP were terrorist attacks, by the Ratio of Damage argument. But what we want to evaluate is the act of setting up the SIOP, not the act of carrying it out. In contemporary moral theory, one evaluates an action by reference to intentions, consequences, and states of character expressed by the action. One could argue that the laudable intention behind the SIOP was the prevention of nuclear attack on the United States; that the laudable consequence of the SIOP was that there was no such attack, even under the pressure of the Cuban Missile Crisis, and that the laudable state of character expressed by the SIOP was a resolute and courageous commitment to do whatever was necessary to defend the United States.

I have considered such arguments at length elsewhere.[17] The problem for this essay is whether nuclear deterrence under this SIOP and its successors indicates an American commitment to terrorism. We are *not* considering the nuclear attack itself, but the threat to launch a nuclear attack under certain conditions. But I believe that the character of a threat to do X, if one is not bluffing, is found in the character of X. The moral character of doing X rubs off on sincere threats to do it. So if it is terrorism to launch a nuclear attack, then it is terrorism to threaten to launch a nuclear attack, provided that threat is no bluff.

Was the American posture under the first SIOP a bluff? Surely the SIOP did not create an automated response, the clearest case of not bluffing. Human beings, the President or his successors, remained in critical positions in the loop. Presumably, if the President chose not to launch a nuclear counter-attack, even after a nuclear attack on the

United States, under the SIOP a nuclear counter-attack would not be launched. (In such circumstances, there might be a pro-response coup, overthrowing the Constitution, but such treason was not part of the SIOP.) For the SIOP to be a bluff, the President would have to have formed a fixed intention, for the duration of his Presidency, not to launch a nuclear counter-attack. I have discovered no evidence, no memoirs written late in life, that either Eisenhower or Kennedy had a fixed and persisting intention *not* to launch a nuclear counter-attack, in the face of a Soviet attack on the United States. Absent such a fixed intention, the threatened counter-attack was no bluff.

The first SIOP was unsubtle and in many ways inefficient. When McNamara was appointed Secretary of Defense in 1961, he set about upgrading efficiency on all fronts, including the SIOP. Daniel Ellsberg was brought in from RAND to design a new SIOP, which became operational in 1963. The new SIOP differed profoundly from its predecessor.[18] The first SIOP called for the same single massive response to any enemy attack that met a defined threshold: 'worthy of nuclear response.' The new SIOP, under the watchword 'flexible response,' called for different responses to different provocations. If the Soviet Union attacked Alaska, there would be a response that left most of the Soviet Union undamaged and most of American nuclear forces in reserve. Should the Soviets respond with an attack on New York, the SIOP called for an even larger, but still less than total, counter-response. Any larger Soviet attack would produce an even larger American response; every gap in the escalation ladder was to be plugged. The Soviets, great chess players, would realize that the end-game belonged to the Americans, and so the game itself blessedly would never start.

Was 'flexible response' still terrorism? Some of the planed responses, those involving limited nuclear war at sea, for example, or those involving attacks on isolated radars in Siberia, would not be terrorist attacks according to the Ratio of Damage Argument. But all other attacks, the vast majority of those planned, would involve great numbers of civilian casualties. By the Ratio of Damage Argument, these 'flexible' responses would be terrorist attacks.

Furthermore, the new flexible SIOP still called for attacks on cities, as attacks on cities are an integral part of the logic of deterrence. If every gap in the escalation ladder has to be plugged, then the top steps will have to consist of very large attacks. The very logic of deterrence calls for this. If the opponent realizes that it can raise the ante until the United States drops out, the capacity to execute limited responses to smaller attacks will fail to deter. Furthermore, except for nuclear attacks at sea, every step in the escalation ladder should be classified as terrorist according to the Ratio of Damage argument.

The SIOP has been revised a number of times since 1963. Nevertheless, the succeeding SIOPs were still governed by the concepts of the 1963 SIOP: 'flexible response,' 'plugging the gaps in escalation ladder,' and so forth. It is sometimes remarked that the new SIOPs, with scenarios for limited nuclear war, were designed to spare civilian life, since the number of civilians killed under flexible response is less than the number of civilians killed under massive retaliation. But the argument for replacing massive retaliation with flexible response sprung from the rationality of deterrence, not from any principle of favoring military targets over civilian targets. I have it on good authority that the Judge Advocate General's Office, during the late 1990s, conducted a legal review of the current SIOP, assessing whether targets listed in the SIOP were compatible with international law, especially laws and conventions inspired by the Principle of Non-Combatant Immunity. This was the first time that such a review had ever been conducted, proof positive that earlier SIOPs were not designed with this thought in mind. Whether the current SIOP reflects the verdicts of JAG review is something for later historians to discover.

Conclusion

There is a continuous line of historical development from Churchill's decision to commence area bombing, to the bombings of Dresden, Tokyo, Hiroshima, and Nagasaki, to Curtis LeMay and SAC plans for nuclear air attacks on Russia, and finally to the American SIOPs for nuclear war. All these bombings and plans for bombings say that in certain circumstances it is acceptable to rain devastation down on a city. The older ideal that soldiers should fight soldiers and military equipment should fight military equipment is cast aside.

I believe that the British policy of area bombing inaugurated a new era in warfare: a kind of state terrorism, now routinely added to the repertoire of policy options of powerful nations. I do not agree with Walzer and others that area bombing is just a new version of the older methods of besieging cities.[19] When the Romans besieged Carthage, when the Crusaders besieged Jerusalem, there were soldiers outside of the city throwing things in and soldiers inside the city throwing things out. A siege was often like a battlefield with a wall in the middle. But when the British bombed Dresden, when the 'Enola Gay' bombed Hiroshima, there was no wall, just the planes above and the city below. If a terrorist is one who prefers killing civilians to damage to soldiers, then most of the older sieges where not terrorism, but most modern 'bombing campaigns' are.

With the world's largest air force and a developing habit of preferring the lives of its soldiers over the lives of non-American civilians, the US Government has become accustomed to raining devastation from the air.[20] I suspect that Americans from 1945 to 2001 approved US bombing campaigns because they themselves had never been targets and had no first hand knowledge of the human results. On September 11, 2001, they experienced, as I did from one kilometer's distance, what a terrorist attack from the air is like. The Americans were correct to judge that the terrorists who flew those planes on September 11 were avatars of evil. What they have not realized is the degree to which their own policies, since January 1945, are more of the same.

Notes

1. For these details see the official history, Sir Charles Webster and Noble Frankland, *The Strategic Air Offensive Against Germany* (London: HMSO, 1961).
2. For Churchill's complicity (and his ability to cover his tracks) see Max Hastings, *Bomber Offensive* (London: Macmillan, 1968).
3. For an English translation of Douhet, see *Command of the Air* (New York: Coward McCann, 1942).
4. For the figure, confirmed by British sources, see Hans Rumpf, *The Bombing of Germany* (London: White Lion, 1963).
5. For these moral accusations and counter-accusations, see Anthony Verrier, *The Bomber Offensive* (London: Collins, 1968).
6. For the steps leading to Dresden see Alexander McKee, *Dresden 1945: The Devil's Tinderbox* (New York: Dutton, 1982).
7. For this and other nasty sides to the campaign, see F.J.P. Veale, *Advance to Barbarism* (London: Thomson and Smith, 1948).
8. See Thomas Coffey, *Decision over Schweinfurt: The U.S. 8th Air Force Battle for Daylight Bombing* (New York: David McKay, 1977).
9. See Arthur Harris, *Bomber Offensive* (London: Collins, 1947) for Harris's battle against Sinclair over oil refinery bombings.
10. Americans with a love of blowing up things can participate (virtually) in these 'dam-busting' raids by purchasing the latest CD-Rom version simulation of these attacks. In the 1954 movie, *Dam Busters*, Michael Redgrave led the raid, with no visible moral qualms.
11. See Martin Middlebrook, *The Battle of Hamburg* (New York: Scribner's 1981) for the firestorm and its sequels.
12. Ibid.
13. For this and the following account of the American raids on Japan, see the official history, *The Army Air Forces in World War II* (Chicago: University of Chicago Press, 1948–58). A good one-volume account is Michael Sherry, *The Rise of American Air Power* (New Haven: Yale University Press, 1987).

14. Martin Caidin, *A Torch to the Enemy: The Fire Raid on Tokyo* (Baltimore, Md: Ballantine Books, 1960).

15. Barton J. Bernstein and Allen J. Matusow (eds.), *The Truman Administration: A Documentary History* (New York: Harper & Row, 1966), pp. 40–1.

16. For this and the ensuing account of the evolution of American nuclear war fighting plans see David Alan Rosenberg's magisterial article, 'The Origins of Overkill,' *International Security* 7 (1983).

17. Douglas P. Lackey, *Moral Principles and Nuclear Weapons* (Totowa, NJ: Rowman and Allanheld, 1984).

18. For Ellsberg and RAND and SIOP-63, see Fred Kaplan, *The Wizards of Armageddon* (New York: Simon and Schuster, 1983).

19. Michael Walzer, *Just and Unjust Wars* (New York: Basic Books, 1977), chapter 10.

20. Bill Clinton, not remembered as a militarist, used air power against the Sudan, Afghanistan, and Serbia, in the last case destroying 30 per cent of Serbian industrial capacity in 1999. Photographs of the devastation have shocked audience and substantially aided Milošević in his defense against war crimes charges at The Hague.

Part IV

Cases

11
Terror Bombing of German Cities in World War II

Stephen A. Garrett

The campaign

In the last week of July 1943, the city of Hamburg was attacked by over 700 aircraft from the Royal Air Force's Bomber Command. A combination of incendiary and explosive bombs was dropped on the central area of the city. Approximately 74 percent of the most densely populated section of Hamburg was destroyed. About 50,000 people were killed in these attacks, and around one million refugees fled to safer outlying areas.[1] Perhaps the most notable aspect of the Hamburg raids was the phenomenon of the firestorm, which produced hurricane-type winds of 150 miles an hour and sucked people, trees, even whole buildings into the center of the flames. The Police President of Hamburg summarized the fate of his city this way:

> Its horror is revealed in the howling and raging of the firestorms, the hellish noise of exploding bombs and the death cries of martyred human beings as well as in the big silence after the raids. Speech is impotent to portray the measure of the horror, which shook the people for ten days and nights and the traces of which were written indelibly on the face of the city and its inhabitants.[2]

The devastation of Hamburg was henceforward referred to by the Germans simply as *die Katastrophe*.

The assault on Hamburg was only one chapter in the RAF's area bombing offensive against Germany. As a method of air warfare, 'area bombing' focused not on specific military or industrial targets but rather on German cities themselves. The targeting instructions given to British aircrew indeed typically designated the center of such cities as the prime 'aiming point.' The RAF launched some 390,000 sorties against Germany in the entire course of the war, and area attacks accounted for about 70 percent of the total effort, with approximately one million tons of bombs being dropped on the enemy. By the end of 1944, around 80 percent of all German urban centers with populations of more than 100,000 had been devastated or seriously damaged. This exercise in destruction continued even into the spring of 1945, with almost 40 percent of British bombing being directed at city targets.[3] It is estimated that overall some 500,000 German civilians lost their lives as a result of the area offensive, and perhaps another 1,000,000 received serious injury. Around three million homes were destroyed.

Can the British area bombing offensive against Germany in World War II be considered a type of 'terrorism' appropriate for inclusion and analysis in the present volume? There are many who would argue against such a proposition, particularly given the nature of the Nazi threat. We typically think of terrorist acts as being directed at innocents, and certainly the Nazi regime could hardly be described as 'innocent.' Some might even extend this point to the broader German society that supported that regime. There were in fact voices in Britain during the war that made precisely this assertion.

Prominent among these was Sir Robert Vansittart, a veteran of the Foreign Office and important diplomatic advisor to the British government, who suggested that throughout history the Germans had been the 'butcher-birds' of Europe, the invariable cause of the trials and tribulations of civilized humanity. Envy, self-pity and cruelty were identified as the fundamental traits of the German people. Even though Vansittart conceded there were a few good Germans, he claimed that for the most part Hitler gave 'to the great majority of Germans exactly what they have hitherto liked and wanted.'[4] Some British newspapers trumpeted the same line at the time. One typical headline was, 'Why all this bosh about being gentle with the Germans after we have beaten them when ALL GERMANS ARE GUILTY!'[5] From this perspective, any measures that promised to contribute to the destruction of the Nazi menace were justified, and more to the point, Bomber Command could hardly be accused of a 'terrorist' enterprise (i.e., an attack on innocents) since all Germans bore guilt for Hitler's program of aggression.

In weighing whether area bombing equaled terrorism, we also have various arguments presented by its proponents at the time that suggested a legitimate (and thus presumably 'respectable') military rationale for its use in wartime. One of these was that it would help to divert German resources from the war on the Eastern Front and the Middle East in order to provide for the air defense of the Reich. Moreover, since German industry was naturally concentrated in and around the major German cities, even so-called indiscriminate attacks on these places were bound to damage or destroy some of the relevant factories. Such attacks would also lead to a shattering of the whole fabric of German civil life, which in turn would create a basic dislocation in war production and the German home front's ability to support the Reich military machine. Sir Arthur Harris, the head of RAF's Bomber Command, was particularly ardent in advancing these propositions and he even went so far as to suggest that if the British Government gave its full support to the bomber offensive, Germany could essentially be defeated by airpower alone.[6]

Despite the above attempts at removing the stain of terrorism in describing the British area bombing offensive, a retrospective examination of that offensive argues strongly that this *was* a variety of terrorism, or, to be more exact, state terrorism. We are accustomed to addressing issues of terrorism in terms of actions taken by a non-state party against a recognized regime, but there seems no reason not to expand the term to include certain measures adopted even in classical inter-state conflict. Fundamental to any working definition of terrorism is that it targets indiscriminately. Michael Walzer speaks of the notion of 'aiming,' and does so in his usual eloquent language:

> [There is] a moral difference between aiming and not aiming – or, more accurately, between aiming at particular people because of things they have done or are doing, and aiming at whole groups of people, indiscriminately, because of who they are. The first kind of aiming is appropriate to a limited struggle directed against regimes and policies. The second reaches beyond all limits; it is infinitely threatening to whole peoples, whose individual members are systematically exposed to violent death at any and every moment in the course of their (largely innocuous) lives.[7]

The essence of the British area bombing campaign was that it did not distinguish between targets reasonably connected to the Nazi military threat – centers of arms production, installations such as airfields, naval assets and command-and-control centers – and the broader society that bore a distant and indirect relationship to the Nazi war machine. Under British air doctrine during World War II, the notion of 'aiming' expanded so that any part or sector of Germany – civilian, military, or indeterminate – became 'legitimate' targets for attack. An assertion of 'collective guilt' on the part of the German people as justifying this lack of discrimination – that is, there *were* really no innocents in Germany – can hardly withstand examination. There may have been a majority of Germans who supported the Nazi regime, but there were also many who did not. That *all* Germans should have been potentially subject to death by bombing simply because of their physical location was at the very least a bizarre reinterpretation of one of the basic moral principles that had heretofore governed (or was supposed to govern) military operations.

Evidence that the British area bombing offensive violated the basic concept of 'aiming' is not hard to find and is reflected in particular in the putative attempt at the time to establish a 'rational' purpose for the destruction of German cities. Chief among the theoreticians of British bombing was Lord Cherwell (F.A. Lindemann), the principal scientific adviser to Prime Minister Churchill. In a famous minute to Churchill on March 30, 1942, Cherwell concentrated on the impact on German morale of a major British area bombing campaign. Based on his analysis of the previous German bombing of British cities, he argued that 'having one's house demolished is most damaging to morale. People seem to mind it more than having their friends or even relatives killed.' He went on from there to estimate that with adequate resources and by concentrating on the 58 major German population centers, Bomber Command could by 1943 render a third of the German people homeless. 'There seems little doubt that this would break the spirit of the people.' The concept of the shattering of the German people's morale, and thus of Germany's will or ability to continue the war, was enshrined henceforth as one of the guiding premises of British bombing policy. As the official history of Bomber Command puts it, 'Because of the position which he occupied and the time at which he submitted his minute, Lord Cherwell's intervention was of great importance. It did much to insure the concept of strategic bombing in its hour of crisis.'[8]

The notion of shattering German 'morale' was inherently a rejection of the principle of discrimination, since the German people themselves now became the main target of British bombing. As it happens, this idea was in itself a chimera (about which more later), but it remains as a prime piece of evidence attesting to what can only be fairly described as a campaign based on terrorizing a whole population into surrender. We also have more specific evidence on this matter, and it comes from Churchill himself. The Prime Minister was careful throughout most of the war to deny that Britain was attempting simply to terrorize the German people into surrender by targeting German cities. He continued to refer to Bomber Command's efforts as being directed solely at the sinews of the German war machine. Following perhaps the most famous (or notorious) British bombing attack of the war, however, he was far more candid in a private memorandum to the air staff.

The case in point was the attack on Dresden on February 13, 1945. Estimates on casualties in this instance vary widely, from a minimal guess of about 35,000 to a more drastic figure of over 200,000. In order to prevent the spread of disease, the authorities cordoned off the center of the city and constructed 25 foot-long grills where thousands of the victims were cremated.[9] The British official history described the Dresden raid as 'the crowning achievement in the long, arduous and relentless development of a principle of bombing [the area offensive].'[10] At this point Churchill evidently decided that Bomber Command's 'crowning achievement' should be left to speak for itself, and he wrote to the Chief of the Air Staff along the following lines:

> It seems to me that the moment has come when the question of bombing of German cities simply for the sake of increasing the terror, *though under other pretexts*, should be reviewed. The destruction of Dresden remains a serious query against the conduct of Allied bombing ... The Foreign Secretary has spoken to me on this subject, and I feel the need for more precise concentration upon military objectives such as oil and communications behind the immediate battle-zone, *rather than on mere acts of terror and wanton destruction, however impressive.*[11]

The sliding scale

In offering an ethical critique of the British bombing offensive against Germany in World War II as a type of state terrorism, one does have to contend with the fact that the putative 'terrorist' in this instance hardly matches our normal image of an individual or group (or nation) committing mayhem for obscure or even irrational causes. As we have already noted, Great Britain was certainly fighting for an eminently just cause at the time, and one whose importance could hardly be clearer: the defeat of a challenge to all basic human values. Given this circumstance, defenders of the morality of the area bombing offensive – both at the time and since – have frequently offered a theory of the 'sliding scale'.

Reduced to its essentials, this suggests that the more just the cause, the greater latitude one has in ignoring or at least temporarily setting aside certain traditional norms in serving that cause (in particular, respect for the rights of innocents). The eminent theoretician John Rawls puts the point somewhat indirectly: 'Even in a just war, certain forms of violence are strictly inadmissible; and when a country's right is questionable and uncertain, the constraints on the means it can use are all the more severe. Acts permissible in a war of legitimate self-defense, when these are necessary, may be flatly excluded in a more doubtful situation.'[12] What this would seem to suggest is that air attacks by Germany against British cities such as London and Coventry during the war can be easily dismissed as morally repugnant whereas the subsequent British area offensive against Germany is far more defensible, since it was in pursuit of a compelling just cause. Noble Frankland, one of the authors of the official British history of the area bombing offensive, makes precisely this argument. In discussing the morality of the area offensive, he suggests that a decisive consideration was 'the causes for which the war [was] being fought and the nature of the enemy, for the means adopted must be in scale with the ends sought.'[13]

There is hardly likely to be any war that provides more comfort and support to the adherents of the sliding scale hypothesis than World War II. Yet two critical objections may be offered to this type of thinking. The unalloyed adoption of the sliding scale would have logically removed any compunctions about the most savage application of military violence to defeat the Nazis. Even the most fervent supporters of Allied air power in World War II would (and for the record did) stop short of such an unvarnished commitment to destruction. Moreover, the argument of the sliding scale ignores the fact that the war against the Nazi regime was after all a defense of certain basic values, among which was a decent respect for the individual. In the ultimate sense this was the political purpose of the war (in the Clausewitzian sense), that is to say, the defense of a whole way of life. One of the leading private historians of the area offensive observes that a great many people (among whom he presumably numbered himself) 'felt that by embarking on a systematic attack on cities ... the Allies sacrificed something of their own moral case and that they contributed substantially to the terrible moral collapse that took place in the Second World War, most especially in the treatment of prisoners and civilians.'[14] To this argument the sliding scale thesis seemingly can present few rebuttals.

Supreme emergency and military necessity

References to the idea of the sliding scale may be found amongst past and present defenders of the area offensive, but the impression is that those making such arguments are generally rather uncomfortable with extending them too far, for perhaps obvious reasons. The supporters of area bombing of Germany, on the other hand, are a good deal less defensive when they discuss two other moral claims for the legitimacy of British air strategy.

The first of these asserts the notion of 'supreme emergency.' The argument is that in such a situation even humane and civilized states may be forced (temporarily) to set aside what Walzer calls the 'war convention' in the interests of survival – and moreover they have a (temporary) right to do so. As Walzer defines it, the war convention consists of 'the set of articulated norms, customs, professional codes, legal precepts, religious and philosophical principles, and reciprocal arrangements that shape our judgments of military conduct.'[15] An important assumption here is that the state is fighting in accordance with the dictates of just war doctrine, that is to say, it is fighting for a just cause. How to define a supreme emergency? Two ingredients seem to be necessary: there must be a clear and imminent danger of defeat by the enemy; and the consequences of such a defeat must appear to be truly catastrophic. In practical terms, this would mean that losing the war would threaten the very essence of the nation, would involve one's society and values being subjugated to a completely repugnant rule, would perhaps even put one's existence as a separate state at risk. Notice that both elements have to be present in order for there to be a supreme emergency: if the threat of defeat is imminent but the consequences of defeat are limited, or if the potential consequences are dire but there is no immediate danger of defeat, then no supreme emergency exists. If such a peril does exist, however, Machiavelli for one argued that with 'the entire safety of our country...at stake, no considerations of what is just or unjust, merciful or cruel, praiseworthy or blameworthy must intervene.'[16]

From the concept of supreme emergency we move to the corollary notion of 'military necessity.' This term is found very widely in all discussions of ethics and military conduct, as well as in various conventions setting out the laws of war. The dilemma has been to interpret the scope and meaning of military necessity, and how it may or may not sanction certain measures that would be unallowable in the absence of it. As a general matter, military necessity may be said to obtain when a certain action bears a legitimate connection to the search for victory and when its non-performance would actively undermine that effort. Even so there are certain military activities that are ruled out regardless of their possible contribution to victory, e.g., the mass slaughter of prisoners. For present purposes I want to attach the notion of military necessity very closely to supreme emergency, and consider both these ideas in the context of the British decision on February 14, 1942 to launch a campaign of indiscriminate bombing of German cities.

The air offensive, according to Directive No. 22 issued by chief of the Air Staff Sir Charles Portal to Bomber Command, was now to be 'focused on the morale of the enemy civil population and in particular of the industrial workers.' In case there was any doubt at Bomber Command headquarters about what was now intended, Portal sent a follow-on communication the next day: 'Ref the new bombing directive: I suppose it is clear that the aiming points are to be the built-up areas, not, for instance, the dockyards or aircraft factories.... This must be made quite clear if it is not already understood.'[17] Sir Arthur Harris, who was to become head of Bomber Command on February 23, indicated that he at least had no misunderstanding on this point.

We can summarize the implicit and, to some extent explicit, rationale of this decision as follows: Britain was indeed facing a supreme emergency in its war with Germany, and directing the RAF's Bomber Command to attack German cities was a military necessity in the sense that Britain had no other significant way at the time of prosecuting the war against the Nazis. Not to prosecute the war was to accept the continuance, and perhaps the actual effectuation, of the supreme emergency, which was intolerable. Therefore, this particular violation of the war convention, that is, indiscriminate killing of German combatants and non-combatants alike, was morally defensible.

In assessing this argument, we need to look closely at both elements of the equation – that is, did a supreme emergency confront Great Britain in February 1942, and was the area offensive a military necessity in that Britain had no other options, or at least none that promised to do significant damage to the Nazi ability to make war?

On the first point, there is no question but that Britain was faced with at least one element of supreme emergency in February 1942. A Nazi defeat of Great Britain, and more especially a Nazi occupation of the British islands, would have ushered in a long night of barbarism which would have threatened all the basic norms of the nation as they had been developed over the past several hundred years. We have plenty of evidence that Hitler planned to remake British society and institutions along lines congenial to the New Order in Europe. This would have begun with a systematic elimination of all the leadership elements in Great Britain (as had earlier happened in Poland, for example). Beyond this there were plans for the mass deportation of British workers to

Germany to work in factories and on farms. An item from the proposed plan of Military Government for England stipulated that the entire 'able-bodied male population between the ages of seventeen and forty-five will . . . be interned and dispatched to the Continent with the minimum of delay.' There was also to be a draconian requisition of foodstuffs and raw materials beyond that required for the bare subsistence of the population. It need hardly be mentioned, finally, that British Jews would have been subjected to the same fate as their co-religionists on the Continent.[18]

But was German victory over Great Britain ever imminent, or more to the point, was it imminent in February 1942, the start of the area offensive? There is a lot to be said for the argument that if a supreme emergency ever did face Great Britain – in the sense of impending defeat by the Germans – it peaked in the summer of 1940 and rapidly ebbed after that time. Even though Britain had managed to extricate over 300,000 men from the beaches of Dunkirk, virtually all of their equipment had been left behind, and the estimate was that there remained only two fully armed divisions in the country itself to resist a German assault. Churchill and his advisers began to consider plans for moving the Government to Canada in such an event. After a brief delay, Hitler ordered that preparations for the invasion of Britain, code-named 'Operation Sea Lion', proceed with all due speed. He established as a prerequisite for the attack, however, that the RAF be essentially eliminated as a threat to the German invasion forces.

In considering the last point it can be argued that September 15, 1940 represented the end of the crisis facing Britain. This was the climactic day in the Battle of Britain, the campaign by the *Luftwaffe* to destroy British airpower, and after Fighter Command had inflicted heavy losses on the attacking German aircraft with comparatively modest damage to its own, Hitler ordered the *Luftwaffe* to concentrate on the bombing of British cities at night rather than targeting the assets of the RAF in daytime. Shortly after September 15, he further directed that all preparations for the invasion be suspended. His mind now became increasingly focused on the campaign against Russia.

In assessing the situation facing Britain in February 1942, then, one might suggest that since any realistic threat of invasion had vanished, so had the specter of supreme emergency. There is still more to the argument, however. The critic might note that even though Britain was at this point free from the peril of actual military occupation, it was questionable how long she could maintain herself in the face of German control of the Continent. Might not her isolated position eventually result in the erosion of her capacity to resist Nazi pressure? In meeting this objection, reference can be made to perhaps the most important week of the entire war, which occurred at the beginning of December 1941. On December 5, the Soviets launched a major counter-offensive in the environs of Moscow, which threw back the *Wehrmacht* from the gates of the city and inflicted the first major defeat of the war on German ground forces. The success of this offensive insured that Hitler's dream of a quick conquest of Soviet Russia in 1941 would prove unavailing. Two days later, on December 7, Japan attacked the United States at Pearl Harbor, which brought the Americans into the war, not only against Tokyo but three days later against the Germans as well. At the dawn of 1942, therefore, it appeared that Russia had survived, the vast might of the Americans was now engaged, and the entire strategic situation had been dramatically transformed. Under the circumstances, the only supreme emergency that loomed was the one the Germans would face sooner or later. Churchill himself happily assessed the entirely changed position:

> So we had won after all! . . . In dire stress, we had won the war. England would live; Britain would live; the Commonwealth of Nations and the Empire would live. . . . Once again in our long Island history we should emerge, however mauled or mutilated, safe and victorious. We should not be wiped out. Out history would not come to an end. . . . Hitler's fate was sealed [and] there was no more doubt about the end.[19]

If any vestige of supreme emergency had passed by February 1942, then this concept cannot be used to justify the initiation of the area offensive, a military strategy that evidently violated one of the principal themes of the war convention, the distinction between combatants and non-combatants. That said, however, there is the second argument advanced in moral support of the area bombing offensive, that of military necessity. Perhaps Britain had indeed been spared from Nazi conquest, but there was still the challenge of actually crushing the Nazis once and for all so that the threat could not be repeated. In these terms, the question that emerges is plain enough: was the bombing of German cities the only realistic military option available to Britain at the time that held out the prospect of doing serious damage to the German war effort? What alternatives were at hand for the British Government in using airpower (or other military resources, for that matter) in the war against Germany? In short, was the area offensive a legitimate military necessity in any real sense of the term?

There seems to be a rather convincing array of evidence that, to the extent Britain was to undertake a strategic bombing offensive against

Germany in the period after February 1942, there was for the foreseeable future little alternative but to concentrate on general city attacks. Bomber Command had earlier attempted a series of daylight raids over Germany, but the losses to aircraft were so prohibitive that these had to be abandoned. Attacks at night then became the chosen alternative, but these too faced a formidable difficulty, which was lack of accuracy. The cover of darkness may have helped in the survival rate of British bombers, but various studies showed that attacks on what were called 'precision' targets, e.g., military installations, munitions factories and the like, were rarely greeted with much success. Given the technical constraints operating on Bomber Command in such operations, then, a large urban area seemed to suggest itself as the only feasible aiming point for the aircrew. The British Bombing Survey Unit summarized the argument after the war: 'The navigational and bombing accuracy actually achieved by Bomber Command in night attacks makes it doubtful whether target systems other than towns could have been effectively bombed before the beginning of 1944.'[20]

If this was the case, obviously the moral argument is strongly affected. Noble Frankland makes the not unreasonable assertion that to criticize the area offensive in the period 1942 to early 1944 on moral grounds is to offer an ethical query quite unrelated to the operational circumstances confronting the decision-makers.

> In the case of bombing, strategic criticism, even when operationally unfounded, often seems to be reinforced by moral indignation and moral indignation often seems to have more to do with the formation of views about strategic bombing than do the strategic pros and cons. This need not be objectionable but it becomes so when, to serve a moral argument, Bomber Command is given in retrospect a function which, operationally, it could not have performed.[21]

This is fine as far as it goes, but of course the issue was more complicated than that. Perhaps the only type of strategic bombing that Britain could do in the middle period of the war was area bombing, but was strategic bombing itself a military necessity? Frankland for one leaves little doubt as to his views on the matter. 'The alternative to area bombing was either no strategic bombing or daylight bombing. In the circumstances of the time, the idea of abandoning strategic bombing was scarcely a practicable proposition.'[22]

This seems pretty strongly stated. *Why* was the idea of abandoning strategic bombing (at least temporarily) such an impracticable proposition?

Consider this comment from a fairly impeccable source, the British Prime Minister. Churchill stated in July 1942:

> In the days when we were fighting alone, we answered the question: 'How are you going to win the war?' by saying: 'We will shatter Germany by bombing.' Since then the enormous injuries inflicted on the German Army and manpower by the Russians, and the accession of the manpower and munitions of the United States, have rendered other possibilities open.[23]

These other possibilities included diverting a significant portion of RAF aircrew employed in attacking Germany to direct support of the ground campaign in North Africa and subsequently in Sicily and Italy, as well as to the destruction of the German U-Boat threat in the North Atlantic. Such a change in strategy could have been even more promising if the vast resources devoted to the building of heavy bombers had been substantially redirected to the expansion of the RAF's tactical capabilities and, even more, to an increase in the assets of the army and navy (the latter a possibility that many, although few within the RAF, strongly supported). Even in terms of strategic bombing itself, there could have been a continued effort to develop improvements in navigation and aiming until a more effective (and certainly more morally attractive) strategy of precision bombing was available for adoption. In the event, such alternatives were basically set aside and the area offensive went ahead unabated.

A consequentialist analysis

In evaluating any resort to force in politics and international affairs, the concept of 'instrumentality' is a critical one, and provides a criterion by which we can offer a judgement on the specific action. Simply put, the 'rational' use of violence is clearly instrumental – that is, has utility – in achieving certain finite political goals. This doesn't mean that we necessarily have to approve of those goals or the means taken to achieve them. It is simply to say that we can understand the connection between the violent act and the desired ultimate end. In these terms a good deal, perhaps a majority, of the terrorist operations today can be regarded as 'useless terror,' since their connection to achieving some finite goal seems either tenuous or quite undemonstrable. A good argument can be made that the assault on the World Trade Center on September 11, 1991 falls in this category. The further point is that non-rational (or non-instrumental) violence is by definition morally repugnant, whereas certain types of instrumental violence may be defended or condemned depending on the circumstances of the particular situation.

What of the 'instrumentality' of the British area bombing offensive against Germany? The evidence is quite strong that the strategy of area attacks in fact had only a very limited utility in contributing to the defeat of Germany.

The notion that German morale could be shattered by a strategy of devastating German cities proved to be an entirely false premise. 'Morale' in this sense basically meant the willingness of the German people to work for and support their government's war effort. For a variety of reasons, the carnage visited on Germany by British bombers never came close to having a real effect in these terms. The British Bombing Survey Unit, established after the war to study the military effectiveness of the area offensive, itself conceded the point: 'The effects of town area attacks on the morale of the German people were . . . very much overestimated by all other ministries and departments through the course of the war. . . . There is no evidence that they caused any serious break in the morale of the population as a whole.'[24] The United States Strategic Bombing Survey (USSBS) offered more or less the same conclusion:

> Under ruthless Nazi control they [the German people] showed surprising resistance to the terror and hardships of repeated air attack, to the destruction of their homes and belongings, and to the conditions under which they were reduced to live. Their morale, their belief in ultimate victory . . . and their confidence in their leaders declined, but they continued to work efficiently as long as the physical means of production remained. The power of a police state over its people cannot be underestimated.[25]

The area offensive also proved generally unavailing in reducing Germany's capability for arms production to feed its war machine. During the first major phase of Bomber Command's assault on Germany, dating roughly from the spring of 1942 to spring 1944, German output of war materials, far from declining, actually increased steadily. For example, construction of aircraft of all types went from approximately 15,000 in 1942 to about 40,000 in 1944. Production of tanks increased six-fold. Overall output of weapons and ammunition peaked in the summer of 1944 and was almost three times the level achieved at the beginning of 1942.[26] Production rates declined rapidly after August 1944, but this was due not to the area offensive but to precision attacks against the German energy and transportation systems (the majority of which were undertaken by the US air force).

Given the above conclusions, how to account for the fact that the area bombing offensive continued virtually to the last days of the war (indeed about 80 percent of all the bomb tonnage dropped on Germany by the Allied air forces came during the last ten months of the war)? It is bizarre to note that as late as mid-April 1945, only three weeks prior to the German surrender, Bomber Command undertook yet another city raid on the Berlin suburb of Potsdam by 500 Lancasters, resulting in around 5,000 civilian fatalities.[27] In addressing the question of why such attacks continued even as the Nazi regime was in its death throes, we can identify various factors, none of which had any direct connection to the notions of instrumentality and utility.[28]

One such factor was simply the force of momentum. By early fall 1944, the effect of earlier decisions taken by the British Government concerning the allocation of military resources to the area offensive began to be fully realized. In 1940 there were only 41 four-engined heavy bombers delivered to the RAF and in 1941 some 500. This increased the following year to about 2,000, and for 1943 and 1944 the figures were 4,600 and 5,500 respectively. At its peak, the Ministry of Aircraft Production was employing about 1,700,000 people.[29]

Bomber Command had over 1,000 heavy bombers in its squadrons as of summer 1944 and frequently more aircrew at its disposal than there were planes to fly. By April 1945 there were some 1,600 bombers available to the RAF, and during the last four months of the war the average daily strength of heavy aircraft was over 1,400.[30] In the face of this enormous surge in the number of aircraft as well as aircrew available to Bomber Command, it became a question of how to employ the vast array of planes and personnel at the disposal of Arthur Harris. It seemed hardly thinkable to allow even part of this armada to stand down since so much political and military authority had previously been committed to the buildup of Bomber Command as a decisive weapon against Germany. Moreover, in line with the past belief in the merits of the area offensive, most aircrew had basically been trained in the techniques of the night-time destruction of cities, and at this stage of the war, neither the pilots nor Bomber Command's leadership had much interest in a fundamental rethinking of bombing strategy.[31]

Moreover, Bomber Command was the one service that seemed to defy the growing American domination of Allied military planning and indeed stood out as the one genuinely independent British contribution to the war effort. From the Prime Minister down, there was an acute and painful realization that Britain's relative position in the world was rapidly being superseded by the much greater power of the United States. Bomber Command's stubborn insistence on going its own way (the Americans were very much on record as doubting the military usefulness of the area offensive) was thus at least a small throwback to an earlier period in which the British writ ruled supreme around the globe.

The concern about Bomber Command's remaining as a symbol of an independent British role in the war effort was especially felt at the higher levels of the British Government, who had to deal with the increasingly assertive Americans on a daily basis. The subtleties of wartime coalition politics presumably were a good deal less central in the life of the average British citizen. At the same time, the man in the street and the Prime Minister did have one thing in common, and that was an admiration for the courage and resoluteness of the aircrew of Bomber Command. Indeed a primary theme of wartime government propaganda in Britain was that these aircrew represented in many ways the quintessential example of British steadfastness and devotion to duty. To introduce a fundamental change in the character of Bomber Command's operations would be to call into question the rationale of its earlier activities, especially since they had been consistently described as having a decisive effect on the German capacity to wage war.

There was also the fact that at this stage of the war, the capacity of Germany to retaliate in kind for the British area offensive was almost non-existent. Once Hitler invaded the Soviet Union, the resources of the *Luftwaffe* were almost entirely redirected to the East, and air attacks on the British islands were no more than a minor annoyance for the remainder of the war, save for the V-1 and V-2 assaults in 1944. Given the fact that the *Luftwaffe* could not (or did not) retaliate in kind for British attacks on German cities, there was little incentive on the part of the British Government to stay their hand with respect to German civilians. London simply recognized that there was little if any real balance between the amount of destruction that Germany could visit on Britain compared to that which Bomber Command was able to inflict on the Germans.

Finally, there may have been a straightforward 'revenge' factor. It is difficult to assess the degree to which such feelings may have caused the area offensive to continue unabated, and leading figures directing that offensive always denied that so ignoble an emotion played any significant role in their calculations. Yet there is various evidence that motivations of revenge did have at least a supporting role in the evolution of British bombing strategy. Early in the war, Arthur Harris himself, after viewing the effects of a German attack on London, remarked that 'they are sowing the wind, and they will reap the whirlwind.' In a press conference on May 25, 1943, Churchill touched on the theme of retribution and in particular the moral lesson of the Germans being hoist on their own petard, receiving in full measure the sort of devastation that they had so coldly meted out to others. The air weapon, he said,

> was the weapon these people chose to subjugate the world. This was the weapon with which they struck at Pearl Harbor. This was the weapon with which they boasted – the Germans boasted – they would terrorize all the countries of the world. And it is an example of *poetic justice* that this should be the weapon in which they should find themselves most out-matched and first out-matched in the ensuing struggle.[32]

Afterword

The head of British Bomber Command, Sir Arthur Harris, was once pulled over by a motorcycle policeman for driving with excessive speed. 'You might have killed someone, sir,' the policeman cautioned. Harris imperiously responded, 'Young man, I kill thousands of people every night.'[33]

Harris's dismissive comment may be taken as a kind of template for the rationale and conduct of the British area bombing offensive against Germany. Reduced to its essentials, the policy of attacking German cities did involve killing thousands of people every night, the vast majority of whom by any measure we would call non-combatants, that is to say, innocents. If one of the basic definitions of 'terrorism' is indiscriminate attacks on innocents, then the area bombing offensive can justly be described as a type of state terrorism.

To be sure, supporters of British air strategy attempted to insulate that strategy from moral criticism by citing its military rationale and its contribution to defeating an unparalleled evil. But the evidence presented here recalls the French aristocrat Boulaye de la Meurthe's famous comment on the execution by Napoleon of the Duc d'Enghien: 'It was worse than a crime, it was a blunder.' If it could be shown that the area offensive was a decisive factor in routing Hitler, and moreover that there were few conceivable alternatives to such a use of British airpower at the time (thus justifying the extraordinary claim on overall British resources that it commanded), then our verdict on it might (possibly) be different. As it is, the area offensive stands as both a crime and a blunder. There were alternative ways in which the RAF could have been employed and military resources allocated away from Bomber Command itself, both of which would have had important effects in successfully prosecuting the war effort.

Such a shift in strategy, moreover, would have had the additional advantage of adhering more closely to the fundamental ethical principle of 'proportionality.' Under its stipulations, the military utility of a given action has to outweigh the evil side-effects of such an action, that is to say, it has to be proportional in balancing the steps taken to achieve victory against the calamities that war can produce. The notion of proportionality continues to provide one of the surest bases on which to judge the moral legitimacy of various measures in wartime, and never more so than when it involves the distinction between combatants and non-combatants.

There were some important developments in the aftermath of the British area bombing offensive in World War II that we should at least touch on, particularly since they provide some hope that in this instance the past would not be prologue to similar measures in wartime. There was first an expanding moral consensus in many countries that what took place over Hamburg and Dresden (as well as Warsaw and Rotterdam) was indeed repugnant to all civilized values. This in turn led to some important developments in international humanitarian law, which further solidified the idea that unrestrained aerial attacks on civilians in wartime clearly lay outside the bounds of the war convention. On the first point, one of the most important – and interesting – pieces of evidence may perhaps be found in the stance taken by the British themselves after the war.

The general picture was one in which both government and society now demonstrated an increasing unease about what had been done in the name of victory. This could be seen especially in the treatment of the great champion of area bombing, Sir Arthur Harris. Given the fact that he was one of the half-dozen principal commanders of British forces in the war, it might have been expected that he would have received honors equal to those bestowed on other famous captains in the great struggle, such as Montgomery, Alanbrooke, and Alexander. In the event, Harris was unique in not receiving such recognition from the British Government. It is true that Churchill recommended that Harris be given a peerage for his service as head of Bomber Command, but the Labour Government of Clement Atlee rejected this proposal. Harris remained in Britain for a time after the war, but when he was offered no continuing employment in the RAF he left for South Africa at the end of 1945 in a not surprising mood of bitterness and feeling of betrayal.

All this suggests that there was at a minimum considerable embarrassment in official circles after the war about the conduct of Bomber Command. The uneasiness that was felt resulted in a calculated effort not to bring attention to its former chief in the form of honors and recognition, since this would have the effect of focusing and perhaps intensifying the emerging public debate on the legitimacy of the area offensive. What we had here in effect was a tacit admission that Britain had seriously violated the war convention, that those in authority knew she had done so, and that many in the broader society were increasingly open to the same conclusion as well.

The specter of indiscriminate aerial attacks on cities that was such a feature of World War II gradually became the subject of such general condemnation that new provisions of humanitarian law now were agreed to which specifically forbade such a strategy. Notable among these was the Additional Protocol I of the Geneva Conventions in 1977. In Article 51 of that Protocol, it is stipulated that 'the civilian population as such, as well as individual civilians, shall not be the object of attack. Acts or threats of violence the primary purpose of which is to spread terror among the civilian population are prohibited.'[34] It would be too much to say that this prohibition has been universally observed since its enactment – witness Russian tactics in Chechnya – but still we have come a long ways from the aerial tactics of World War II, even if more remains to be done in specifying the details of the above norm. The level of discrimination employed in the use of air power in the Kosovo conflict as well as the more recent war in Iraq may be taken as testaments to this fact. To be sure, there are legitimate criticisms that may be offered of specific targeting choices in each of these campaigns. At the same time, the civilians most directly effected, as well as the international community generally, could take some satisfaction in the fact that a repeat of Hamburg was not only not attempted but would have seemed unthinkable today.

Notes

1. The standard treatment of the attack on Hamburg remains Martin Middlebrook's *The Battle of Hamburg* (London: Allan Lane, 1980).
2. Martin Caidin, *The Night Hamburg Died* (New York: Ballantine Books, 1960), p. 9. Caidin reports without comment that the British employed phosphorus bombs in considerable quantities over Hamburg because of their 'demonstrated ability to depress the morale of the Germans.'

3. Basil Liddell Hart, *History of the Second World War* (New York: G.P. Putnam's Sons, 1970), p. 609.
4. Sir Robert Vansittart, *The Black Record* (London: Hamish Hamilton, 1941), pp. viii, 4–5, 18–20.
5. Angus Calder, *The People's War* (New York: Pantheon Books, 1969), p. 490; Max Hastings, *Bomber Command* (New York: Simon and Schuster, 1987), p. 174.
6. Arthur Harris, *Bomber Offensive* (London: Collins, 1947), pp. 74–5, 113.
7. Michael Walzer, *Just and Unjust Wars* (New York: Basic Books, 1977), p. 200.
8. Noble Frankland and Charles Webster, *The Strategic Air Offensive against Germany 1939–1945*, Vol. I (London: Her Majesty's Stationery Office, 1961), pp. 331–6 (hereafter SAOG).
9. David Irving, *The Destruction of Dresden* (New York: Holt, Rinehart and Winston, 1963).
10. SAOG, Vol. III, p. 109.
11. Ibid., p. 112 (emphasis added).
12. John Rawls, *A Theory of Justice* (Cambridge: Harvard University Press, 1971), p. 379.
13. Noble Frankland, *The Bombing Offensive against Germany* (London: Faber and Faber, 1965), pp. 113–14.
14. Max Hastings, *Bomber Command* (New York: Simon and Schuster, 1987), p. 124.
15. Walzer, *Just and Unjust Wars*, p. 44.
16. J.E. Hare and Carey B. Joynt, *Ethics and International Affairs* (New York: St. Martin's Press, 1982), p. 70.
17. SAOG, Vol. I, pp. 323–4.
18. Peter Fleming, *Operation Sea Lion* (New York: Simon and Schuster, 1957), pp. 260–4.
19. Winston S. Churchill, *The Grand Alliance* (Boston: Houghton Mifflin Company, 1951), pp. 606–7.
20. Norman Longmate, *The Bombers* (London: Hutchinson, 1983), p. 354.
21. Frankland, *Bombing Offensive*, p. 96.
22. Ibid., pp. 61–2.
23. Winston S. Churchill, *The Hinge of Fate* (Boston: Houghton Mifflin Company, 1950), p. 770.
24. Longmate, *The Bombers*, p. 356.
25. United States, *Strategic Bombing Survey, Overall Report, European War* (Washington: Government Printing Office, 1945), p. 108.
26. P.M.S. Blackett, *Military and Political Consequences of Atomic Energy* (London: Turnstile Press, 1948), p. 195.
27. Martin Middlebrook and Chris Everitt, *The Bomber Command War Diaries* (London: Viking, 1985), pp. 683, 695.
28. For a more detailed discussion of these factors, see my *Ethics and Airpower in World War II* (New York: St. Martin's Press, 1996), pp. 183–97.
29. Longmate, *The Bombers*, pp. 166, 169–73.
30. John Campbell, *The Experience of World War II* (New York: Oxford University Press, 1989), p. 112.
31. I am grateful to Don Kerr, a career (and now retired) RAF navigator at the International Institute of Strategic Studies in London, for suggesting these particular points during a personal interview.

32. Martin Gilbert, *The Second World War* (New York: Henry Holt and Company, 1989), p. 433 (emphasis added).
33. H.R. Allen, *The Legacy of Lord Trenchard* (London: Cassell, 1972), p. 103.
34. Dietrich Schindler and Jiri Toman (eds.), *The Laws of Armed Conflicts*, third revised edition (Geneva: Henry Dunant Institute, 1988), p. 53.

12
Violence and Terrorism in Northern Ireland[1]

Peter Simpson

Introduction: basic principles

For the purposes of this case study I shall be using the principles of just war theory, in particular that armed force is justified only in defense of the common good and that only just and proportionate means may be used for this purpose. Wars between countries, as well as acts of rebellion or revolution within countries, will thus be just or unjust depending on whether they are in accord with these principles. Terrorism, on the other hand, I regard as always unjust. It is distinctive of terrorism that it consists of acts of indiscriminate violence directed at civilian or non-hostile personnel, in order to terrorize them, or their governments, into carrying out or submitting to the demands of the terrorists. Terrorism in this sense may be performed by private individuals and groups, by rebels and revolutionaries, and also by governments. It thus has a broad connotation in the way I use it here.

As so characterized, terrorism is necessarily unjust. This is not a matter of definition, but it is a necessary inference. Justice is giving each their due; the deliberate infliction of harm is not due to the innocent; therefore terrorism, which deliberately attacks innocents, is unjust. The term 'innocence' has to be taken in a strict and even formal sense. It does not mean that victims of terrorism are innocent of all crimes whatsoever. Some among them may indeed be wrongdoers of one sort or another (thieves, embezzlers, adulterers, perjurers, and so forth). It means, rather, that these victims are innocent in the precise sense in which they are attacked. For they are attacked as civilians or non-hostile personnel going about their day-to-day tasks (walking along the street, waiting for a bus, getting into a car, sitting at a desk), and these tasks are not as such offenses against anyone, least of all against the terrorists. The terrorists anyway have no authority to judge or punish any crimes of which their victims might, incidentally, be guilty.

Note that, in adopting just war theory, I am adopting a non-consequentialist account of wrong action. The injustice of deliberately attacking the innocent is not a matter of the overall badness of the consequences thereby produced. It is a matter of the repugnance to reason of the act as such. Any act has, as the act it is, a specific nature or description, and this nature will or will not cohere with reason. Theft, for instance, is the taking of what belongs to another, or the making to belong to oneself what in fact does not belong to oneself, which is manifestly unreasonable. The same is true of attacking the innocent, which is the infliction of harm on someone who does not deserve harm (or does not deserve it from the one doing the inflicting). All such acts are contradictions, and as contradictions are absurd in thought so are they absurd in deed. Of course, that something is absurd does not prevent one from believing or doing it (or at least from trying to do so), but it does prevent that something from being good to believe or to do. For, in the case of creatures who, like ourselves, have rational natures, to do something opposed to reason is to do something opposed to what we are, and nothing that opposes what we are can possibly be part of our good. On the contrary it can only destroy our good by destroying, as far as it goes, what we are.

Justice and the common good in Northern Ireland

Justice in the case of just war is understood in terms of the common good, and since the common good is the good of all in the community, the first question that arises about just war in Northern Ireland is what the relevant community is.[2] In the broadest sense, of course, we might say that the whole of mankind constitutes a single community, and there certainly are questions of justice that arise in the context of the globe as a whole. One thinks in particular of keeping the environment healthy and fruitful for all and of the fair use and apportionment of natural resources. But while some aspects of the situation in Northern Ireland may have a global dimension, the fundamental problems of justice there arise from and are internal to that particular community.

What then is this community? Is it Northern Ireland by itself? Is it the whole island of Ireland? Is it the United Kingdom? Is it all the British Isles together? No little controversy about justice begins right here. That Northern Ireland is currently a province within the United Kingdom is not by itself determinative. It is determinative, no doubt, for Unionists in Northern Ireland and for most people in the United Kingdom generally, but for Nationalists in Northern Ireland, as well as for multitudes of Irishmen the world over, it is not determinative at all. These latter hold that the relevant community is rather the whole island of Ireland and that justice and injustice must be assessed starting from the fact that Northern Ireland is an artificial abstraction, a forced, not to say illegal, splitting of a part from its whole. Ireland was, after all, a single unit under British rule before it was partitioned into north and south, and partition came about contrary to the wishes of the majority of Irishmen as expressed in a national ballot (the election of 1919 which, in Ireland, was won decisively by the Nationalist party, Sinn Féin). Against this, however, one must note that the acknowledged authority of the day, the British Government in London, whose job it was to give proper expression to the wishes of Irishmen as expressed in the ballot and which was, as a matter of fact, charged with the care of the common good for the United Kingdom, including Ireland, did decide, with Parliamentary approval, to divide Ireland and to give Home Rule to each of its parts in separation. Since Ireland was, at the time, ruled through Parliament and did elect its own Parliamentary representatives, it would seem that the decisions of Parliament, and not the votes of Irishmen (whether in north or south or both), should be held decisive – as in fact Parliamentary decisions are held decisive in the United Kingdom still. Representative democracy is, after all, not a way of translating votes into legislation, but a way of translating votes into legislators, and it is the job of the legislators, not the voters, to decide what is best for the whole and the parts alike.

I am inclined, therefore, to think that the view of Nationalists, that the Ulster Protestants had no legal or moral right to form a separate province contrary to the majority wishes of Irishmen, is incorrect. The Protestants certainly had the legal right, since it was given them by Parliament, and, if Parliament was justly ruler, they can hardly be denied the moral right too. But this only throws the dispute about Northern Ireland back to the further questions of whether the British Parliament was justly ruler and of whether, when Parliament did decide, it decided justly. As to the former of these two questions, note first that British rulers acquired authority over Ireland in different ways at different times, and the rule they exercised varied from benign to indifferent to criminal. In short, British rule in Ireland shows the same features that rule any-where by anyone has shown throughout human history. Thus it was sometimes justly exercised and justly acquired and sometimes it was neither, but when precisely it was each and when something mixed or in between is perhaps beyond human power fully to decide. But so it is, I wager, of all rule everywhere, including the rule exercised by the government of the Republic of Ireland. The sensible course, then, and the course universally followed in international practice and law, would be to accept the presumption of legitimacy. Whoever is in fact in control anywhere is legitimately in control unless or until there is compelling evidence to the contrary. Justice itself, moreover, would seem to counsel this approach. For since justice is the common good, and since the common good requires that someone exercise authority, there can be no just reason to reject or overthrow the existing ruler, whoever it is, unless that ruler is manifestly destroying the common good instead of fostering it. We must therefore presume that the British Parliament was justly ruler at the time of the partitioning of Ireland. The immediate upshot of this is that the answer to what the relevant community is when it comes to judging the common good in Northern Ireland is the community of Northern Ireland itself. The community of Southern Ireland (also created by the act of partition) is thus a separate community with a separate common good under a separate authority. This is not to say that the two communities do not have many common interests, but it is to say that, from the point of justice, they are two communities and not one. Their interrelations fall under the heading of foreign and not domestic affairs.

This brings us, however, to the second of the two earlier questions: did Parliament decide justly when it decided for partition? As regards formal procedures, there can be no doubt that it did. The decision was made by vote in Parliament in the prescribed way. That none of the representatives from the south of Ireland had taken their seats in Parliament at the time is not to the point, for they could have taken their seats if they had wanted to. That they set up their own Parliament in Dublin and refused to attend Parliament in London was their own choice and can be neither put to London's charge nor used to delegitimate London's decision. The more important question, and the one on which the issues concerning justice and force in Northern Ireland depend, is the question of whether the partition London set up was just and was designed to promote the common good of the people there.

This question itself has two parts, since there are two ways in which the common good may be opposed or oppressed: either by an alien and occupying power, or by an indigenous power that is tyrannical. As regards the first part, note that since, as has just been argued, Northern Ireland is both legitimately separate from the rest of Ireland and legitimately part of the United Kingdom, it is impossible to describe the situation there as one of occupation and rule by an alien power, whether this alien power be identified with the Protestant Unionists or with British troops and government officials. The presence in Northern Ireland of British troops and officials is no more alien than is their presence in Scotland or Wales. The Protestant Unionists too, as British citizens, have as much right to be there as to be anywhere else in the United Kingdom. That most Ulster Protestants are descended from settlers brought over from other parts of the United Kingdom during the seventeenth century, and that such settlements involved injustice (the forced dispossession of the indigenous inhabitants) are besides the point. We should, here as elsewhere, proceed according to the presumption of legitimacy and accept what is now unless this is clearly unjust (which it is not – the mere existence of Protestants in Northern Ireland is not contrary to the common good). In addition trying to put the clock back and returning things to what they were several hundred years ago is manifestly absurd and cannot be considered a requirement of justice. There are populations all over the world who are where they are now as a result of earlier invasion or colonization. To suppose it necessary to uproot them all and force them back to where they came from is a recipe for global unrest and confusion. Some compensation or rectification may be needed, to be sure, but beyond that justice would seem to require only that existing populations, whatever their origins, work together for the common good of all. What it was unjust to do in the past is not necessarily just to undo in the present. Fortunately, in the case of Northern Ireland, this is not a matter of dispute. That the Protestant population is legitimately part of the community there is accepted by everyone, including the IRA and Sinn Féin. Consequently, it is no part of anyone's policy to expel the Protestant population from Northern Ireland.

One important implication of all this, since neither the British nor the Protestant population are an occupying power in Northern Ireland, is that violent resistance to them as if they were is not justifiable. Accordingly, violent attempts to secure a United Ireland are not justifiable either. One may, to be sure, use political and peaceful means to attain this goal, but not violent ones. Violence would only be justified if the very existence of partition were somehow unjust. The decision, the legitimate decision, about the unity of Ireland belonged not to the voters but to those for whom the voters voted, and they decided against the unity of Ireland.

There remains then the second part of the question, whether rule in Northern Ireland as set up by partition, though not that of an alien and occupying power, was nevertheless that of a tyrannical power. A power or regime may be tyrannical as regards the legitimacy of its rule (because it possesses power unjustly), or as regards the exercise of this rule (because it uses power unjustly). The regime in Northern Ireland would seem, from the evidence recorded by historians,[3] to be tyrannical in both these ways.

I will take first the question of the legitimacy of rule. The particular partition set up by the British Parliament and the kind of self-rule established in Belfast were, in the first place, achieved in no small part by threats of force by Protestant Unionists. Parliament had initially intended to set up Home Rule for the whole of Ireland as one unit but the vehemence of Unionist opposition prevented that. In the second place, the non-Unionist population in Ulster were not consulted, nor were they given any say, let alone any power of veto, over the ultimate decision reached.[4] In the third place, the goal of the partition for Unionists was openly sectarian. The aim was to keep as many Protestant families and as much Protestant land as possible out of the clutches, as they saw it, of rule by Catholic Dublin. Ulster was to become a Protestant enclave run for and by Protestants. Such facts make it clear that partition, despite the ultimate backing of Parliament, was unjustly carried out. It did not have the common good of all as its motive or its aim. But note that, as argued earlier, there was nothing wrong or illegitimate *in principle* about Parliament partitioning Ireland. Such actions fell properly within its competence as the legitimate authority in Ireland at the time. The unjust or tyrannical nature of partitioning lay not in the fact *that* a partition was made but in *what sort* of partition was made.

Turning next to the actual exercise of rule in Northern Ireland once it had been set up, the same conclusion follows. The Unionists not unexpectedly ran Ulster as a Protestant enclave since that was what they had aimed at in the first place. There was deliberate and systematic exclusion of Catholics from all walks of life. They were denied any share in political life, whether at the center in Stormont or in the several counties and towns. Gerrymandering was liberally indulged in to ensure Protestant domination in local councils even where Catholics were the majority. The police force (the Royal Ulster Constabulary) was heavily if not exclusively Protestant. Discrimination against Catholics in employment was rife, notably in the Belfast shipyards, as well as in housing, education, and health.[5] In short, the Unionist majority secured for themselves a partisan, despotic state where the large Catholic minority was denied the benefits and rights of citizenship.[6] The requirement of justice, that rule be for the common good of all, was not merely ignored; it was directly opposed. Parliament in London was not free of blame for this result. It failed to stand up to Protestant threats when deciding on partition (indeed, in the case of the Conservative Party, these threats were actively seconded); it connived at the sectarian regime that was created in Ulster; it ignored its duty, as the superior authority, and did nothing to rectify the evil until more or less forced into it by the violence in the 1960s and 1970s.

Just and unjust uses of force in Northern Ireland

The argument so far given is sufficient to show that the political situation in Northern Ireland as constituted by Parliament and as carried out by the Unionists was unjust and tyrannical. The question that must now be asked is what uses of force are justifiable or not justifiable as a result. This question relates principally to what uses of force on the part of the oppressed party, the Nationalists, are justifiable. But it also relates, as will appear, to what uses of force on the part of the oppressing party, the Unionists and the British Government in London, are justifiable.

   Let us begin with the easier and intuitively more obvious case of the oppressed party, the Nationalists. It is evident that these are under no obligation of justice to support or uphold the Unionist regime in Northern Ireland. Since this regime systematically denied them their share of the common good, they were justified, in sheer self-defense, to take matters into their own hands and do what they deemed necessary to secure their just rights. Of course, the Unionist regime was not going to let them do this, or not going to let them do it without a fight. To the extent, therefore, that the attempts of Nationalists to escape the oppression of Unionist rule were met by force on the part of the Unionists, whether police or others, to that extent the use of force by Nationalists to oppose this force was just. Conversely, the force used by the Unionists was unjust. There is no right to tyranny and, *a fortiori*, no right to use force to impose it. In fact Unionist force could, to this extent, be regarded as a sort of state terrorism. It amounted to attacks, in many cases indiscriminate attacks, on innocents in order to cow them into submission. And even if some of these attacks could be regarded less as acts of terrorism and more as regular acts of police or even of war, they would still be unjust. For, being contrary to the common good, they manifestly failed the principles of just war theory.

   It is important to note that Nationalist uses of force against Unionist attempts to impose and maintain tyranny are justified not so much because they are responses to injustice as because they are responses to the violence used to enforce the injustice. Were it simply a matter of injustice there might be need to calculate whether force was the only or the right response or whether peaceful means might be more appropriate instead. As it is, however, the right of self-defense, of using force to repel force, comes immediately into play. The only calculation concerns whether the force used in defense is sufficient to repel the attack. Let me give some instances. The Nationalist community may rightly repel by force army or police patrols that tour and sometimes terrorize Nationalist neighborhoods. They may anticipate such patrols by sabotaging police or army equipment, by blowing up surveillance or observation towers, and by attacking the barracks where the patrols originate. They may do the same as regards any private or unofficial individuals or groups that undertake the same assaults. They may bodily remove themselves from the control of the regime by setting up no-go areas as in Derry, by entering into alliance (open or secret) with friendly powers, by destroying the regime's infrastructure and other instruments of rule. They may also repel by force attempts by the regime to win these no-go areas back. They may seek support, financial or otherwise, from sympathizers around the world and smuggle necessary equipment into the country. They may expel from their midst any agents of the regime or any who, whether knowingly or not, are the means of the regime's control over Nationalist areas. And they may do anything else of like nature. In short, whatever uses of force are necessary to escape the injustice of the regime, or to create alternative political arrangements that will better promote the common good, are just.

There are, however, other uses of force which are not justifiable. To begin with, as already noted, force to set up a United Ireland or to expel the British from Ulster is not justifiable. The oppressed Nationalists have the right, under self-defense, to resist the oppressing Unionists, but they do not have the right to impose on the whole of Ulster, let alone the whole of Ireland, another regime of their own devising. A regime that is just for all, whether in Ulster or in Ireland generally, could not justly be set up except by the common consent of all. It could not justly be set up by the forced action of a few. Other instances of unjustifiable force would be violence outside the borders of Northern Ireland. Since the use of force is justified only as a defense against the regime's violent imposition of despotism, where this despotism is not being imposed there is no place for defense against it. So the bombings carried out in mainland UK (or elsewhere outside Ulster for that matter) are unjust. Indeed, since these bombings were indiscriminate and directed against innocents (in the sense explained earlier), such as drinkers in bars or shoppers in department stores, they were clearly terrorism. The same goes for acts of violence committed in the Republic of Ireland, such as armed robberies and kidnappings to help finance violence in the north, or the assassination of prominent UK figures vacationing there. These too are terrorism. They are manifestly not acts of defense against tyranny (as resistance to patrols in Belfast might be), and they are indiscriminate and directed against innocents.

Not all violence within Northern Ireland can be justified either. Targeted assassinations and tit-for-tat killings are not justifiable, nor are the killings of members of the police or security forces when these are off-duty or directing traffic and the like. For no such killings can be construed as acts of self-defense against tyranny. In addition, acts of intimidation against Protestant neighbors, either as revenge or in order to drive them away from Nationalist areas, are not justifiable. Unless such neighbors are in some way instruments of government oppression or are engaged in acts of oppression of their own they are innocent and not deserving of attack. Uses of force against them, not being required by self-defense, would clearly be terrorism again. In addition to these uses of force by Nationalists against those on the opposite side of the political divide, as it were, there are also uses of force against other Nationalists. I particularly have in mind acts of intimidation and punishment, so-called, carried out by the IRA and its offshoots against those deemed not to have been sufficiently Nationalist or not to have toed the IRA line. Paramilitary groups everywhere have a tendency to become as ruthless in their dealings with those whom they profess to represent as with their alleged enemies, and this seems to be as true of paramilitaries in Northern Ireland, whether Nationalist or Unionist. True, if Nationalists set up no-go areas, as they justly might, they will need to set up some security and police apparatus too. But this does not give anyone the right to despotize over these no-go areas or to lay down the law there as he alone sees fit. All members of a given community have a right to shares in rule. Members of paramilitary groups have no greater right here than others, and perhaps they have less right if their natural disposition is towards abuse. Anyway in Northern Ireland there has always been the possibility of Nationalists ruling themselves under the auspices of the SDLP (Social and Democratic Labour Party) or other non-violent parties. For the IRA to impose itself on Nationalist communities regardless of the wishes of these communities is already tyranny, and for it to enforce its rule by violence is at least gangsterism if not also terrorism.

So much, then, may be said about justifiable and non-justifiable uses of force by the Nationalists. Turning next to uses of force by the Unionists and the British, the main point to note here is that no use of force to impose or retain tyrannical control can be just. Force is only just insofar as it serves the common good, and the use of force in the service of tyranny opposes this good. So any uses of force by the oppressing party to enforce its control over Nationalist areas or to hinder their setting up relations with the neighboring Republic of Ireland are necessarily unjust. On the contrary, the Unionists and the British should, in this matter, simply let the Nationalists go. The Northern Ireland regime has done this, however, and on a massive scale. It has done it, moreover, beyond what the limits of justice would allow even to a non-tyrannical regime. For instance, evidence has recently surfaced to confirm long-standing Nationalist charges that the British security services have colluded with Protestant paramilitaries in targeted killings of Catholics.[7] To enforce tyrannical rule is bad enough; to enforce it by systematic murder is worse.

Still, if the uses of force by Unionists and the British so far mentioned are unjustifiable, not every use of force need be. There remains in Northern Ireland, as elsewhere, the need to preserve the ordinary and day to day elements of civil peace, as the direction of traffic, the protection of property, the control of crowds, and the like. In so far as force is applied to achieve these ends and these ends alone (and not to uphold tyranny) it is just. It will be especially just if the application of force is by Unionists and the British against Unionist or British troublemakers. A regime may certainly restrain by force those whom it does not oppress. It may, and indeed should, restrain them by force from committing acts of oppression against others. When British troops were introduced into Northern Ireland in the early 1970s after the suspension of direct Unionist rule, the restraint of acts of oppression by Unionists against Nationalists was their chief task. This restraint first concerned acts of oppression carried on through the laws, and some considerable progress has been made over the years in ridding Northern Ireland of the instruments and effects of Unionist tyranny. But it soon had to concern acts of oppression carried on outside the laws, in particular the acts of Protestant paramilitaries who resorted to violence to retain what they could of former Unionist dominance.

The emergence of Protestant paramilitaries in Northern Ireland is a phenomenon of special interest. Their violence is principally directed against the Nationalist paramilitary groups because these groups repres-ent, as Unionists see it, the vanguard of militant Nationalism that wants to impose a united Ireland on the North by force. To this extent, indeed, one can even regard Protestant paramilitaries as not wholly unjust. A forced United Ireland would no more be just than the current forced Union with the United Kingdom is, and if Nationalists may rightly resist the latter, Unionists may rightly resist the former. This partial excuse or justification for Protestant paramilitaries arises, as I have said, from the injustice of the aims of Nationalist paramilitaries. It is a striking example of how a just cause cannot be served by injustice. The Nationalists have a just cause in resisting Unionist and British tyranny, but they do not have a just cause in fighting for a United Ireland, and the injustice they commit in this latter cause makes the achievement of the former cause much harder. For the Protestants have not only, and up to a point justly, been provoked into paramilitary activity of their own, but they seem to have become more hardened against admitting any justice to the Nationalist cause. Injustice used even in a just cause prepares its own revenge and its own defeat. One might add too that, to the extent Nationalist paramilitary activity is unjust or even terrorism, the British have a right in justice to resist and suppress it. And this leads them, as it leads the Unionists more generally, into falsely supposing that the suppression of Nationalist paramilitaries is just altogether.

Such a list of legitimate and illegitimate acts of violence in Northern Ireland is not meant to be exhaustive. It is meant to be illustrative only, in order to give some concrete idea of how the principles of just war and the idea of terrorism would be applied in practice. One must, besides, keep always in mind the changing situation on the ground, for as this changes so will the judgments that one must form about it. In particular one must consider the change brought about by the Good Friday Agreement. This was signed by parties from all sides in 1998, and is now, despite setbacks, the effective program for peaceful coexistence and shared governance in Northern Ireland.[8] The Nationalist and Protestant paramilitaries have also declared cease-fires. These efforts to achieve a peaceful reconciliation of differences are much to be welcomed. While they are being pursued with good faith on both sides, and in particular while the powers that be are not engaging in any oppressive activity, there can be no case for violence. The principles of just war do not justify violence in circumstances of truce and good faith undertakings of peace and shared pursuit of the common good.

Nevertheless, these principles will justify violence again if the current arrangement breaks down and things return to what they were before. The way things were before was fundamentally unjust, and only the sorts of mutually agreed corrections and revisions of the Good Friday Agreement, or of some agreement like it, could be such as to remove the case for violence in Northern Ireland. This fact is what in particular justifies the reluctance of Nationalist paramilitaries immediately to decommission all their arms and to renounce violence. Nationalists are entitled to arms as a simple matter of self-defense and they may keep them, and may remain ready to use them, as long as those against whom they may need to defend themselves also have arms which they are ready to use in oppressive ways. The same goes, incidentally, for Unionists insofar as they too might have cause to fear attempts by Nationalists to force them into a United Ireland. On the other hand, justice forbids any return to the actual use of force unless and until the common good or one's share in it is directly under attack again.

Conclusion and a suggestion

I have argued that some uses of violence in Northern Ireland, both by the security forces and the paramilitaries, are just. The guiding principle to determine which these are is that neither a United Ireland nor an Ulster in Union with the United Kingdom are legitimately objects to be pursued or preserved by force and, hence, that attempts to do either may legitimately be opposed by force. Of course it would be better if force were avoided altogether and the several sides agreed to solve their differences peacefully. Such a possibility is now available through the Good Friday Agreement. The question is whether this possibility will be fully exploited. Only time will tell, of course, but there is one suggestion I would like to make in the meantime which, while seemingly outrageous, may, on reflection, be the way to tip the balance decisively in favor of peace.

The suggestion is that the British Government should give up its responsibility for Northern Ireland and hand over political control to some international body, say the EU or the UN. I say political control rather than control simply, for there is no reason that civil aspects of government, such as those to do with social services or the maintenance of the currency or the issuing of passports or the other duties and privileges of citizenship, should not be left in the hands of departments run by the British Government. Of course some of these things might be better handled by local or devolved institutions, but those that could not may fairly be left to decision in London. What, however, would not be left to London (though London would not be deprived of consultation) would be matters of security or police or the resolution of political disputes between rival parties. All these would be taken away and handed over to some neutral third party.

The main objection to such a move would naturally be that it is a denial of British sovereignty. The Good Friday Agreement raised the question of sovereignty and affirmed that there would be no derogation from the sovereignty of either the British or Irish Government. My suggestion, however, is not about derogating from sovereignty altogether, but about limiting its application in a certain geographical area. Anyway, I think it is an error of modern political thought and practice to regard national sovereignty as an absolute right. It is, I agree, a right, but only a presumptive right. One presumes that governments and nations have the right of sovereignty, and one only questions or denies this in particular cases and for particular and compelling reasons. The most obviously compelling reason is that the government or nation in question is, with respect to a whole or a part of its ordinary jurisdiction, engaging in acts of despotism and tyranny. Should such acts be serious enough, the government or nation has, by the very requirements of political justice, lost the right to exercise rule. Rule exists for the common good of the whole people and not for the pleasure or indulgence or interest of some.

There is, anyway, a further reason that the British Government should not have ultimate political authority for Northern Ireland. This reason is that it gives unequal support to Unionists and takes from them an important motive for serious implementation of the Agreement.[9] For the Unionists know that if the Agreement fails, or if, as is now temporarily the case, the shared Assembly is suspended, rule will return to London and the Union will be preserved. In other words the Unionists will suffer no penalty for intransigence or insincerity. They may, to be sure, lose devolved power in this way, but they will never lose the Union, and it is the latter loss they most fear. The British Nation, unlike the Irish Republic or some third party, is beholden to the Unionist community in Northern Ireland by many ties of interest and partiality, not least those of religion and history. Both remain fundamentally Protestant and both were, for several centuries, militantly Protestant, imposing on Catholics and others severe civil and political penalties. Both have generally shared the same political and imperial aspirations, and members of the Unionist community took a full part in maintaining the British Empire as well as in sacrificing themselves for that empire during two World Wars. The fierce loyalty still felt by Unionists for the British Crown owes not a little to these facts – facts that remain at the basis of the self-understanding and identity of Unionism. If, however, the Government in London gave up its position as the ultimate political authority in Northern Ireland (albeit for a trial period), the Unionists would lose this, their one sure path of retreat. Only in serious and well-intentioned implementation of the Agreement could they continue to enjoy control over their own affairs. A failure in the Agreement would mean, not a return to Union with London, but submission to a neutral third party that had no more sympathy for their history and traditions than for those of the Nationalists. Such a suggestion is eminently practicable, especially if the EU, of which the United Kingdom and both parts of Ireland are already members, were to be the neutral third party. Whether it will be put into effect I rather doubt. I make it anyway, if only because I think philosophers should be able to give practical advice. Contemplation may be better, but it is not always sufficient.

Notes

1. I first dealt with this question in 'Just War Theory and the IRA,' *Journal of Applied Philosophy* 3 (1986). My ideas have not fundamentally changed in the meantime, though here I express them rather differently.
2. I must thank Paul Gilbert, 'Just War: Theory and Application,' *Journal of Applied Philosophy*, 4 (1987), for drawing my attention to the need expressly to address this question.
3. M. Laffan, *The Partition of Ireland 1911–1925* (Dublin: Dublin Historical Association, 1983), passim. See also R.F. Foster, *Modern Ireland* (Harmondsworth: Penguin, 1988), part 4; and A.C. Hepburn, *The Conflict of Nationality in Northern Ireland* (New York: St. Martin's Press, 1980), passim.
4. Laffan, *The Partition of Ireland*, pp. 78–9, 88, 90, 102.
5. Ibid., pp. 106–10. See also the Cameron report summarized, along with several others of interest, in A. Maltby, *The Government of Northern Ireland 1922–1972: A Catalogue and Breviate of Parliamentary Papers* (New York: Barnes and Noble, 1974), pp. 212ff.
6. Laffan, *The Partition of Ireland*, pp. 109, 124, and also 5–6.
7. As related in the Stevens Report; see *The Stevens Enquiry*, April 2003, Metropolitan Police Service, London.
8. See *The Belfast Agreement*, Command Paper Cm 3883, April 1998, Northern Ireland Office, London.
9. I am grateful to Mark McEnvoy of the Department of Philosophy at Hofstra University for discussion of this matter.

13
Terrorism in the Arab–Israeli Conflict
Tomis Kapitan

Introduction

Terrorism is politically motivated violence directed against non-combatants. It is no doubt as ancient as organized warfare itself, emerging as soon as one society, pitted against another in the quest for land, resources, and dominance, was moved by a desire for vengeance, or found advantages in operations against 'soft' targets. While terrorist violence has been present in the conflict between Jews and Arabs over Palestine for over eighty years, the prevalence of the rhetoric of 'terror' to describe Arab violence against Israeli and Western targets, is a more recent phenomenon. This rhetoric has fostered the popular perception that Arab terrorism is the central problem in the Middle East crisis, and that once solved, progress can be made on other issues.

Nothing could be more illusory. The Western obsession with Arab terrorism not only overlooks the fact that terrorist activity has been reciprocal, but, more generally, that attempts to remove an effect without touching its causes are utterly futile. Terrorism between Arabs and Israelis is the *product* of deep divisions, entrenched strategies, and fundamental grievances, and it will not disappear so long as both sides cling to their present political ambitions and convictions. No informed discussion can ignore its historical and political context. At the same time, terrorism is the most noticeable and tragic aspect of a bitter struggle, and any serious attempt to grasp the goals, methods, and passions of either party must realize that it has been central in giving the conflict the shape it has.

The core of the Israeli–Palestinian conflict

The conflict between Israeli Jews and Palestinian Arabs is fundamentally a struggle over land, over who is to reside in, own, and possess sovereignty over the territory that is variously called *Palestine* and *Israel*. Prior to 1948, the conflict concerned the entire 10,000 square mile area of Palestine as defined in the 1922 League of Nations Mandate, but since 1967, the conflict has been focused on the remaining 22 percent of the area that was not incorporated into the state of Israel as delimited in the 1949 armistice agreements. Anyone familiar with this conflict knows that more than land is at stake: both Israeli Jews and Palestinian Arabs are conscious that their very identity is bound up with that land, its terrain, cities, villages, and monuments. Both have been jealous in their attachments and have denigrated the claims of the other.

The reasons for these mutual attachments reach far back into the history of both peoples, but the conflict dates from the inception of the Zionist movement in late nineteenth-century Europe that called for the establishment of a Jewish state in the historic homeland of the Jewish people, Palestine. From the outset, Zionism faced a moral problem, namely, that its vision of a Jewish state *with a decisive Jewish majority* could be fulfilled only at the expense of another people, the Arab inhabitants of Palestine. In 1897, Palestine contained approximately 600,000 people, 95 percent Arab and 5 percent Jews. Faced with this imbalance, how was the Zionist vision to be achieved? Zionist leaders like Theodor Herzl came to favor a two-step program for demographic change: first, to promote massive Jewish immigration into Palestine, and second, to encourage the emigration of the Arabs into the neighboring countries.[1]

In late 1917, the British, whose forces now controlled Palestine, pledged to facilitate establishment of a Jewish national home and open the doors of Palestine to Jewish immigration. As a result, Jews went from 8 percent of the population in 1918 to 20 percent by 1931, and by 1948, after three decades of British rule, Jews made up one-third of the two million people in Palestine.[2] Inducing the Arabs to emigrate proved more difficult. Official Zionism advocated peaceful coexistence with the Arabs, insisting that there was ample room in Palestine for both peoples, that the Jews had no intention of dispossessing people of their property and that the Arabs stood to benefit by cooperation with the Jews. But the maximalist idea – that there is no room for two peoples sharing sovereignty in Palestine – predominated among Zionist leaders, such as Chaim Weizmann, Israel's first president, and David Ben-Gurion, Israel's first Prime Minister,[3] and with it, the prospect of forcibly transferring the

Arabs came to be seen as the 'obvious and most logical solution to the Zionist's demographic problem'.[4]

In 1918, it became clear to the British authorities in Palestine the Arabs were opposed to Zionism and would resort to violence in order to prevent a Jewish state from being established. One Palestinian, Pasha Dajani, summed up the Arab attitude in 1919: 'If the League of Nations will not listen to the appeal of the Arabs, this country will become a river of blood'.[5] Men like Ben-Gurion understood this as well and began preparing the Jewish community for armed conflict and forcible transfer.[6] 'I am for compulsory transfer,' he declared, 'I don't see anything immoral in it.'[7] His view was echoed by his political rival, Vladimir Jabotinsky, who stated that intentional demographic change was a necessary evil that was neither unprecedented nor a historical injustice.[8]

Forcible removal of a population constitutes violence against civilians, and hence, the mechanism of demographic change that came to be pursued by Zionist leaders was – and continues to be – terrorism. Attempts at transfer would expectedly evoke outrage, resistance, and similar terrorism by Arabs against Jews. Jabotinsky predicted this, but seeing no other alternative, he insisted that the tit-for-tat violence was something that the Jewish community had to endure. Since the *end* of Zionism is moral, he contended, so are the *means* necessary to achieve it, even if this requires an 'iron wall' of military might to prevail against Arab opposition. In a nutshell, this reasoning is the most simple and straightforward Zionist attempt to show that terrorism is not only rational, but also morally justifiable.

Terrorism

While all terrorism is the deliberate, politically motivated use, or threat, of violence against non-combatants, there are different kinds depending on facts about the agents and the modes and mechanisms whereby harm is threatened or carried out. Terrorism is *strategic* if violence or coercive threat is part of a plan to achieve a political goal, but *reactive* if it derives only from an emotional response to politically induced grievances, e.g., vengeance. Of course, since strategy and emotion can be jointly operative, and actions can have multiple agents, a given act might manifest both modes of violence.

A second contrast concerns the causal route whereby harm is inflicted. An act of *direct violence* consists in assault or an immediate threat to do so, for example, killing or maiming someone or giving the orders to do so. However, violence can be committed by other means, say, by imprisoning people, depriving them of essentials, like clean water, food, or necessary medical supplies, or by damaging the institutional fabric of their society, e.g., hospitals, schools, factories and businesses, through legal and other authoritative mechanisms. States in particular accomplish such *structural terrorism* by forcibly implementing or impeding institutions, laws, policies, and practices that result in harm to non-combatants.

A final contrast depends upon the identity of the perpetrators. In Western media, 'terrorism' is regularly used to depict the violence of individuals or groups pursuing specific political agendas, not that inflicted by states or governments.[9] This restriction is questionable as a reportive definition since, etymologically, the root, 'terror', implies nothing about its cause, and, historically, 'terrorism' has been applied to states. Moreover, given that the term is *the* expression of choice for illegitimate violence, exempting states from being agents of terrorism yields an unfair rhetorical advantage to established governments, especially since states usually inflict greater harm upon civilians than do non-state agents. One could always yield this point and employ a different term to describe politically motivated violence against civilians by states, but apart from propaganda concerns, we may speak of the latter as 'state terrorism'.[10]

'A miraculous clearing of the land'

It is idle to speculate on who initiated terrorist violence or in describing one side as engaging in 'terrorism' and the other in 'retaliation.' In the broad perspective, the Zionists have been the aggressors in the territorial conflict,[11] but, from the outset, both sides have been quick to resort to the gun to settle differences. Already in 1921, 62 Arabs and 90 Jews were killed in intercommunal violence,[12] and in 1929, fighting in Jerusalem and surrounding towns resulted in the deaths of 120 Arabs and 133 Jews, including 64 native Palestinian Jews in Hebron.[13] Although a British commission blamed demonstrations by Zionist factions advocating a Jewish state, Britain continued to promote Jewish immigration and land settlement.

By 1935, Jewish immigration reached 60,000 per year, and as land sales to Jews increased, Arab tenant farmers were turned off the lands and forced into cities under deteriorating economic conditions. Their discontent was fertile ground for the revolutionary ideas of men like Sheikh Izzeddin Al-Qassam, who was among the first to call for an Islamic-based resistance to Zionism. His 'martyrdom' in November 1935 sparked a three-year campaign of attacks upon Jewish settlements and British forces. In response, some Jews formed an underground group, the *Irgun Zvai Leumi*, in 1937. Its ideologue, Jabotinsky, urged 'retaliating' against Arabs who had targeted Jews and Jewish property, and denied that there was a choice between pursuing 'bandits' and punishing a hostile population. Instead, the choice is between 'retaliating against the hostile population or not retaliating at all'.[14] The Irgun planted bombs in Arab marketplaces that killed 77 Arabs in three weeks in 1937,[15] and in the summer of 1938 massive marketplace bombs in Haifa, Jerusalem, and Jaffa killed over 100 Arabs; the most devastating bomb killed 53 Arabs in Haifa. Arabs began to imitate these actions by bombing Jewish civilians. Approximately 5,000 Palestinians and at least 463 Jews were killed in the fighting before British forces crushed the Arab revolt in 1939.

Britain abandoned its policy of establishing a Jewish state in 1939, and began restricting further Jewish immigration, bringing itself into direct conflict with the Jewish community after World War II. Jewish underground groups once again employed terrorism, and in the single most spectacular incident, the Irgun, under the leadership of Menachem Begin, bombed the British Headquarters in Jerusalem's King David Hotel killing about 90 people, many of them civilian workers.

In November 1947, after the UN General Assembly recommended partitioning Palestine into two states, terrorism between Arabs and Jews occurred with greater frequency and on a larger scale than ever before. On April 9, 1948, the Irgun and Lehi militias attacked the Palestinian village of Deir Yassin on the road between Tel Aviv and Jerusalem killing about 120 Arab villagers, and parading the survivors in Jerusalem while urging the Arab residents to flee. Arabs exacted revenge a few days later by killing some 70 Jewish medical and university personnel in a convoy on its way to Mount Scopus. But Deir Yassin and other similar massacres precipitated a flight of over 300,000 Arab villagers and townspeople from their homes into what they felt would be safer areas.[16] By the time the state of Israel was declared on May 14, the better armed and better organized Jewish forces had crushed the Palestinian resistance, and after soldiers from five Arab countries entered the fray, more Palestinians were forcibly expelled from their homes by the Israeli Defense Force (IDF). When an armistice was signed in 1949, Israel controlled over 77 percent of Palestine and approximately 750,000 Arabs had fled or been expelled from what was now Israel.[17]

Here was strategic terrorism at its most effective; through violence, Zionists had taken a decisive step forward in solving the demographic problem and ensuring a decisive Jewish majority in the newly formed Israel. After the war ended, Begin wrote, 'Of the about 800,000 Arabs who lived on the present territory of the State of Israel, only some 165,000 are still there. The political and economic significance of this development can hardly be overestimated'.[18] For Chaim Weizmann, the exodus of the Arabs was 'a miraculous clearing of the land: the miraculous simplification of Israel's task'.[19]

'The gun and the olive branch'

With three-quarters of their homeland taken, and well over half their numbers in refugee camps, the Palestinians were initially too stunned and scattered to mount any attempt at reconquest or reprisal. Apart from sporadic cross-border raids, an organized Palestinian resistance did not emerge until the 1960s. Armed violence by *fedayeen* (those who sacrifice themselves) accelerated after the 1967 war as Palestinians realized that they could not wait for Arab governments to solve their political problems. While Yassir Arafat's *Fatah* initially claimed that it would not target Israeli civilians, especially not women and children, this guideline was often ignored. One *Fatah* fighter, captured in 1968, told an Israeli court that he had been ordered to sabotage everything he could. Asked whether that meant the killing of children too, he replied, 'Yes, to destroy everything, because we haven't forgotten Deir Yassin.'

As attacks against the Israeli military proved ineffective and PLO fighters were expelled from the West Bank in 1968, some Palestinians resorted to more sensational terrorist tactics, including rocket attacks on Kiryat Shemona, plane hijackings, and most spectacularly of all, taking Israeli athletes hostage during the 1972 Munich Olympics during which nine Israelis and five Palestinian *fedayeen* died. In 1974, there were two highly publicized attempts to take Israeli hostages and exchange them for Palestinians held in Israeli prisons, resulting in the deaths of eighteen Israelis in Kiryat Shemona, twenty young Israelis in Ma'alot, and the six Palestinian *fedayeen*.

Palestinian violence had its own Machiavellian logic. Despite being exiled through a massive injustice, Palestinians, like all other peoples, retain rights of self-defense and self-determination in their traditional homeland. In an imperfect world, these rights cannot be won peacefully, and facing a vastly superior Israeli military, they must demonstrate that they can do enough damage by other means so that their grievances will be addressed and their rights secured. Terrorism would achieve three important intermediary steps in working towards this goal. First, by demonstrating an ability to strike against their enemies, a sense of unity and confidence would be heightened within their own community, thereby strengthening its will to resist. Second, through violence against civilians, the Israeli sense of security would be undermined and Israeli leaders would be forced to consider the high price of continued occupation.[20] Third, through spectacular violence, the Palestinians could draw attention to their cause, neglected for over two decades by the world community. Here, they succeeded dramatically; probably some 500 million people witnessed the events in Munich on television as 'the Palestinian people imposed their presence on an international gathering that had sought to exclude them'.[21]

Though repelled by their tactics, people began to ask why the Palestinians had suddenly appeared on the world stage in so violent a manner. What are their grievances? What are their aims? Having grabbed the spotlight, in 1974 the PLO indicated willingness to work towards a negotiated resolution of the conflict. They were granted official recognition in many of the world's capitals, and the PLO leader, Arafat, addressed the UN General Assembly, declaring that he carried a 'freedom fighter's gun' in one hand, and warning not to let the 'olive branch' in his other fall to the ground. Despite the setbacks of the 1980s, the PLO emerged as a partner in the negotiations that led to the signing of the Oslo Accords in 1993. As Begin had done fourteen years earlier, Arafat underwent the miraculous metamorphosis from strategic terrorist to Nobel Peace Prize laureate.

Structural violence in the occupied territories

In the 1967 war, the remainder of Palestine came under Israel's control and has remained so ever since. Israel argues that its presence in the West Bank and Gaza Strip is necessary to ensure its security in the absence of an overall peace settlement in the Middle East. 'Security' has largely been a ruse, however, for successive Israeli governments have embarked upon a massive transformation of these territories by progressively confiscating both public and private lands for the expansion of Jewish settlement.[22] Currently, satellite images show 282 Jewish built-up areas in the West Bank, including East Jerusalem and 26 in Gaza, excluding military sites. The settlements surround every major Palestinian population center, are connected to each other and to Israel via a road network spanning almost 400 kilometers, and are situated to ensure Israeli authorities maximal surveillance and control over movement in the territories. Some of the settlement blocs sit astride major West Bank aquifers from which Israel currently draws one-third of its water supply. They are home to over 400,000 Jewish settlers, of which nearly 200,000 are in the neighborhoods surrounding East Jerusalem, while another 7,000 settlers live in the Gaza Strip. While most settlers are ordinary Israelis taking advantage of subsidized housing, a good many are armed zealots who openly advocate expulsion of the Palestinians and justify it in religious terms.[23]

The settlements are weapons in a campaign of structural terrorism against the Palestinians, ultimately aimed at incorporating the territories, or large segments thereof, into the Jewish state. To maintain and protect them, Palestinians have been subjected to a vast institutional framework that features economic control, land expropriation, destruction of property, and regulation of Palestinian movement. Their protests against this creeping usurpation of their land and restrictions on their lives have been routinely met with more direct forms of violence which have included house demolitions, destruction of trees, curfews, deportations, detention without trial, torture, and killings. For example, during the first Palestinian *intifada* (1987–93), at least 1,283 Palestinian civilians were killed by the IDF, over 130,000 were injured, over 2,500 houses were demolished, and thousands of trees were uprooted. Of the Palestinians fatally shot, 271 were 16 years of age or younger, and this age group constituted almost 40 percent of the total number of Palestinians injured.[24] The *intifada* and the iron-fisted response with which it was met would be unintelligible apart from the underlying structural terrorism.

The reign of 'terror'

Because terrorists are perceived as breaking the *jus in bello* principle of discrimination, the term 'terrorism' and its cognates have acquired an intensely negative connotation in contemporary discourse. This has provided governments with a powerful rhetorical tool for discrediting those who forcefully oppose their policies. The 'terrorist' label automatically places actions and agents outside the norms of acceptable behavior, and consequently erases any incentive an audience might have to question the nature of their grievances and the possible legitimacy of their demands.[25] The rhetoric effectively stifles political debate, repudiates calls for negotiation, and, consequently, paves the way for state-sanctioned violence.[26]

The Palestinians' resistance fell victim to this rhetoric, for while their violence succeeded in placing their cause on the world agenda, too often their complaints were overshadowed by the sensationalism of their deeds. In the minds of many, disgust with the means outpaced sympathy with the plight of Palestinian refugees and trumped the patience needed to understand the root causes of the conflict. As the 1970s wore on, and various leftwing groups in Europe and elsewhere made headlines with similar sorts of violence, the 'terrorists' came to be viewed as a new type of barbarian whose willingness to hijack planes, take hostages, and carry their struggle into foreign lands placed them beyond the bounds of civilized behavior.

Israeli officials quickly employed the rhetoric of 'terror' to deflect attention away from their own controversial policies in the occupied territories and towards the more spectacular reactions by Palestinians. They realized that it would be to their advantage to portray 'Arab terrorists' as the enemies not only of Israel, but of the entire Western world, and to depict the causes of their actions as something other than victimization by Israel. A prime example of this is a book entitled *Terrorism: How the West Can Win* by former Israeli Prime Minister, Benjamin Netanyahu, who wrote that the 'root cause of terrorism lies not in grievances but in a disposition toward unbridled violence' traceable to 'certain ideological and religious goals' that 'demand the shedding of all moral inhibitions'.[27] In calling for a vigorous political, economic, and military response to any act of terrorism against 'the West', Netanyahu insisted that 'there is certainly no moral imperative to confine the retaliation to the actual perpetrators,' and that the only way to combat terrorism is 'to weaken and destroy the terrorist's ability to consistently launch attacks,' even at the 'risk of civilian casualties'.[28]

By classifying Palestinian resistance to Israeli policies as 'terrorism' and by portraying 'terrorists' as monsters unworthy of moral dialogue, it became easier for Israel to implement the 'reprisal' policy enunciated by Ben-Gurion in 1948 by which 'there is no need to distinguish between guilty and innocent'.[29] Three days after the Munich killings, for example, Israeli air raids took the lives of between 200 and 500 Arab villagers.[30] After Ma'alot, Israeli air raids killed 200 people in Lebanese villages and Palestinian refugee camps, and after a bus hijacking in central Israel on March 1978 resulted in the deaths of 38 Israelis, the IDF occupied southern Lebanon killing over 2,000 people in the process and causing several thousand Lebanese to flee northward.[31]

In 1982, in an effort to crush the PLO, Israel invaded Lebanon again, taking the lives of nearly 20,000 Lebanese and Palestinians, 90 percent of them civilians. The most devastating use of the 'terrorist' rhetoric to justify terrorism occurred in early September after PLO fighters had been evacuated from West Beirut. Israeli officials contended that some '2,000 terrorists' remained in the Sabra and Shatilla refugee camps in southern Beirut, a claim repeated in the Israeli press. On September 15, three days after the assassination of the Lebanese Phalangist leader, the Israeli Defense Minister, Ariel Sharon, authorized entry of members of the Lebanese militia into the camps which were surrounded by Israeli tanks. For the next 38 hours, aided by Israeli flares at night, the militia raped, tortured, mutilated, and massacred Palestinian civilians, killing between 2,400 and 3,000.[32] Though Sharon was subsequently removed as Defense Minister because of 'indirect responsibility' for the massacre, four years later he was able to set a new standard for *chutzpah* in an op-ed piece entitled 'It's Past Time to Crush the Terrorist Monster,' in which he called upon Western countries and Israel to stage a coordinated 'war on terrorism' through pre-emptive strikes on 'terrorist bases' and sanctions against the state supporters of terrorism.[33]

Twenty years later, the rhetoric of 'terror' was once again a prelude to violence against Palestinians, as Sharon unleashed the IDF to destroy the 'terrorist infrastructure' in the occupied territories. What transpired was a wholesale assault not only upon militants, but also the political, cultural, informational, and medical institutions that form the core of Palestinian civil society. The events of September 11, 2001 made it easier to cloak Israeli state violence as part of the ongoing 'war on terrorism.' Although human rights groups around the world, including in Israel, accused the Israeli Government of military excesses and war crimes, the rhetoric dominating the mainstream media led the Israeli public and the American Congress to approve of Sharon's offensive against 'terrorism.'

The rhetoric of 'terror' is itself a mechanism of state terrorism, enabling Israel to consolidate its hold on the territories by emphasizing the need for Israel's 'security' in the face of Arab terrorism, while submerging any consideration of the Palestinians' own security concerns. Because terrorists are portrayed as irrational beings devoid of a moral sense and beyond all norms, Israel has found it easier to justify military responses that deface the distinction between the agents of terrorist actions and the populations from which they emerge. The logic of the strategy is simple: to get away with a crime, demonize your victims.

Terrorism begets terrorism

In February 1994, a settler from Kiryat Arba, Baruch Goldstein, massacred 29 Palestinian worshippers at the Ibrahimiyya mosque in Hebron. His suicidal terrorism was both reactive and strategic, for, while motivated to avenge the deaths of Jews at the hands of Arabs, Goldstein also wanted to undermine the Oslo peace process which he feared would lead to a withdrawal from the occupied territories. His action precipitated a like response by Palestinian militias such as Hamas. Founded in

1988, Hamas initially confined its resistance to what it regarded as legitimate military targets in the occupied territories, but after the Goldstein massacre and the failure of the Israeli Government to respond to its May 1994 offer of an 'armistice' in which civilians would be immune from violence,[34] Hamas launched a wave of suicide bombings that took the lives of scores of Israeli civilians.

Like Jewish zealots, Hamas offers a religious justification for violence, but it also justifies its actions through the familiar self-defense argument. The Zionists are intent upon dispossessing the Palestinians of the remaining 22 percent of their homeland, and its occupation is 'downright terrorism.'[35] By all laws, human and divine, people have a right to defend themselves against those who employ violence to dispossess them of their homeland. Since appeals to justice and the world's conscience are futile in stopping determined aggressors, and since attacks against the Israeli military are insufficient to stop Israel's expansionism or force the rest of the world to intervene, then making Israel suffer by striking at civilian targets is the principal mechanism Palestinians have left for self-defense. The effect of striking at 'the most vulnerable spot in the Zionist body' will be to exhaust Israel and weaken both its tourism and immigration programs. Like Goldstein's, the terrorism of Hamas has been reactive as well as strategic, for Hamas routinely maintains that specific operations are carried out to avenge massacres and assassinations.[36]

Hamas has been at the forefront of armed resistance in the second *intifada* which started after the collapse of the Oslo peace process. Sharon's visit to the Jerusalem mosques on September 28, 2000 began a round of terrorism by both sides that eclipsed any previous level of violence seen during the previous 33 years of occupation. Young Palestinians, finding little hope for improvement in their situation, began volunteering for suicide missions, and in time, women joined the ranks the martyrs. 'She is the first, but not the last,' said a teacher who knew the first of these women. 'You shouldn't think we don't love life and don't want to live. We do this only because it is the last thing we can do.' A student of psychology at the Islamic University in Gaza put it this way: 'The arbitrary killing that we've experienced during the *intifada* has caused every young person to say, "If in any case I am destined to die, why shouldn't I die with dignity?" '[37]

Facing a greater proportion of armed Palestinians in this second *intifada*, the IDF has responded with more firepower than ever before, employing Merkava tanks, F-16 fighter jets, and Apache attack helicopters. Implementing Sharon's directive to eliminate the 'terrorist infrastructure' has involved it more deeply in a war against a civilian population.[38] In the process, the casualty rates have increased on both sides, this time with more deadly ratios from the Israeli point of view. In the first *intifada*, there were eleven dead Palestinians for every dead Israeli, but during the second, this figure has approached a three to one ratio.[39] The Israeli Government justifies its violent response by invoking its right to defend its citizens from the threat of Palestinian terrorism, and the only effective means for this is a massive military crackdown in the form of checkpoints, curfews, house to house searches, detentions, interrogations, house demolitions, and targeted killings. Yet, just as Hamas had its Palestinian critics, some Israelis have dissented from this policy, including members of the Israeli military,[40] and four former heads of Shin Bet (Israel's domestic security service), who claimed that the Sharon's government will 'gravely damage' Israel unless it stops its 'immoral treatment' of the Palestinians.[41] At the end of the IDF offensive in late April 2002, the Israeli Defense Minister Ben-Eliezer admitted that 'it is impossible to eradicate the terrorist infrastructure,' and that 'military actions kindle the frustration, hatred and despair that are the incubators for the terror to come'.[42] More than a year later, this view was echoed by the Israeli Chief of Staff, Lt. Gen. Moshe Ya'alon, who claimed that Israel's military tactics against the Palestinian population were fomenting explosive levels of 'hatred and terrorism' that might become impossible to control.[43]

Concluding observations

Moral conjectures are nearly unavoidable in any philosophical scrutiny of terrorism. The suggestions I offer are preliminary, since a thorough moral assessment requires a more extensive study than allowed here. Still, I think that the facts point to the following conclusions.

First, the burden of ending this tragic violence lies primarily with the stronger party, Israel, especially since the Palestinian leadership and the Arab states have repeatedly expressed their willingness to accept a compromise that would recognize Israel in exchange for a Palestinian state in the occupied territories. Because of this, the maximalists in charge of Israeli policy and their supporters in the United States and elsewhere are chiefly to blame for the ongoing cycle of violence. The Jewish desire for security is a powerful one, and fully understandable in light of the prejudice, discrimination, and persecution that Jews have experienced, but it is doubtful that long-term security is best achieved through continued brutality.

Second, the rhetoric of 'terror' obscures the causes of violence and stifles the sort of critical examination and humanitarian concern that might create political pressure for a negotiated solution. Since news reports influence decision-makers and those who place them in power, the obligation of the media is to produce accurate and unprejudiced representations of what has happened. Because a term like 'terrorism' suggests an unlawful and immoral act in a way that 'retaliation', 'resistance,' or 'self-defense' do not, then to use the former in labeling the actions of one party and the latter in describing the same actions of another, is an obstacle to understanding. To reach sound judgments about this conflict, we are better off using terms like 'terrorism' clearly and consistently, or avoiding them altogether.

Third, four powerful emotions, humiliation, outrage, vengeance, and hopelessness – derived from a sense of justice and honor, and from the experience of more than 36 years under occupation – ensure that Palestinians' violence will continue if their situation is not rectified. And, when members of a society repeatedly resort to acts of suicidal vengeance, we must not fall for the incredible suggestions that it is because of their cultural or religious beliefs, or, even more ludicrously, because of an 'unbridled disposition' towards violence. That Palestinians have availed themselves of such a desperate expedient over the years indicates that something is seriously wrong with the political conditions under which they live. Rather than heap blame upon suicide bombers, it is more accurate to say their actions are a tragic testimony to the political failure of international diplomacy and the moral failure of the world community.

Fourth, it is tempting to make a sweeping denunciation of all terrorism on the grounds that it violates the rules of *jus in bello*, fails to treat people as moral persons,[44] and undermines trust and the possibility of future coexistence. Yet, it is not obvious that these considerations trump all others if terrorism is the *only* means available to secure an overridingly justifiable end. As indicated above, there are those on both sides who have found terrorism *rational* in the self-defense of an entire people, and, given their conviction in the morality of this goal, they have also argued their violence to be *justifiable*. The real question is whether their respective ends of national self-preservation confer *overriding* moral significance upon their chosen means.

This question cannot be answered here, but I close by recalling Kant's injunction that violence can be justified only if it is expected to contribute to future peace. In the long run, terrorism may be a strategy that backfires since the hatred and vengeance it generates raise the frightening possibility that genocidal annihilation of one or both parties might be the only way to end violence. Intense struggles have never ceased to produce astonishing outcomes. While Palestinians have gained recognition and a place at the negotiating table, it is too early to tell whether their recourse to violence will secure their self-determination in Palestine, or even their survival as a distinct people. Similarly, while Israeli Jews presently enjoy a strong, vigorous state, it cannot yet be determined whether Zionism's expansionism by force can be long tolerated or sustained.

Notes

1. In his diary Theodor Herzl wrote: 'We shall try to spirit the penniless population across the border by procuring employment for it in the transit countries, while denying it any employment in our own country.... Both the process of expropriation and the removal of the poor must be carried out discreetly and circumspectly'. In Raphael Patai (ed.), *The Complete Diaries of Theodor Herzl* (New York: Herzl Press and Thomas Yoseloff, 1960), vol. I, p. 88.
2. Currently, the population is approaching nine million, with approximately five million Israeli Jews, four million Palestinian Arabs (about one million of whom are Israeli citizens, 1.9 million in the West Bank and East Jerusalem, and 1.2 million in the Gaza Strip).
3. Benny Morris, *Righteous Victims: A History of the Zionist-Arab Conflict 1881–1999* (London: John Murray, 1999), pp. 140–1.
4. Benny Morris, 'Revisiting the Palestinian Exodus of 1948,' in Eugene Rogan and Avi Shlaim (eds.), *The War for Palestine: Rewriting the History of 1948* (Cambridge: Cambridge University Press, 2001), p. 40. See also Morris, *Righteous Victims*, p. 91 on Ben-Gurion's realization of an unbridgeable gulf between Arabs and Jews on Palestine, and also on the views of Moshe Shertok (Sharret), Israel's second prime minister. For more on the normative debate concerning rights to Palestine, see Tomis Kapitan (ed.), *Philosophical Perspectives on the Israeli-Palestinian Conflict* (Armonk, NY: M.E. Sharpe Inc., 1997), pp. 9–11, 19–24.
5. Morris, *Righteous Victims*, p. 91.
6. Morris, Revisiting, the Palestinian Exodus,' pp. 42–3.
7. Simha Flapan, *The Birth of Israel* (New York: Pantheon, 1987), p. 103; and see Morris, *Righteous Victims*, p. 659. Tom Segev writes that despite attempts by Ben-Gurion's biographers to distance Ben-Gurion from the idea of forcible transfer, his 'stand on deportation, like that of other Zionist leaders is unambiguous and well-documented' (*One Palestine, Complete*. New York: Metropolitan Books, 1999, p. 407).
8. Yosef Gorny, *Zionism and the Arabs* (Oxford: Clarendon Press. 1987), p. 270.
9. In the United States Code, for example, it is stipulated that terrorism is committed only by 'sub-national groups' or 'clandestine state agents,' never by the official military organizations of states (title 22 of the *United States Code*, Section 2656f(d)).
10. For example, Robert Ashmore, 'State Terrorism and Its Sponsors, in Tomis Kapitan (ed.), *Philosophical Perspectives on the Israeli-Palestinian Conflict*

pp. 105–32; Igor Primoratz, 'State Terrorism and Counter-terrorism,' Chapter 9 in this volume.

11. In 1938, addressing the Mapai Political Committee, Ben-Gurion said, 'When we say that the Arabs are the aggressors and we defend ourselves – that is only half the truth. As regards our security and life we defend ourselves . . . politically, we are the aggressors and they defend themselves' (Flapan, *The Birth of Israel*, p. 141).

12. David Hirst, *The Gun and the Olive Branch: The Roots of Violence in the Middle East*, second edition (London: Faber and Faber, 1984), pp. 48–55.

13. Charles Smith, *Palestine and the Arab-Israeli Conflict*, fourth edition (New York: Bedford/St. Martin's Press, 2001), p. 130; Morris, *Righteous Victims*, p. 114.

14. Joseph Schechtman, *Fighter and Prophet: The Vladimir Jabotinsky Story* (New York: Thomas Yoseloff, 1961), p. 485.

15. Smith, *Palestine and the Arab–Israeli Conflict*, p. 143.

16. Benny Morris, *The Birth of the Palestinian Refugee Problem, 1947–1949* (Cambridge: Cambridge University Press, 1987); and idem, 'Revisiting the Palestinian Exodus.'

17. As a consequence of a Cabinet decision in June 1948, Israel rejected UN-GA Resolution 194 calling for the repatriation of these refugees (Morris, 'Revisiting the Palestinian Exodus,' p. 38). The UN negotiator, Count Folke Bernadotte, was murdered by members of the Lehi militia in September 1948.

18. Menachem Begin, *The Revolt* (New York: Nash Publishing Corporation, 1951), p. 164.

19. Hirst, *The Gun and the Olive Branch*, p. 143.

20. Khalid Hroub, *Hamas: Political Thought and Practice* (Beirut: Institute for Palestine Studies, 2000), p. 248.

21. Abou Iyad with Eric Rouleau, *My Home, My Land: A Narrative of the Palestinian Struggle* (New York: Times Book, 1981), pp. 111–12.

22. The Zionist movement had long held that the outmost chains of Jewish settlement would mark the frontiers of the Jewish state (Morris, *Righteous Victims*, p. 653).

23. See Robert Friedman, *Zealots for Zion* (New York: Random House, 1992).

24. See James Graff, 'Targeting Children: Right versus *Realpolitik*,' in Tomis Kapitan (ed.), *Philosophical Perspectives on the Israeli-Palestinian Conflict*, p. 157, and reports issued by Physicians for Human Rights USA, Amnesty International, Human Rights Watch, and the Israeli human rights group B'tselem.

25. See Tomis Kapitan, 'The Terrorism of "Terrorism",' in James P. Steba (ed.), *Terrorism and International Justice* (New York: Oxford University Press, 2003), pp. 47–66. The strategy of discouraging inquiry into causes is typified in Alan Dershowitz, *Why Terrorism Works* (New Haven: Yale University Press, 2003), p. 24, who writes: 'We must commit ourselves never to try to understand or eliminate its alleged root causes, but rather to place it beyond the pale of dialogue and negotiation.'

26. The general strategy is nothing new; it is part and parcel of the war of ideas and language that accompanies overt hostilities. The term 'terrorism' is simply the current vogue for discrediting one's opponents *before* the risky business of inquiry into their complaints can even begin.

27. Benjamin Netanyahu, *Terrorism: How the West Can Win* (New York: Farrar, Straus & Giroux, 1986), p. 204.

28. Ibid., pp. 202–5. See the assessments of Netanyahu's book in Edward Said, 'The Essential Terrorist,' in Edward Said and Christopher Hitchens, *Blaming the Victims: Spurious Scholarship and the Palestine Question* (London: Verso, 1988), pp. 149–58. See also Avishai Margalit, 'The Terror Master,' *New York Review of Books*, October 5, 1995, pp. 17–18; and Kapitan, 'The Terrorism of "Terrorism"'.

29. Robert Ashmore, 'State Terrorism and its Sponsors,' p. 107. This policy was followed in a 1953 raid on the West Bank village of Qibya, by a military unit commanded by Ariel Sharon, in which 66 men, women, and children were killed. Discussions of the policy occur in Hanan Alon, *Countering Palestinian Terrorism in Israel: Toward a Policy Analysis* (Santa Monica: Rand Corporation, 1980)which mentions that Israeli policy includes the proviso that civilian populations that 'shelter anti-Israeli terrorists' will not be immune from punitive action. Noemi Gal-Or 1994 also discusses this aspect of Israeli policy, in 'Countering Terrorism in Israel,' in David A. Charters, ed., *The Deadly Sin of Terrorism* (Westport Conn.: Greenwood Press 1994), pp. 137–72; as does Barry Blechman's earlier study, 'The Consequences of Israeli Reprisals: An Assessment,' PhD dissertation, Georgetown University (1971).

30. Hirst, *The Gun and the Olive Branch*, pp. 251, 314.

31. Alfred Lilienthal, *The Zionist Connection* (New Brunswick: North American Inc., 1982), p. 388.

32. Hirst, *The Gun and the Olive Branch*, pp. 422–8; Swee Chai Ang, *From Beirut to Jerusalem* (London: Grafton Books, 1989).

33. Sharon's article appeared in the *New York Times* on September 20, 1986. The rhetoric of 'terror' extends beyond the mainstream media and corporate 'think tanks.' Academics also employ it, e.g., Harvard Law professor Alan Dershowitz, who calls for the organized destruction of a single Palestinian village in retaliation for every terrorist attack against Israel. 'It will be a morally acceptable trade-off even if the property of some innocent civilians must be sacrificed in the process' ('A New Way of Responding to Palestinian Terrorism,' *The Jerusalem Post*, March 18, 2002).

34. Hroub, *Hamas*, p. 246.

35. Yonah Alexander, *Palestinian Religious Terrorism: Hamas and Islamic Jihad* (Ardsley, NY: Transnational Publishers, 2002), p. 346.

36. Hroub, *Hamas*, pp. 245–51.

37. *Ha'aretz*, July 17, 2002.

38. *Ha'aretz*, March 9, 2003.

39. In the first three years of the Al-Aqsa *intifada* which began on September 29, 2000, at least 870 Israelis lost their lives, and approximately 71 percent of these were civilians. Over 2,600 Palestinians were slain, three-quarters of whom were non-combatants. Well over 5,000 Israelis and 22,000 Palestinians have been injured in the ongoing violence. These figures have been compiled from various sources, including the Israeli Ministry of Foreign Affairs at www. israel-mfa.gov.il, the Israeli human rights group, B'tselem, at www.btselem. org, the Palestine Monitor at www.palestinemonitor.org, and Miftah at www. miftah.org.

40. *Ha'aretz* supplement, September 14, 2001.

41. *Yedioth Aharonoth*, November 14, 2003.

42. Stephen Zunes, *Tinderbox* (Monroe, ME: Common Courage Press, 2003), p. 149.
43. *Washington Post*, October 31, 2003.
44. Haig Khatatchadourian, *The Morality of Terrorism* (New York: Peter Lang, 1998).

14

The Catastrophe of September 11 and its Aftermath*

Burton M. Leiser

For most of us, memories of the catastrophe of September 11, 2001 consist of images of airliners crashing into giant skyscrapers, of flames and smoke shooting from them, and of thousands of terrified people fleeing from the area as those great structures crumpled into themselves amid roiling clouds of smoke and ash. But the events of that day cannot be reduced to those images; for they resulted in thousands of individual tragedies whose consequences continue to reverberate in the lives of those most immediately affected and in the lives of thousands more throughout the world.

The enormity of that awful day encompasses the cumulative effects of thousands of discrete events knitted together in time and space by the horrendous explosions that tore through the twin towers of the World Trade Center in New York, the Pentagon in Washington, and a field in Pennsylvania. Box cutters and airliners were converted into weapons of mass destruction by a band of terrorists bent on the annihilation of human beings on a scale rarely seen in human history. Millions viewed the events behind the protective glass shields of their television sets, watching them unfold as if they had been produced by special effects artists in a particularly awful horror film. An air of unreality clung to those images. Like viewers of horror movies, most of us soon went back to our daily lives and allowed the emotional impact of those awesome hours to fade into distant memories.

For some, however, the memories will never fade. Wives, mothers, and friends throughout the New York metropolitan region, as well as around the country, received phone calls from loved ones stranded in the Twin Towers. Lisa Jefferson, on duty at the in-flight service of the GTE telephone company, took a call from Todd Beamer, a passenger on United Flight 93, who described the situation to her. Passengers on that flight witnessed the slaughter of at least two people – probably the pilot and co-pilot – with knives and box cutters. Their bodies lay in the aisle in front of the cockpit door. Beamer told her, 'I know I'm not going to get out of this,' and asked her to call his wife if the worst happened, and to pray with him. He told Ms. Jefferson *sotto voce* that he and others were going to try to overpower the hijackers; then he said, 'Let's roll!' Lisa and others who had received calls from passengers on the plane listened as passengers screamed and glass and china were smashed. Then all the phones went dead.

Anna Egan, who had watched the first plane crash into the North Tower, reacted with joy when her husband, Michael, called. He had been shepherding workers from the 104th floor to the 78th floor of the South Tower, where they waited to catch express elevators down to the lobby. Michael assured Anna in a calm voice that there was nothing to worry about, that he was safe, and that he was going back up to rescue more people. She pleaded with him to get out of the building. During his last call, from the 105th floor, he told her that things did not look good, the heat was unbearable, windows had blown out, he couldn't breathe. And then, as she watched her TV in horror, she saw the second plane heading towards the South Tower. Evidently he too saw the plane approaching, for he said, 'Oh, God! I love you, darling. Kiss the boys – ' And the phone went dead.[1]

The tragedy of September 11 was not just the 3,000 fatalities. It was the loved ones left behind – co-workers, spouses, parents, children, and children yet unborn who would never meet their fathers. The terrorists who murdered those innocent victims on September 11 left in their wake tens of thousands, possibly hundreds of thousands of grieving loved ones whose lives were changed forever. People who lived and worked in lower Manhattan were traumatized by the horrendous vision of planes flying into the Twin Towers, the flames and smoke, the men and women falling or jumping from immense heights, plummeting to their deaths on the pavement below.[2] Small children attending school not far from the World Trade Center witnessed horrors that no child should ever have to see.

The death, destruction, and the psychological trauma inflicted on those who witnessed those dreadful events, and those who suffered personal losses in the flames that day, were by far the worst immediate effects of that act of terrorism; but they were by no means the only ones.

The financial damage

The financial damage inflicted upon the United States is difficult to estimate, but some reasonable approximations have been made:[3]

Lost future income of those killed in New York City	$7.8 billion[4]
Cleanup, rebuilding, replacement of WTC	$18 billion[5]
Rebuilding of subways, utilities	$3.7 billion[6]
Lost wages in New York	$6.4 billion
Repairs to the Pentagon	$700 million[7]
Net jobs lost	$1.3 million[8]
Decrease in gross domestic product	$150 billion[9]
Lost airline revenues	$11 billion
Government bailout of two airlines that were bankrupted	$15 billion
New border security expenses (federal government)	$38 billion
State expenses for homeland security	$1.3 billion
Protective services paid by private companies	$33 billion

These sums are almost too vast to comprehend. Not including the millions of jobs lost, they add up to about $285 billion, far more than the entire gross domestic product of most nations. They do not include the cost to the world economy, factoring in stock market losses, business and leisure travel canceled or deferred, goods not sold, and other losses still not calculable. More than two and a half years after the tragedy of September 11, its reverberations are being felt throughout the world. As I write these words on Christmas Day, 2003, the United States has been put on high alert for terrorist incidents; Air France has canceled a number of flights scheduled to take place between Paris and Los Angeles because of terror alerts, stranding hundreds of passengers in Europe and in North America; casualties are inflicted almost every day in the hot war against terrorism in Afghanistan and Iraq; relations among Western allies have never been more strained; and although the world economy is recovering from the impact of the attacks on the United States, it has yet to return to its previous levels.

The impact on public opinions and attitudes

These vast losses of life, property, and income made an enormous impact on the American psyche. September 11 produced changes in the attitudes of Americans toward their own country and toward those they perceived to be their enemies far more powerful than any I have seen in my lifetime, except perhaps the aftermath of the Japanese attack on Pearl Harbor in December 1941. People who had never displayed the national flag and disliked nationalism and chauvinism suddenly found themselves wanting to wear tiny American flags on their lapels. Manufacturers of larger flags for display on homes and public buildings could not keep up with the demand. Americans had virtually lost, or at least suppressed, such feelings during the Vietnam War and the civil rights struggles of the 1960s and 1970s. They had recovered a degree of restrained patriotism during the Reagan administration. But the attacks on the United States on September 11 surged through the population like electrical shocks, awakening feelings of patriotism that had been dormant in a substantial part of the population – especially among intellectuals – for more than thirty years. There arose a surge of pride in government leaders like Mayor Rudolph Giuliani of New York, who had many detractors prior to the attacks but virtually none afterward, and President George W. Bush, who had barely won election to the White House less than two years before.

Even more than national pride and patriotism, however, the terrorist attacks produced anger and fear – anger at those who perpetrated such devastation on their nation and fear that they or others might try to repeat such attacks. Such emotions in themselves may not have great significance. But this case had worldwide implications. Although Americans have generally been inclined, since the days of George Washington,[10] to be isolationist and non-interventionist, violent attacks have always been sufficient to arouse the people and their leaders to action, and September 11 certainly did that. President Bush's immediate response was to call upon Congress to support a war against terrorism, bringing the war to Al-Qaeda's hideouts and training grounds in Afghanistan and to the Taliban rulers of that country who had sheltered them. The American people made a dramatic turn, rallying behind the President's response to the terrorists almost without dissent. Surprisingly, his approval ratings have remained remarkably high throughout the wars on Afghanistan and Iraq. President Bush's belligerence clearly reflected the feelings of the American people.

American attitudes toward the United Nations and international relations

The international impact of September 11 went beyond the American-led wars on Afghanistan and Iraq. International alliances have suffered significantly.

The American administration became convinced that it was necessary to invade Iraq in order to remove Saddam Hussein from power. It saw 'regime change' as the only way to prevent him from using weapons of mass destruction (i.e., nuclear, biological, and chemical weapons) that he was believed to possess or providing them to terrorist organizations that could use them against American targets. The United States invoked its right of self-defense under Article 51 of the UN Charter and sought the aid of its NATO allies and the Security Council in order to mount a concerted effort to remove a brutal dictatorship and to put in its place some form of democratic government. In the Security Council, the Bush administration cited Iraq's failure to comply with numerous Security Council resolutions calling on it to dispose of all of its weapons of mass destruction and to give unhampered access to the UN weapons inspectors who had been dispatched to verify Iraq's claims that it was disposing of those weapons.

In the end, several members of the Security Council and three of the permanent members – France, Russia, and China – opposed military action against Iraq. Inasmuch as no Security Council resolution could pass over the veto of any of the permanent members, the United States withdrew its resolution and proceeded to act unilaterally, together with its ally, Great Britain, and other nations in a coalition to oust Saddam Hussein with a view to replacing him with a democratic government in Iraq.

Critics of the United States have accused it of inflicting enormous damage on the United Nations through its unilateral actions, unauthorized by the Security Council. By the same token, the reaction within the United States to the UN's failure to come to its aid in what was seen as a time of crisis was anger and growing hostility to the UN.

The United States is by far the greatest financial supporter of the United Nations, contributing more than $3 billion in 2002 to the UN and its various programs and operations, which amounts to 22 percent of the UN's total operating budget and 27 percent of its peacekeeping operations. In addition to its assessments, the United States' voluntary contributions to the World Food Program come to 51.4 percent of the program's total budget, helping to feed 72 million people in 82 countries. The United States provides similar generous support to numerous other UN programs.[11] The disillusionment that set in after the Security Council's rejection of US appeals for support on the Iraq issue seriously jeopardized future appeals for aid from the United Nations and its agencies. The United States Congress, which must appropriate the funds, is highly sensitive to popular sentiment among its constituents. If the current hostile climate persists, there is a strong likelihood of future cuts in US contributions to the organization.

A reassessment of the UN Charter and self-defense

Behind the impact of US disillusionment with the United Nations and its 'allies,' however, there may lie a significant misunderstanding of the UN Charter. To understand the limitations the Charter is assumed to place on member states, it might be useful to consider its origins. The Charter was signed in San Francisco, California, on June 26, 1945, and came into force on October 24 of that year. Hitler's suicide had occurred less than two months earlier, and Germany had surrendered on May 7, 1945. Meanwhile, the war against Japan was continuing in the Pacific.

The principal authors of the Charter were the five nations still struggling to win a war that had wrought death and destruction across all of Europe, Asia, the islands of the Pacific, and other parts of the world. By that time, the United States was fighting virtually alone in the Pacific. The Soviet Union entered the war against Japan only in the last few days before the Japanese surrender. The Allies brought the United Nations into being as a means of preventing such a destructive war from breaking out in the future. At the time, they were in the process of defeating three of the most violent and evil regimes in the history of mankind – the Axis powers of Germany, Italy, and Japan – and their allies. In the all-out war that they were fighting to liberate the enslaved masses of Europe, Asia, and the Pacific, they employed every military means at their disposal. It is inconceivable that the Allied leaders would have willingly adopted measures that would constitute an absolute legal bar to any of them ever going to war in the future without the acquiescence of all of the others. They were at that very moment intent on destroying the armies and navies of those evil empires, opening the gates and tearing down the concentration camps, the slave labor camps, and the extermination camps. That they would have adopted a Charter that could later be invoked to prevent them from defending themselves against future dangers, or from coming to the aid and rescue of persecuted people, while the horrors were being revealed during the liberation of the camps, defies belief. At such a moment in history, Truman, Churchill, Stalin, Chiang, and de Gaulle would not have considered tying the hands of their successors so that they could not stave off the evil intentions of future tyrants.

In view of the circumstances of its birth, it would be preposterous to suppose that the UN Charter was intended to be a bar against a nation's doing what it deemed necessary to preserve the lives of its own citizens, to defend its sovereign territory against wanton aggression, or to save innocent people from gross violations of basic human rights and genocide.

The claim that Iraq posed no 'imminent' threat to the United States because it did not yet have the means to deliver the weapons of mass destruction against American targets holds no water. A century or two ago, 'imminent' meant 'instant, overwhelming, leaving no opportunity to seek another solution.' At that time were no jet planes, no guided missiles, no nuclear weapons, in short, none of the weapons that modern technology has enabled nations or terrorists to wield against other nations. A state that was about to come under attack had time enough to prepare against an imminent attack. Like a homeowner concerned about his safety when a trespasser intruded into his home, a state could wait until it was reasonable to anticipate that an attack was imminent, i.e., that it was likely to be mounted within an instant. But that is no longer the case. Even a homeowner is not expected to wait until an armed intruder has pulled the trigger before taking appropriate action to defend himself. The law has always recognized his right to resort to deadly force if that was reasonably necessary to ward off an imminent attack.

But today, 'imminent' cannot have such a narrow definition. An imminent threat may properly be considered to exist weeks or even months before the missiles are launched. It may be recalled that President John F. Kennedy was prepared to launch World War III during the Cuban missile crisis to defend against what he perceived to be an imminent threat against the United States. The Soviets were then in the process of delivering and installing on Cuba missiles capable of delivering nuclear warheads to targets throughout the United States. The missiles were not yet armed, much less prepared for launching. But the threat was so grave that Kennedy and his advisers concluded that they could not take the risk that the Soviets might launch nuclear weapons against the United States from Cuban soil, just 90 miles off the coast of Florida. International law does not stipulate that a state must risk its own destruction in order to observe legal niceties. If it did, it would become utterly meaningless and useless, for no responsible national leader would have the slightest inclination to follow it.

The United States did not need the 'authorization' of the Security Council before it could go to war against Iraq. A necessary condition for a party to be *authorized* to do something is that there be some *higher authority* to which that party is *subordinate*. Neither the United States

cafés, restaurants, buses, and discos where they blow themselves up with shrapnel-laden explosive belts, causing as many deaths and serious injuries as possible.

Indeed, terrorism becomes habitual, inuring those who belong to communities where it is practiced to the suffering of victims, as illustrated by the celebrations that spontaneously broke out in Palestinian communities immediately upon hearing the news of the damage inflicted upon the United States by the Al-Qaeda terrorists. Palestinian authorities attempted to suppress news and photographs of the celebrations by threatening to kill journalists who reported them, not out of shame, but because they feared the impact such reports and photos would have in the rest of the world.[19]

For centuries, pirates plied the seas, attacking ships of all nations, murdering their crews and passengers at will or selling them in the slave markets, and plundering their cargoes. Some pirates and their patrons demanded 'tribute,' ransom for their hostages' release. Because their depredations were considered to be so disruptive of civilized travel and commerce, the law from ancient times treated them as *hostes humani generis*, enemies of mankind. As such, it was held that any nation that captured them had jurisdiction over them and could apply its own law to them. As Chief Justice Story wrote, such jurisdiction is justified because pirates commit 'hostilities upon the subjects and property of any or all nations, without any regard to right or duty, or any pretense of public authority.'[20] In sentencing some defendants convicted of piracy, the Chief Justice of the Province of Carolina said of their crime:

> It is so destructive of all trade and commerce between nation and nation, that pirates are called enemies to mankind with whom no faith or oath ought to be kept; and they are termed in our law brutes and beasts of prey, and therefore it is in the interests, as well as the duty, of all governments to bring such offenders to punishment.[21]

The term 'enemies of mankind' was interpreted to mean that they had forfeited the protection of any government and of any law whatever, for they acknowledged the authority of no law and acted as if they were a law unto themselves. As Thomas Hobbes put it, a person who refuses to abide by the laws of society is 'left in the condition of war he was in before [civilized society came into being], wherein he might without injustice be destroyed by any man whatsoever.'[22]

To be sure, the analogy between today's terrorists and the pirates of yore is not exact, but it is close enough to be useful. They respect no international boundaries. The laws of no nation are sacred in their eyes. Flying from one nation to another, they spread death and destruction, not only recklessly murdering men, women, and children who are utterly innocent of any offense, but deliberately seeking them out in order to garner maximum publicity for their cause. As President, Thomas Jefferson was confronted with a demand by Barbary pirates who had captured an American vessel and demanded tribute. He responded by saying that since the usual alternative offered by the pirates was tribute or war, 'why not build a navy and decide on war?'[23]

Terrorism has precisely the same consequences upon the world community as piracy. It disrupts international commerce; it deprives people of the right to travel and participate in innocent activities free of the fear that they may be put in deadly peril for no other reason than that they happen to be there when the attacker chooses to strike; they hamper the free exchange of ideas by placing psychological obstacles in the way of tourists, scholars, and scientists who are deterred from attending international congresses by their fear of possible attack; and most important of all, they subject persons to terrifying ordeals, using them as unwilling pawns in deadly political games, assaulting them, kidnapping them, and murdering them. Terrorists commit their crimes with the same callous disregard for their victims and the consequences that befall others.

Therefore, Al-Qaeda and other terrorist organizations should be regarded, like the pirates, as *hostes humani generis*, enemies of mankind, with all that that entails, both in law and in morals. Like all other cold-blooded killers, the 'justifications' they offer for their depredations should be discounted, they should be deemed to have forfeited the rights that they would otherwise have enjoyed, and any state that is able to capture them should be deemed to have proper jurisdiction over them.

Responses to terrorism

We may note at the outset what will *not* be helpful in the war on terrorism. The paralysis of the United Nations with regard to terrorists is complete, and no solution can possibly come from it.[24] Therefore, individual states must take unilateral actions, or make multilateral alliances with like-minded states, to deal forcefully with this scourge.

All states should declare that terrorists and terrorist organizations are implacable foes that must be eliminated as a threat to every state's very existence. They are a menace to world peace and order and a threat to civilization.

There should be steadfast resistance to any temptation to negotiate with terrorists. This would obviously include negotiations with such long-time terrorists as Yasser Arafat. Thus far, the effort to impose such a requirement has been notably unsuccessful, with only a handful of nations adopting this policy.

Every state should consider itself duty bound to pursue terrorists wherever they are. Where appropriate treaties exist, they should be extradited for prosecution to the states most affected by their depredations. But they may be prosecuted and punished by any state that apprehends them.

States should be free to pursue terrorists wherever they may flee. Hot pursuit across international boundaries should be deemed to be legal with or without the consent of the state whose boundaries are crossed whenever there is good cause to believe that the state concerned will not act effectively to bring the criminals to justice. Similarly, destruction of terrorist camps and operations across international borders should be considered no offense if the state harboring them does not do so of its own accord. The evil of harboring terrorists is far greater than the harm done by brief sorties that violate international boundaries. Terrorists should not be able to enjoy the protection of their host states with impunity. Nor should their hosts be permitted to give them safe harbor without risking incursions to root out their unwelcome guests.

Granting refuge to terrorists who have engaged in destructive acts against other states is an act of war. No self-respecting power should shrink from its national and international responsibilities by not responding forcefully to acts of war that threaten its stability, its national security, its citizens' lives, and its territorial integrity.

Suspected terrorists are entitled to a fair trial, humane treatment during confinement before trial, and no cruel and inhuman punishment. This does not preclude the imposition of the death penalty for those convicted of particularly heinous crimes. Nor does it preclude trials before military tribunals, or special tribunals set up for that purpose. Nor, finally, is a person captured in an international anti-terrorist operation entitled to all of the rights and privileges that are accorded to domestic defendants under Constitutional law.

Obviously, those caught in the act of terrorism may properly be stopped by any means necessary, including the use of deadly force, like any other violent criminals. Until a person is found to have participated in terrorism, he is entitled to the benefits of criminal due process, both because he has not yet been found to have forfeited the rights to which he would otherwise be entitled, and because a civilized society owes it to itself and to its citizens to adhere to proper procedures before condemning even the most abhorrent persons to criminal punishment.

Various attempts have been made through the years to appease terrorists of all stripes, to persuade them to join the community of nations and to work out their grievances through negotiation and compromise. Although such efforts have not been altogether fruitless, they have not been particularly successful either. Some people are simply not open to genuine negotiations. Whether they say so or not, their demands are non-negotiable. Too often their 'negotiations' are a sham, designed to leave the way open for the next step in their march toward total victory, giving them both the time to prepare for their ultimate triumph and room to deploy their propaganda machines to win the sympathies of the naïve and vulnerable. This has clearly been the methodology of the Palestine Liberation Organization and its various offshoots. While smiling, shaking hands, and promising compromise, they march on toward their ultimate goal, the total destruction of the State of Israel. Al-Qaeda, on the other hand, makes no secret of its ultimate goal, and is utterly uncompromising. It sees itself as at war with all Christians and Jews. Its vision is of a world united under the banner of Islam. As Omar Abdel Rahman, the blind sheikh, said in 1993 after the first World Trade Center bombing which he helped to engineer:

> There is no solution for our problems except jihad for the sake of God.... There's no solution, there's no treatment, there's no medicine, there's no cure except with what was brought by the Islamic method which is jihad for the sake of God.... We welcome being terrorists.... And the Koran makes it, terrorism, among the means to perform jihad for the sake of Allah, which is to terrorize the enemies of God who are our enemies, too.[25]

Rahman added that this jihad was not fasting and prayer, but bullets and bombs.

Islamic jihadists have been predicting for years that there would be a great apocalypse that would involve the slaughter of 'infidel collaborationist governments' and 'their ignorant masses' that conspire with the Jews to deceive and seduce the Muslim world and ride the Crusader (Christian) horse against Islam. The great apocalyptic war will lead to the conquest of Rome and all of Europe and America by Islam. This war will be centered primarily in New York, because Jews and 'their banks, their political foundations which control the entire world (the U.N., the Security Council, the International Monetary Fund, the World Bank, and the principal media networks)' are centered there and because 'there is no evil greater than in New York in any other place on the inhabited earth.'[26]

In his *fatwa* 'Declaration of War against the Americans Occupying the Land of the Two Holy Places [Saudi Arabia],' Osama bin Laden went beyond threats against America and Israel to threaten Arab leaders who collaborate with them as well. The royal house of Saudi Arabia is singled out for having failed to expel the 'polytheists' from its country.[27]

After the destruction he and his minions wrought on September 11, bin Laden explained that the events that transpired that day made it clear that 'the West in general, led by America bears an unspeakable Crusader grudge against Islam.' He described the actions of the hijackers as messages that resounded throughout the world, and were leading to mass conversions of infidels to Islam in China, in Holland, and even in America. The attacks on the West were just retribution for 'the tragedy of al-Andalus,' the defeat of the Muslims in Spain by Christian armies in 1492, and the abolition of the caliphate in 1924.[28] Thus, bin Laden's war is against the entire Judeo-Christian world and an attempt to re-establish the caliphate and spread Islam throughout the world.

Bin Laden's campaign recognizes no limits on the methods to be employed in bringing that Islamic world about. This form of militant Islam is a threat to civilization as we know it, and must be fought by every means at our disposal.

That is the battle that will occupy the world for the foreseeable future, and the legacy of the bombers of September 11, 2001.

Notes

1. Recounted in Gail Sheehy, *Middletown America: One Town's Passage from Trauma to Hope* (New York: Random House, 2003), pp. 5ff.
2. My colleagues and students at the main campus of Pace University, three blocks from the World Trade Center, were among them.
3. *Wall Street Journal*, September 11, 2003, A12.
4. Federal Reserve Bank of New York.
5. Ibid.
6. Ibid.
7. US Congress.
8. Milken Institute.
9. Ibid.
10. In his Farewell Address, delivered in 1796, he said: 'The great rule of conduct for us in regard to foreign nations is in extending our commercial relations, to have with them as little political connection as possible... Why, by inter-eaving our destiny with that of any part of Europe, entangle our peace

and prosperity in the toils of European ambition, rivalship, interest, humor or caprice? It is our true policy to steer clear of permanent alliances.' See the entire text at www.yale.edu/lawweb/avalon/washing.htm.

11. U.S. Participation in the UN – Financial Contributions, United States Department of State, September 22, 2003.

12. Richard Falk, *The Great Terror War* (Brooklyn, New York: Olive Branch Press, 2003), p. 33.

13. Ibid., p. 34.

14. Ibid., p. 35.

15. Franklin Delano Roosevelt, Address to Congress, December 8, 1941. Available at http://bcn.boulder.co.us/government/national/speeches/spch2.html.

16. See, for example, *United States v. Verdugo-Urquidez*, 494 U.S. 259 (1989), holding that the Fourth Amendment guarantee against warrantless search and seizure does not apply to property of a nonresident alien located in a foreign country.

17. Note that Saddam was funding terrorist organizations and offered $25,000 to every family whose son or daughter became a 'martyr' in a suicide bombing against Israeli targets.

18. A series of coordinated attacks in 1971 was said to be so severe that they were compared to the blitz in Belfast in 1941. Richard Clutterbuck, *Protest and the Urban Guerrilla* (London: Cassell, 1973), p. 132.

19. See yesha.org, imra.org, and Catherine Donaldson-Evans, September 13, 2001, at foxnews.com/story/0.2933.34346.00.

20. 2 How. 210 (1844), at 232.

21. 15 How. 1286 (1718).

22. *Leviathan*, ed. Herbert W. Schneider (Indianapolis: Bobbs-Merrill, 1958), p. 146.

23. T. Harry Williams et al., *A History of the United States* (New York: Alfred A. Knopf, 1959), p. 248. The US Marines, whose hymn begins, 'From the halls of Montezuma to the shores of Tripoli,' played a major part in ridding the world – at least temporarily – of the plague of Middle Eastern piracy/terrorism.

24. I have taken the liberty of quoting myself. This sentence, and much of what is included in this and the preceding section, is drawn from my book, *Liberty, Justice, and Morals: Contemporary Value Conflicts*, second edition (New York: Macmillan, 1979), pp. 393ff. Sadly, nothing has occurred in the last 25 years to change my mind on this subject.

25. Cited in Daniel Benjamin and Steven Simon, *The Age of Sacred Terror: Radical Islam's War against America* (New York: Random House, 2003), pp. 16f.

26. Abdullah Yusuf Ali, *The Holy Qur'an: Text, Translation and Commentary* (New York: Tahrike Tarsile Qur'an, Inc., 1987), 46:21–6, 22:1, cited in Benjamin and Simon, *The Age of Sacred Terror*, pp. 92f.

27. Issued on August 23, 1996. Cited in Benjamin and Simon, *The Age of Sacred Terror*, p. 142.

28. Al Jazirah broadcast of bin Laden's recorded statement, 27 December 2001, cited in Benjamin and Simon, *The Age of Sacred Terror*, pp. 158ff.

Selected Bibliography

Books

Corlett, J. Angelo, *Terrorism: A Philosophical Analysis* (Dordrecht: Kluwer, 2003)

Gilbert, Paul, *Terrorism, Security and Nationality* (London: Routledge, 1994)

Gilbert, Paul, *New Terror, New Wars* (Edinburgh: Edinburgh University Press, 2003)

Khatchadourian, Haig, *The Morality of Terrorism* (New York: Peter Lang, 1998)

Wilkins, Burleigh Taylor, *Terrorism and Collective Responsibility* (London: Routledge, 1992)

Collections

Coady, Tony and Michael O'Keefe (eds.), *Terrorism and Justice* (Melbourne: Melbourne University Press, 2002)

Frey, R.G. and Christopher W. Morris (eds.), *Violence, Terrorism, and Justice* (Cambridge: Cambridge University Press, 1991)

Laqueur, Walter (ed.), *The Terrorism Reader: A Historical Anthology*, revised edition (New York: New American Library, 1987)

Rapoport, David C. and Yonah Alexander (eds.), *The Morality of Terrorism: Religious and Secular Justifications*, second edition (New York: Columbia University Press, 1989)

Sterba, James P. (ed.), *Terrorism and International Justice* (New York: Oxford University Press, 2003)

Articles

Ashmore, Robert B., 'State Terrorism and Its Sponsors,' in Tomis Kapitan (ed.), *Philosophical Perspectives on the Israeli–Palestinian Conflict* (Armonk, NY: F.E. Sharpe, 1997)

Coady, C.A.J., 'The Morality of Terrorism,' *Philosophy* 60 (1985)

Corlett, J. Angelo, 'Can Terrorism Be Morally Justified?', *Public Affairs Quarterly* 10 (1996)

Fullinwider, Robert, 'Understanding Terrorism,' in Steven Luper-Foy (ed.), *Problems of International Justice* (Boulder, Col.: Westview Press, 1988)

George, David A., 'Distinguishing Classical Tyrannicide from Modern Terrorism,' *Review of Politics* 50 (1988)

George, David A., 'The Ethics of IRA Terrorism,' in Andrew Valls (ed.), *Ethics in International Affairs* (Lanham, Md: Rowman & Littlefield, 2000)

Gregor, A. James, 'Some Thoughts on State and Rebel Terror,' in David C. Rapoport and Yonah Alexander (eds.), *The Rationalization of Terrorism* (Frederick, Md: Aletheia Books, 1982)

Hughes, Martin, 'Terrorism and National Security,' *Philosophy* 52 (1987)

Khatchadourian, Haig, 'Terrorism and Morality', *Journal of Applied Philosophy* 5 (1988)

Leiser, Burton M., 'Terrorism, Guerrilla Warfare, and International Morality,' *Stanford Journal of International Studies* 12 (1977)

Louch, Alfred, 'Terrorism: The Immorality of Belief,' in David C. Rapoport and Yonah Alexander (eds.), *The Rationalization of Terrorism* (Frederick, Md: Aletheia Books, 1982)

Nielsen, Kai ,'Violence and Terrorism: Its Uses and Abuses,' in Burton M. Leiser (ed.), *Values in Conflict* (New York: Macmillan, 1981)

Primoratz, Igor, 'The Morality of Terrorism,' *Journal of Applied Philosophy* 14 (1997)

Simpson, Peter, 'Just War Theory and the IRA,' *Journal of Applied Philosophy* 3 (1986)

Valls, Andrew, 'Can Terrorism Be Justified?', in Andrew Valls (ed.), *Ethics in International Affairs* (Lanham, Md: Rowman & Littlefield, 2000)

Wallace, Gerry, 'Area Bombing, Terrorism and the Death of Innocents,' *Journal of Applied Philosophy* 6 (1989)

Wallace, Gerry, 'Terrorism and the Argument from Analogy,' *International Journal of Moral and Social Studies* 6 (1991)

Walzer, Michael, 'Terrorism: A Critique of Excuses,' in Steven Luper-Foy (ed.), *Problems of International Justice* (Boulder, Col.: Westview Press, 1988)

Wellman, Carl, 'On Terrorism Itself,' *Journal of Value Inquiry* 13 (1979)

Wellmer, Albrecht, 'Terrorism and the Critique of Society,' in Jürgen Habermas (ed.), *Observations on 'The Spiritual Situation of the Age'*, trans. Andrew Buchwalter (Cambridge, Mass: MIT Press, 1984)

Young, Robert, 'Revolutionary Terrorism, Crime and Morality,' *Social Theory and Practice* 4 (1977)

Index